FOR DUMMIES®

COMPUTER
BOOK SERIES
FROM IDG

LotusScript™ For Dummies®

MW01012210

Common Error Messages and How to Fix Them

(Some of these error messages use sample data, like the word "day.")

Error Message	What to Look for to Fix the Error
Type mismatch	Reference to a variable's data type that doesn't match its declared data type.
Instance member does not exist	Use of OOP objects that aren't defined in terms of a class.
Class or type name not found	Typing errors in LotusScript keywords.
Unterminated string constant	Omission of ending quotation marks (").
Unexpected: Bogart; Expected: End-of-Statement, Operator	Omission of both quotation marks (" ... ").
Not a sub or function name: Endif	Spaces missing in LotusScript keyword (End If).
Unexpected: Print; Expected: End-of-Statement	More than one LotusScript statement on one line.
Unexpected: day; Expected: Identifier	Variable name identical to a LotusScript keyword.
Unexpected: Code; Expected: (;End of Statement; ,;AS;LIST	Spaces in a variable name.
Unexpected: &; Expected: Statement	Omission of line continuation character.

Handy Keyboard Shortcuts for Working with LotusScript

Keyboard Shortcut	What It Does
F1	Brings up LotusScript Help files. When the cursor is in a keyword, brings up Help on that keyword.
F2	Performs line-by-line syntax checking of Globals.
Shift + F2	Checks all scripts for the current document.
F3	Creates a Sub.
Shift + F3	Creates a Function.
F5	Runs the current sub.
F6	Switches between the Script Editor and another IDE panel (Breakpoints, Browser, Output, or Variables).
+ (plus) or - (minus)	Expands or collapses items in an outline list.
Tab or Shift+Tab	Moves forward and backward between fields in a panel.
Ctrl+PgDn or Ctrl+PgUp	Moves the insertion point to the previous or next procedure that contains user-defined scripts.

...For Dummies: #1 Computer Book Series for Beginners

COMPUTER
BOOK SERIES
FROM IDG

LotusScript™ For Dummies®

Cheat Sheet

Good Scripting Practices

1. Declare your variables at the beginning of the script.
2. Give your variables meaningful names.
3. Put one script statement per line.
4. Test changes to your script right away.
5. Use lots of subs.
6. Use `Call` statements for your subs.
7. Give your variables data types when you declare them.
8. Declare data types for the arguments that go along with your functions.
9. As much as possible, use subs instead of nested Ifs.
10. Avoid endless loops.

Handy Mouse Shortcuts

To expand or collapse list items in the Browser panel, click the expand symbol or the collapse symbol.

To choose a command from the Browser, click on it and then click Paste Name.

To set a breakpoint on a script line in the Script Editor, click at the far left of the line in the area known as the *breakpoint gutter*.

To clear a breakpoint, click the breakpoint icon that appears at the far left of the script line in the breakpoint gutter.

To disable or enable a breakpoint, simultaneously press Ctrl and click the breakpoint.

To change the size of IDE window panels, drag the pane splitter.

To restore IDE window panels to their previous size, double-click the pane splitter.

To easily open the IDE, click on its SmartIcon (which you have to put on the Universal SmartIcon Bar yourself).

Reading Syntax Diagrams

Ignore everything in [brackets] — at least at first.

Remember that the words in *italics* are the elements supplied by the scripter.

Skip the Syntax Diagram and read the example, which is easier to follow.

The One Command You Can't Live Without

`Dim`

LotusScript Numeric and String Data Types — for Variables and Arguments

Data Type	Value	Data Suffix Character
Integer	A whole number in the range -32,768 to 32,767	% (percent)
Long	A whole number in the range -2,147,483,648 to 2,147,483,647	& (ampersand)
Single	A *floating-point* value — that is a really large number (10 or 15 digits), or a really small number (10 or 15 digits to the right of a decimal point)	! (exclamation point, or *bang* to programmers)
Double	Like a Single, but twice as much	# (pound sign)
Currency	A number representing a monetary value, calculated to four decimal places	@ (at sign)
String	A series of letters, numbers, even punctuation marks. For example, `Rag` is a string; so is `rage#*`, `ty`.	$ (dollar sign)

IDG
BOOKS
WORLDWIDE

...For Dummies: #1 Computer Book Series for Beginners

LOTUSSCRIPT™
FOR
DUMMIES®

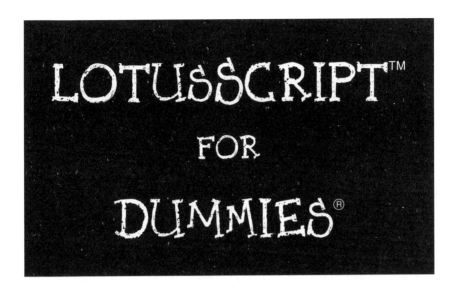

LOTUSSCRIPT™ FOR DUMMIES®

by Jim Meade

Foreword by
Chris Smith

IDG Books Worldwide, Inc.
An International Data Group Company

Foster City, CA ♦ Chicago, IL ♦ Indianapolis, IN ♦ Southlake, TX

LotusScript™ For Dummies®

Published by
IDG Books Worldwide, Inc.
An International Data Group Company
919 E. Hillsdale Blvd.
Suite 400
Foster City, CA 94404
`http://www.idgbooks.com` (IDG Books Worldwide Web site)
`http://www.dummies.com` (Dummies Press Web site)

Library of Congress Catalog Card No.: 96-77703

ISBN: 1-56884-638-X

Printed in the United States of America

10 9 8 7 6 5 4 3 2 1

IO/RR/QT/ZX/IN

Distributed in the United States by IDG Books Worldwide, Inc.

Distributed by Macmillan Canada for Canada; by Contemporanea de Ediciones for Venezuela; by Distribuidora Cuspide for Argentina; by CITEC for Brazil; by Ediciones ZETA S.C.R. Ltda. for Peru; by Editorial Limusa SA for Mexico; by Transworld Publishers Limited in the United Kingdom and Europe; by Academic Bookshop for Egypt; by Levant Distributors S.A.R.L. for Lebanon; by Al Jassim for Saudi Arabia; by Simron Pty. Ltd. for South Africa; by Pustak Mahal for India; by The Computer Bookshop for India; by Toppan Company Ltd. for Japan; by Addison Wesley Publishing Company for Korea; by Longman Singapore Publishers Ltd. for Singapore, Malaysia, Thailand, and Indonesia; by Unalis Corporation for Taiwan; by WS Computer Publishing Company, Inc. for the Philippines; by WoodsLane Pty. Ltd. for Australia; by WoodsLane Enterprises Ltd. for New Zealand. Authorized Sales Agent: Anthony Rudkin Associates for the Middle East and North Africa.

For general information on IDG Books Worldwide's books in the U.S., please call our Consumer Customer Service department at 800-762-2974. For reseller information, including discounts and premium sales, please call our Reseller Customer Service department at 800-434-3422.

For information on where to purchase IDG Books Worldwide's books outside the U.S., please contact our International Sales department at 415-655-3023 or fax 415-655-3299.

For information on foreign language translations, please contact our Foreign & Subsidiary Rights department at 415-655-3021 or fax 415-655-3281.

For sales inquiries and special prices for bulk quantities, please contact our Sales department at 415-655-3200 or write to the address above.

For information on using IDG Books Worldwide's books in the classroom or for ordering examination copies, please contact our Educational Sales department at 800-434-2086 or fax 817-251-8174.

For authorization to photocopy items for corporate, personal, or educational use, please contact Copyright Clearance Center, 222 Rosewood Drive, Danvers, MA 01923, or fax 508-750-4470.

 is a trademark under exclusive license to IDG Books Worldwide, Inc., from International Data Group, Inc.

About the Author

Jim Meade likes to think of himself as a dummy. He started out that way as a child and likes to be true to his roots. Nevertheless, he is a dummy who has written an awful lot of computer books — 16 so far — including *Word Pro For Windows 95 For Dummies* and its popular predecessor *Ami Pro For Dummies* (both published by IDG Books Worldwide, Inc.). Jim's other leading titles include *Using PowerPoint* and *Using Ami Pro*.

A former in-house writer with Digital Equipment Corporation, Meade founded his own writing enterprise, Meade Ink, Inc., in 1984. Jim's company is based in Fairfield, Iowa, and provides writing services to companies such as DEC, Lotus, and MCI. As a magazine writer as well as a book author, Jim has contributed to *PC Magazine* and dozens of trade magazines, including *Data Communications* and *HR Magazine* (in which he writes regular software reviews).

He coaches eighth-grade basketball but would rather play, and he regrets rules stipulating that, to play at that level, you have to be in eighth grade.

ABOUT IDG BOOKS WORLDWIDE

Welcome to the world of IDG Books Worldwide.

IDG Books Worldwide, Inc., is a subsidiary of International Data Group, the world's largest publisher of computer-related information and the leading global provider of information services on information technology. IDG was founded more than 25 years ago and now employs more than 8,500 people worldwide. IDG publishes more than 275 computer publications in over 75 countries (see listing below). More than 60 million people read one or more IDG publications each month.

Launched in 1990, IDG Books Worldwide is today the #1 publisher of best-selling computer books in the United States. We are proud to have received eight awards from the Computer Press Association in recognition of editorial excellence and three from *Computer Currents'* First Annual Readers' Choice Awards. Our best-selling *...For Dummies*® series has more than 30 million copies in print with translations in 30 languages. IDG Books Worldwide, through a joint venture with IDG's Hi-Tech Beijing, became the first U.S. publisher to publish a computer book in the People's Republic of China. In record time, IDG Books Worldwide has become the first choice for millions of readers around the world who want to learn how to better manage their businesses.

Our mission is simple: Every one of our books is designed to bring extra value and skill-building instructions to the reader. Our books are written by experts who understand and care about our readers. The knowledge base of our editorial staff comes from years of experience in publishing, education, and journalism — experience we use to produce books for the '90s. In short, we care about books, so we attract the best people. We devote special attention to details such as audience, interior design, use of icons, and illustrations. And because we use an efficient process of authoring, editing, and desktop publishing our books electronically, we can spend more time ensuring superior content and spend less time on the technicalities of making books.

You can count on our commitment to deliver high-quality books at competitive prices on topics you want to read about. At IDG Books Worldwide, we continue in the IDG tradition of delivering quality for more than 25 years. You'll find no better book on a subject than one from IDG Books Worldwide.

John Kilcullen
CEO
IDG Books Worldwide, Inc.

*Eighth Annual
Computer Press
Awards ≥1992*

*Ninth Annual
Computer Press
Awards ≥1993*

*Tenth Annual
Computer Press
Awards ≥1994*

*Eleventh Annual
Computer Press
Awards ≥1995*

IDG Books Worldwide, Inc., is a subsidiary of International Data Group, the world's largest publisher of computer-related information and the leading global provider of information services on information technology. International Data Group publishes over 275 computer publications in over 75 countries. Sixty million people read one or more International Data Group publications each month. International Data Group's publications include: **ARGENTINA:** Buyer's Guide, Computerworld Argentina, PC World Argentina; **AUSTRALIA:** Australian Macworld, Australian PC World, Australian Reseller News, Computerworld, IT Casebook, Network World, Publish, Webmaster; **AUSTRIA:** Computerwelt Österreich, Networks Austria, PC Tip Austria; **BANGLADESH:** PC World Bangladesh; **BELARUS:** PC World Belarus; **BELGIUM:** Data News; **BRAZIL:** Annuário de Informática, Computerworld, Connections, Macworld, PC Player, PC World, Publish, Reseller News, Supergamepower; **BULGARIA:** Computerworld Bulgaria, Network World Bulgaria, PC & MacWorld Bulgaria; **CANADA:** CIO Canada, Client/Server World, ComputerWorld Canada, InfoWorld Canada, NetworkWorld Canada, WebWorld; **CHILE:** Computerworld Chile, PC World Chile; **COLOMBIA:** Computerworld Colombia, PC World Colombia; **COSTA RICA:** PC World Centro America; **THE CZECH AND SLOVAK REPUBLICS:** Computerworld Czechoslovakia, Macworld Czech Republic, PC World Czechoslovakia; **DENMARK:** Communications World Danmark, Computerworld Danmark, Macworld Danmark, PC World Danmark, Techworld Denmark; **DOMINICAN REPUBLIC:** PC World Republica Dominicana; **ECUADOR:** PC World Ecuador; **EGYPT:** Computerworld Middle East, PC World Middle East; **EL SALVADOR:** PC World Centro America; **FINLAND:** MikroPC, Tietoverkko, Tietoviikko; **FRANCE:** Distributique, Hebdo, Info PC, Le Monde Informatique, Macworld, Reseaux & Telecoms, WebMaster France; **GERMANY:** Computer Partner, Computerwoche, Computerwoche Extra, Computerwoche FOCUS, Global Online, Macwelt, PC Welt; **GREECE:** Amiga Computing, GamePro Greece, Multimedia World; **GUATEMALA:** PC World Centro America; **HONDURAS:** PC World Centro America; **HONG KONG:** Computerworld Hong Kong, PC World Hong Kong, Publish in Asia; **HUNGARY:** ABCD CD-ROM, Computerworld Szamitastechnika, Internetto online Magazine, PC World Hungary, PC-X Magazin Hungary; **ICELAND:** Tolvuheimur PC World Island; **INDIA:** Information Communications World, Information Systems Computerworld, PC World India, Publish in Asia; **INDONESIA:** InfoKomputer PC World, Komputek Computerworld, Publish in Asia; **IRELAND:** ComputerScope, PC Live!; **ISRAEL:** Macworld Israel, People & Computers/Computerworld; **ITALY:** Computerworld Italia, Macworld Italia, Networking Italia, PC World Italia; **JAPAN:** DTP World, Macworld Japan, Nikkei Personal Computing, OS/2 World Japan, SunWorld Japan, Windows NT World, Windows World Japan; **KENYA:** PC World East African; **KOREA:** Hi-Tech Information, Macworld Korea, PC World Korea; **MACEDONIA:** PC World Macedonia; **MALAYSIA:** Computerworld Malaysia, PC World Malaysia, Publish in Asia; **MALTA:** PC World Malta; **MEXICO:** Computerworld Mexico, PC World Mexico; **MYANMAR:** PC World Myanmar; **NETHERLANDS:** Computer! Totaal, LAN Internetworking Magazine, LAN World Buyers Guide, Macworld Netherlands, Net, WebWereld; **NEW ZEALAND:** Absolute Beginners Guide and Plain & Simple Series, Computer Buyer, Computer Industry Directory, Computerworld New Zealand, MTB, Network World, PC World New Zealand; **NICARAGUA:** PC World Centro America; **NORWAY:** Computerworld Norge, CW Rapport, Datamagasinet, Financial Rapport, Kursguide Norge, Macworld Norge, Multimediaworld Norge, PC World Ekspress Norge, PC World Nettverk, PC World Norge, PC World ProduktGuide Norge; **PAKISTAN:** Computerworld Pakistan; **PANAMA:** PC World Panama; **PEOPLE'S REPUBLIC OF CHINA:** China Computer Users, China Computerworld, China InfoWorld, China Telecom World Weekly, Computer & Communication, Electronic Design China, Electronics Today, Electronics Weekly, Game Software, PC World China, Popular Computer Week, Software Weekly, Software World, Telecom World; **PERU:** Computerworld Peru, PC World Professional Peru, PC World SoHo Peru; **PHILIPPINES:** Click!, Computerworld Philippines, PC World Philippines, Publish in Asia; **POLAND:** Computerworld Poland, Computerworld Special Report Poland, Cyber, Macworld Poland, Networld Poland, PC World Komputer; **PORTUGAL:** Cerebro/PC World, Computerworld/Correio Informático, Dealer World Portugal, Mac*In/PC*In Portugal, Multimedia World; **PUERTO RICO:** PC World Puerto Rico; **ROMANIA:** Computerworld Romania, PC World Romania, Telecom Romania; **RUSSIA:** Computerworld Russia, Mir PK, Publish, Seti; **SINGAPORE:** Computerworld Singapore, PC World Singapore, Publish in Asia; **SLOVENIA:** Monitor; **SOUTH AFRICA:** Computing SA, Network World SA, Software World SA; **SPAIN:** Communicaciones World España, Computerworld España, Dealer World España, Macworld España, PC World España; **SRI LANKA:** Infolink PC World; **SWEDEN:** CAP&Design, Computer Sweden, Corporate Computing Sweden, Internetworld Sweden, it.branschen, Macworld Sweden, MaxiData Sweden, MikroDatorn, Natverk & Kommunikation, PC World Sweden, PCaktiv, Windows World Sweden; **SWITZERLAND:** Computerworld Schweiz, Macworld Schweiz, PCtip; **TAIWAN:** Computerworld Taiwan, Macworld Taiwan, NEW ViSiON/Publish, PC World Taiwan, Windows World Taiwan; **THAILAND:** Publish in Asia, Thai Computerworld; **TURKEY:** Computerworld Turkiye, Macworld Turkiye, Network World Turkiye, PC World Turkiye; **UKRAINE:** Computerworld Kiev, Multimedia World Ukraine, PC World Ukraine; **UNITED KINGDOM:** Acorn User UK, Amiga Action UK, Amiga Computing UK, Apple Talk UK, Computing, Macworld, Parents and Computers UK, PC Advisor, PC Home, PSX Pro, The WEB; **UNITED STATES:** Cable in the Classroom, CIO Magazine, Computerworld, DOS World, Federal Computer Week, GamePro Magazine, InfoWorld, I-Way, Macworld, Network World, PC Games, PC World, Publish, Video Event, THE WEB Magazine, and WebMaster; online webzines: JavaWorld, NetscapeWorld, and SunWorld Online; **URUGUAY:** InfoWorld Uruguay; **VENEZUELA:** Computerworld Venezuela, PC World Venezuela; and **VIETNAM:** PC World Vietnam.   2/14/97

Dedication

For Elinor:

My dad's sister, forever loyal

Author's Acknowledgments

It's fun to be associated with something big. And the . . .*For Dummies* books are big. I want to thank everybody who has had anything do with making them what they are (with special mention to Dan Gookin), and I want to give a special thanks to the people who gave me the chance to do this book: Milissa Koloski, Diane Steele, Mary Bednarek, and Tammy Goldfeld.

Two very special people guided me as I was attempting to guide you, the reader. I want to thank my diligent, gentle, insightful Project Editor, Leah Cameron. And thanks to someone I never met who watched over technical matters and offered gentle suggestions as needed, Tech Editor David Medinets. Thanks to all the IDG people listed on the Publisher's Acknowledgments page. You people rule!

You don't realize how many programmers you know until you write your first programming book. I asked a lot of questions. I especially want to thank Foy Shiver and Chris Smith at Lotus, who may have gotten tired of my asking things but who always came across with the goods. Also, thanks to Cheryl Fields and Bob Norton at Lotus. I want to mention my friends Tom Harper, Ed Kingsbury, John Stamm, Susan Westlake, Wayne Blair, Jeff Welch, Bob Williams, and David Ledina. And thanks to fellow author John Walkenbach.

I want to thank my family — Nina, Molly, Ben, and Josh — for dragging me away from this project and, basically, feeding me, making me watch TV, playing with me, stuffing newspaper into my shoes unexpectedly, eating my share of the pie, and generally maintaining me as the dummy my readers expect to see when they read this book.

Finally, thanks to everybody I should have thanked but forgot.

Publisher's Acknowledgments

We're proud of this book; please send us your comments about it by using the Reader Response Card at the back of the book or by e-mailing us at feedback/dummies@idgbooks.com. Some of the people who helped bring this book to market include the following:

Acquisitions, Development, & Editorial

Senior Project Editor: Leah P. Cameron

Acquisitions Editor: Tammy Goldfeld

Technical Editor: David Medinets

Editorial Manager: Mary C. Corder

Editorial Assistant: Chris H. Collins

Production

Project Coordinator: Cindy L. Phipps

Layout and Graphics: Brett Black, Cameron Booker, Valery Bourke, Linda M. Boyer, Elizabeth Cárdenas-Nelson, J. Tyler Connor, Dominique DeFelice, Maridee V. Ennis, Todd Klemme, Drew Moore, Anna Rohrer, Brent Savage, Gina Scott, Michael A. Sullivan

Proofreaders: Kathy Layna, Joel K. Draper, Rachel Garvey, Nancy Price, Rob Springer, Ethel Winslow

Indexer: Sherry Massey

Special Help: Stephanie Koutek, Proof Editor Constance Carlisle, Copy Editor Patricia Yuu Pan, Copy Editor

General and Administrative

IDG Books Worldwide, Inc.: John Kilcullen, CEO; Steven Berkowitz, President and Publisher

IDG Books Technology Publishing: Brenda McLaughlin, Senior Vice President and Group Publisher

Dummies Technology Press and Dummies Editorial: Diane Graves Steele, Vice President and Associate Publisher; Judith A. Taylor, Brand Manager; Kristin A. Cocks, Editorial Director

Dummies Trade Press: Kathleen A. Welton, Vice President and Publisher; Stacy S. Collins, Brand Manager

IDG Books Production for Dummies Press: Beth Jenkins, Production Director; Cindy L. Phipps, Supervisor of Project Coordination, Production Proofreading, and Indexing; Kathie S. Schutte, Supervisor of Page Layout; Shelley Lea, Supervisor of Graphics and Design; Debbie J. Gates, Production Systems Specialist; Tony Augsburger, Supervisor of Reprints and Bluelines; Leslie Popplewell, Media Archive Coordinator

Dummies Packaging and Book Design: Patti Sandez, Packaging Specialist; Lance Kayser, Packaging Assistant; Kavish+Kavish, Cover Design

◆

The publisher would like to give special thanks to Patrick J. McGovern, without whom this book would not have been possible.

◆

Contents at a Glance

Cartoons at a Glance

By Rich Tennant • Fax: 508-546-7747 • E-mail: the5wave@tiac.net

page 125

page 225

page 81

page 169

page 7

page 263

Table of Contents

Part IV: Claiming New Territories: Scripting Lotus Products *169*

Chapter 14: They Call This *OOPs*. It Must Be for Me! 171

Chapter 15: Attaching to Events: In Our Main Event 185

Foreword

· ·

You have this big fancy computer, so why do you still have so much work to do? Wasn't the idea that the computer would do all the work? The software helps you do much more than you could ever do without the computer, yet so much is still repetitive. The more specific a chore is to your business, the less the machine seems ready to help with it. If only there was a way to build into the software the things that only *you* do. . . .

That's what LotusScript is all about. Software developers like Lotus build software that gets 80 percent of the job done for 80 percent of the people. The closer the developers get to solving all the problems for all the people, the closer to astronomical the price of the software becomes. LotusScript represents a set of powerful tools for customizing and automating our software so that you can get the extra 20 percent, and the computer can do more of what is specific to your work.

We designed LotusScript's tools to fit well into the hand of those who are typically engaged in crafting custom software solutions: programmers. We built the LotusScript software that way; we wrote the LotusScript documentation that way. For the non-programmer, it may seem like we left out a lot of the introductory material. That's because we did.

Now you know what this book is all about. Jim Meade's *LotusScript For Dummies* gives you what you need to know to get started. He builds you the bridge to get you from the concepts and vocabulary of an everyday computer user to the wonderful world of programming. Yes, there are new concepts, and lots of new jargon. He'll take you step by step, and there is plenty of interesting scenery along the way. So don't worry; it's great fun when you get there. And soon, your computer will be doing all the work instead of you. Isn't that the way it was supposed to be?

Chris Smith
Senior Product Manager
SmartSuite Integration
Lotus Development

Introduction

*W*elcome to *LotusScript For Dummies*! I'm delighted to tell you that, by picking up this book, you're taking the first step in an exciting journey. You're obviously an adventurous soul — with the desire to begin your own expedition into the LotusScript territory.

This book can help you find the easier paths on your trek into the world of writing LotusScript scripts. Scripting is simply a form of programming, you know, so this book enjoys the awesome task of guiding your journey into the wilderness of programming concepts, too. But have no fear! *LotusScript For Dummies* stays right with you when you wander off the path a bit.

About This Book

I would like this book to be the special programming book that everybody gives to their scripting-challenged friends.

How can *LotusScript For Dummies* be that special gift book, any more than a lot of good programming books already out there? Well, this is truly a book that I could write only once in my lifetime — as I was learning to program.

At the beginning of this project, I was (literally) a nonprogrammer. When I read documentation that said something like *a variant is a variable that has no assigned data type,* I started to get a headache. The pain didn't get any better when I read that *a constant is also a variable.* I mean, what I was reading didn't make sense. (If it's constant, how can it be variable?) And I remembered that headache and tried to explain the whole topic of constants and variables to you in such a way that you feel just fine — no headache!

You know that old saying, "Those who can . . . do; those who can't . . . teach." I always suspected that the saying was true, but I thought that it was a put-down to teachers. Now I've discovered new meaning in the old adage. Maybe having all those can't-quite-do-it people in the classroom is good. Who makes up their class, after all? All those people who (as of yet, at least) can't-quite-do-it-either. Assuming that the pedagogue has prepared the lesson and knows a little something, that teacher is perfectly positioned to understand where the student is coming from and provide sympathetic guidance.

Having worked through the material for this book, I may now know too many things and take them for granted. I know how important variables are. I know what a concatenation operator is, and a containment hierarchy, but I didn't know these things when I started using LotusScript. And I believe that my initial ignorance of programming may be the inspiration that makes this book truly useful to other people starting out in scripting.

Can a dummy write a book . . . *For Dummies*? I hope so, because that happened here.

How to Use This Book

. . .*For Dummies* books are different from the many other computer books out there. Instead of trying to force you to be good, logical, hard working, and disciplined, these books let you read the way a human being probably wants to read — unpredictably, at random, by fits and starts, and never the same way twice.

My recommended guidelines for reading this particular book are as follows:

- ✔ First, flip through and look at all the cartoons. (You're going to do that anyway. Why fight the inevitable?) The cartoons only make comments about what's in the book and may teach you nothing about scripting. But enjoy . . . and come back after you've read them.

- ✔ Flip through and read all the "Test your newfound knowledge" quizzes. (You find these quizzes in sidebars at the end of several chapters.) They may sound pretty silly, but you'll probably pick up a bit of useful information, if that's okay. And these quizzes have more jokes per line than any other part of the text. So, read them early.

- ✔ Next, start at the end. (Why not? This is a . . .*For Dummies* book.) Read through "The Part of Tens." Every book should have a section like this one, and I'm talking from *Moby Dick* right on down. In this part, you truly get the gist of things — the few basic commands you need to know (out of the thousands available), an understandable meaning for scripting terms like *variable* and *property* (that can drive you nuts if you think these words mean what they mean in English), and other fundamental things like that. Cut out Part VI and carry it around in your pocket, purse, backpack, shoe, or whatever.

- ✔ Read whatever else you want, in whatever order you want. Try out any examples that you want, whenever you want, in whatever order you want.

    ✔ Sit back somewhere — on the beach, on the commuter train, on the sofa on a Sunday — and read for enjoyment. "Yeah, right," you're saying, "A computer book I'd read for enjoyment." Maybe not, but it's just a thought.

    ✔ Toss the book on the desktop by your computer — not too far away — and turn to it whenever you need help with LotusScript. Not every LotusScript detail is in *LotusScript For Dummies*, but you can find enough to get you going in the right direction on most topics. And you find out how to get the most out of a LotusScript syntax statement, for that random occasion when you must turn to the LotusScript Help files.

Who This Book Is For

This book is *. . .For Dummies* — it says that, right on the cover. Do you know what I find, though? All of us have subjects for which we think that we're *dummies*. And when I say that I've written a book *for dummies*, I always hear the same response: "That sounds like the right book for me!" I've had an internationally acclaimed scholar say that to me; I've heard it from an experienced programmer and consultant . . . that same phrase has come from lots of high-tech wizards, from top business people, and even from my mother.

Often, people who are new to some interesting topic want to begin with a book that's easy, and maybe one that isn't stiff and formal all the time. This book on LotusScript — relaxed, a little bit funny here and there — is for *everybody*, really. But it's especially for everybody whose mood supports an easy approach to the subject of LotusScript.

What about experienced programmers? Would such people find value in this book? Hey, I'm not ready to surrender that audience completely either. It's not likely that even a programmer has been over the full breadth of LotusScript. And some programmers aren't yet experienced in working with OOP (object-oriented programming). So if you're a programmer, you can get a quick, plain-English introduction to OOP and a great overview of LotusScript's capabilities in the different Lotus products.

This book, then, is *. . .For Dummies*. If you're wondering whether that includes you, well sure, why not?

How This Book Is Organized

You don't have to read this book in order, you know. I wrote it with the idea of *skipping-around* in mind. For example, you don't get a bunch of definitions in Chapter 1 that you then need in all the rest of the chapters. You can skip around to find what you need. I did try to put the easier stuff near the front of the book and the harder stuff later, but the truth is: It's all kind of hard. And I did try (somewhat) to put topics into an *order of utility* so that you can find out about things in more or less the order you're likely to use them. I know that what one person needs isn't necessarily what another person needs; therefore, if the order-of-utility system breaks down for you, just skip around to find what you need.

The following shows you the parts of the book with a brief summary of what's in them.

Part I — Reading the Compass: Getting Oriented in LotusScript

Part I is kind of like a head start. You get your bearings in LotusScript and find out where you'll be going on your scripting journey. And you can get a taste of real scripting by writing a couple of basic scripts. You also find out about LotusScript's integrated development environment — the so-called IDE — the windows that you work in as you script.

Part II — Getting Your Equipment in Order for the Trek

Do you want to know what you work with all the time when you're scripting . . . the one thing you work with to get your results? Variables. In Part II, you find out about variables and their associate scripting elements: operators, key-words, statements, expressions, comments, and so on. You get an introduction to another scripting tool, the Dialog Editor, too.

Part III — Lost in the Wilderness: Loops, Ifs, Subs, and So On

If statements. You're not really a scripter until you write them. And if you get serious about scripting, you write If statements all the time. In Part III, I give you a chance to get tangled up in your first one. You also get a chance to wander through other programming structures: loops, subs, and functions. Of course, you can make ever fancier scripts as you go!

Part IV — Claiming New Territories: Scripting Lotus Products

Hey, face it. LotusScript is for Lotus products, not for creating neat stand-alone programs. Finding out about OOP (object-oriented programming) in Part IV gets you ready for working with the whole family of products.

The statements in LotusScript are the same in all products. Other things may be different, though. In Part IV, I help you find out how to use LotusScript in Word Pro and Approach.

Part V — Claiming More New Territories: Scripting Other Lotus Products

In Part V, you get the big skinny on using LotusScript with Lotus 1-2-3, Freelance Plus, and Notes.

Part VI — The Part of Tens

I love this part. I can think of all kinds of things that I want to summarize for you, to make your life easier — things I wish somebody had summarized for me. The summaries are in Part VI: the most important statements, the confusing error messages, the terms that ought to mean one thing but mean something else to LotusScript. I hope you get a chance to, at least, scan this part.

Icons Used in This Book

I find this fact kind of interesting: When I wrote a . . .*For Dummies* book on Word Pro (*Word Pro For Windows 95 For Dummies,* IDG Books Worldwide, Inc., 1995), I was forever offering *Tips.* With this book, I had to put in a lot of icons that notify you of *Technical Stuff.* That is, the stuff that's just hard enough that I wanted to give you the option of skipping it (in the interest of keeping your sanity).

Actually, I use several icons throughout the book to point out some particularly good, scary, important, or otherwise significant bit of information:

LotusScript comes with little shortcuts that can make your life a lot "pleasanter" if you use them. Tips are things you don't have to know to get your work done, but you're usually glad if you do know.

This book may as well have a Technical Stuff icon right on the cover. I mean, the whole book is technical stuff. Some material is particularly tricky, convoluted, confusing, or otherwise hard. Sometimes that same stuff is pretty essential, though. When I talk about it, I tack one of these icons in front of it, and you can know what to skip. Or, you can read at your own risk.

Certain areas of LotusScript can be a bit unnerving and may create extra confusion. Or maybe LotusScript ought to do certain things that it just doesn't. I slap on this Warning icon to try to save you from a Catch-22.

The Good to Know icon marks the end of chapter quizzes that help you "Test your newfound knowledge."

Certain things about LotusScript are just really important to remember.

I take great delight in using the Programmerese icon to point out the peculiar language of programmers, or the terms and structures that are common to all kinds of programming languages.

I like to tell stories about my own misadventures in scripting, or about some great scripting discovery that I've made. Somebody decided to put an icon in front of stories like that, and the idea stuck, so you'll see these icons, too.

Where to Go from Here

To the cartoons.

Part I
Reading the Compass: Getting Oriented in LotusScript

The 5th Wave   By Rich Tennant

"This system came bundled with a suite of office products and some kid called a "scripter.""

In this part . . .

Before you head out on your expedition, you may want to lay out your equipment, check your maps, and have a good orientation meeting with a naturalist of some sort. Part I gets you oriented for your scripting adventures. You find out why you want to go on this journey. You write a small program (sort of a test journey, where you keep the campgrounds in sight). You write a little-bit-bigger program. You check out valuable equipment — the LotusScript Script Editor. And you find out how to solve problems, which inevitably come up . . . on an expedition or in scripting.

Chapter 1

Why Would You Want to Write Scripts Anyway?

*A*s you contemplate your approach to the LotusScript programming language, do you find yourself asking this question: "Why would I want to write a script anyway?"

"After all," your question to yourself continues, "in these computer programs, like Word Pro and Notes, I can already find a million more things to do than I want to do, just on the menus. Why would I want to write a script and give myself more choices?"

As one small example, in Word Pro, you can already — oh, I don't know — create a table with as many rows and columns as you want and color some of the rows green (*any* shade of green). You can drag and drop the rows or just what's in the rows. Nowadays, you can seemingly do about anything in any of the Lotus SmartSuite programs. As for the whole suite, well, it has more options than anyone can even contemplate using. The scope is downright bewildering. Even the people who *write* the programs can't keep track of all you can do with them.

So, if you can do so much with these Lotus programs already, why would you want to write a script in the first place? Let's face it — lots of people don't. Scripting is too hard. What are subroutines, variables, and all those programming things? The truth of the matter is this: People *do* want and need scripts . . . even though, to be honest, most people would rather have somebody else write the scripts for them.

In this chapter, I show you the long-term, real-world benefits of learning and applying such admittedly hard stuff as scripts. I include specific examples, tell you which Lotus software packages make use of LotusScript, and describe everyday activities that use scripting within and among these packages. In the process, I help you answer the question posed at the beginning of the chapter, "Why would I want to write a script anyway?"

People are Lazy, and Scripts Love to Work

The fact is that we, as people, are just plain lazy. Therefore, we want scripts. True, making the script in the first place may take a little brain juice. We're so lazy, though, that we're willing to invest a little now so that we can kick back later.

Laziness may not be a popular term to apply, but I'm just trying to get your attention. So I'll rephrase: People love efficiency. They hate doing repetitive tasks. People want to please their employers and fellow workers by doing the best job possible in the shortest possible time. There! Is that a more acceptable way of putting it? I like the first way, though — I believe people are lazy and, in my opinion, have every right to be. Why should they waste time doing some menial task that the computer can do for them?

Heading toward custom automation

Whoever designed the program that you're using — Freelance Graphics, Word Pro, or whatever — can't know the special things that you are going to do with it. Sure, the Freelance designers can assume that you're going to do a slide presentation. But they don't know that the presentation is for the National Association of Hospital Employees and that you want to put in statistics that you've compiled in Lotus Notes on how many breaks hospital workers take each day (and how many of them go outside to smoke cigarettes during that time). Only you know that.

If you want to pull in statistics on hospital worker smoking habits and project these statistics into a screen show at the press of a single key, you have to set up the script for that task yourself. The market for such a script isn't big enough for the Lotus people to build it into the program. (Besides, the Lotus in-house programmers just can't think of everything.) The program developers can only automate so far, and you have to do the rest. That's where scripts come in.

Looking at LotusScript in a nutshell

In a nutshell, I believe that using LotusScript has these advantages for you:

- ✔ It helps you save time by automating repetitive or redundant tasks.
- ✔ It helps you combine the information and resources from different programs.
- ✔ It helps you create easy-to-use applications with increased interactivity.
- ✔ It lets you be lazy without getting into trouble for it.
- ✔ It serves as a great introduction to concepts and terms that are common to many programming environments.

And you can integrate all the following products by using LotusScript:

- ✔ All the Lotus SmartSuite 97 programs
  - Lotus 1-2-3 97
  - Lotus Approach 97
  - Lotus Freelance Graphics 97
  - Lotus Organizer 97
  - Lotus Word Pro 97
- ✔ Lotus Notes Release 4

Setting Your Sights on Scripting

Scripting is a pretty neat name. It sounds like what Shakespeare did, or what modern screenwriters do, too. It sounds adventurous and creative. The person using LotusScript can devise a whole intelligent creation where mere flatness existed before.

Or, to come down to earth a little, the person writing a script can do a little bit now that saves a lot of work later, and scripts can do things for people that they may not know how to do for themselves. Suppose that a person wants to pull sales data from Lotus Notes into Freelance and present it all using the same SmartMasters that the company always uses in those presentations. Well, maybe the person doesn't know how to pull in the data from Notes, and maybe that eager presenter doesn't know which *SmartMaster* (kind of like a template) is the standard.

LotusScript can be right there doing the work so that the presenter doesn't have to know. He just has to interpret the data, saying such things as, "Boy, we sure don't sell many chrysanthemum bulbs in January, as you can see from this data. Maybe we should give our sales people a pep talk."

Some real people who write real LotusScript applications for real companies have been kind enough to share information with me about what they do, or plan to do, with scripts.

Everyday examples — timesheets and expense reports

I have a friend who regularly keeps track of his billable time in Lotus Notes. Before he wrote a script to automate the task, he had to reenter data for the projects he worked on before he could bill his client. That is, he reentered the same time information (that was already in Lotus Notes) into a Lotus 1-2-3 spreadsheet and gave the spreadsheet to the client along with his invoice.

Now, whenever anybody rekeys anything, a light bulb goes on in someone's head. "Wait a minute . . . I see wasted effort here. Somebody could use a script to do this."

My friend is now writing a script where he begins in Word Pro, pulls in the time data from Lotus Notes, and places it into a table in Word Pro. "The output will be slicker than it was from my old spreadsheet," he tells me, "and I will not have to reenter my times and work descriptions." He's a LotusScript guru at his company. After he gets the application done, other members of his company can use it as well. None of them has to keep reentering information, and they can all have that slick Word Pro output. You could call it laziness. Or smartness. Or good business. Using LotusScript for this application automates what was pretty automated already — Lotus Notes, 1-2-3, and Word Pro.

Is the urge starting for you? When you hear about people doing these time-saving things, do you just naturally begin to itch a little bit to do them for yourself? Maybe you can automate everything but your own creative thinking and spend the whole business day doing just that (which is precisely why I'm talking about these things in the first chapter of the book — to inspire you to derive some of the benefits of LotusScript).

I have yet another example from my same friend, the programmer analyst. When he travels, he has trouble (and who among us doesn't?) keeping track of what expenses he has and hasn't been reimbursed for. He used to put all his expenses into a Lotus 1-2-3 spreadsheet and just hope he could remember what he had submitted already. But now, he's designing a Lotus Notes database that tracks expenses and readily separates the submitted expenses from the unsubmitted ones. Then, by using LotusScript, he plans to build an interface with Word Pro so that he can submit the expenses on a beautiful-looking form.

(He also told me, ambitiously, that he's designing a script that makes use of the complete Notes suite. That will be cool to see. . . .)

Another example — questionnaires

Okay, this scripting example may not relate so much to *laziness* as to *keeping people out of your hair*. (Same difference, really.)

In one project at a large government organization, employees with very little computer experience have to fill out forms on the computer for people applying for financial assistance. The managers of these information-takers want the employees to record the right information, put it in the right places, and do it fast . . . all without having to go through special training or bothering somebody else who is an expert on filling in computer forms.

So, the managers bring in a forms expert at the beginning of the whole project and have that expert use LotusScript to make all aspects of filling out the computerized form as easy as possible. A script can help with the form-filling task in the following ways:

- ✔ **By recommending responses:** When the person entering data comes to a field on the form that says `Highest educational level`, the LotusScript program can pop up a list with the three or four appropriate choices. The person can click on a choice from the list to fill in that field.

- ✔ **By automatically moving through the form:** After the form-filler completes each field, the script moves on to the next appropriate blank to fill in on the form.

- ✔ **By verifying that the form is complete:** When the form-completers think that all needed information is filled in, they try to file the form permanently. Then, the LotusScript script can check over the form to see whether the nonexpert completing the form has done everything that the experts who designed the form wanted done. That is, a LotusScript script can look over the form and tell the user about any information that may be missing.

In this example, a well-designed LotusScript script can take the place of a forms expert, a social issues expert, and a computer expert — right there holding the hand of the person filling in the form on the computer.

Enabling smart investing

Another friend of mine is a programmer/analyst at a brokerage firm in New York. He's so busy that I haven't been able to get him to tell me exactly what applications he develops for the brokers he serves. He does admit to me, though, that these highly paid, motivated brokers line up at his desk and use all kinds of tricks to get him to develop scripts for them. They want to save time and get results fast . . . so they can make more money.

They may want scripts to pull in stock quotes automatically over the Internet and put them right into 1-2-3, where they can "crunch" them and gain an edge over their competitors. They may want standardized sales letters that automatically pull in clients' names and enticing information (stored in Lotus Notes) about future investments for them.

I'm not sure exactly what they want, but I can't get the picture out of my mind of these crackerjack Wall Street types lined up at the desk of the LotusScripter just waiting their turn for his help. Scripting must have real value in the real world, or those people wouldn't be waiting in line.

Doing whatever, whenever

Finally, another power-programmer friend wrote to me (eight months after I asked him for input) to confess that he didn't know at first what he wanted to do with LotusScript. But he liked the fact that he could do *whatever* he wanted, *whenever* he wanted. (Such freedom is power, and after all, he is a power programmer.)

My friend's large, international company hires hundreds of people per month and automates everything that happens to the new hires within the first couple of days. These happenings include issuing security badges, scheduling new-hire briefings, coordinating telephone and LAN connections, and lots of stuff. For the hundreds of employees that leave the company, similar kinds of things happen — turning off phones and LAN connections, turning in ID badges, scheduling extended benefits briefings, and so on.

The company uses a combination of Lotus Notes and Lotus SmartSuite applications. When the Human Resources person puts a new employee into the database (or takes one out), this database activity serves as the trigger for other little programs to accomplish all the scheduling, coordinating, connecting, and everything. As my programmer friend sees it, LotusScript provides the perfect flexibility in this situation. Whenever an unanticipated need arises for the HR department or the new employee — something that Lotus Notes or Lotus SmartSuite doesn't already automate — my friend can easily write a script to meet the need.

Scripting — Adventures in Programming Land

Of course, to accomplish all the automating that it does, LotusScript would have to be a lot like a programming language — a lot like one. In fact, you may as well face it now: LotusScript *is* a programming language. As a form of the good, old BASIC programming language (that you've at least heard of), LotusScript has all the usual things that go into programming languages — subs, variables, functions, loops, and even the very modern objects. LotusScript is an adventure . . . full of fun rides, amazing discoveries, and a few pitfalls.

A down side to all of this scripting – downsizing

Of course, I can hear the objections coming up. The down side to automating is always that it can lead to downsizing. It can cost people their jobs. Before the capabilities of scripting, somebody had to track down all the information from the database and key it into the spreadsheet. Now, the script transfers the data, and somebody loses a few minutes of paying work (and at larger companies, perhaps someone loses a job).

Before the capabilities of scripting, an office employee had to take those calls from people filling in unintelligible computerized forms. Now, with a LotusScript script recommending responses to the questions on the form, you don't need the employee to do it.

Before the capabilities of scripting, stock brokers and salespeople needed assistants to help them gather information and handle client contact. Now, with a LotusScript script automatically downloading data and creating personalized correspondence, the need for assistants decreases.

I can hear the objections. Look, I don't want to appear politically insensitive or anything, but, hey, you know, I can't really get into a discussion like that. It's hard enough getting the scripts to work; I can't be deciding whether, in the overall order of the universe, scripts may be costing some people their jobs.

I'm guessing that scripting will create some jobs here and there — for the scripters. And scripting may create jobs for the companies that grow really fast because their scripts make them competitive. Scripting may create some jobs, and it may eliminate some. But after all, this is just a . . .*For Dummies* book about how to script. I don't expect to solve a major economic issue of our time.

Chapter 2

"Good-bye, Cruel World": Writing Your Really Basic BASIC Program

● ●

In This Chapter

▶ Beating the system by scripting without typing in commands

▶ Running that script you wrote

▶ Writing the world's simplest script

▶ Getting your script to do something to your document

● ●

*A*fter playing with scripts a bit in preparation for this chapter, I can sort of see why, until the . . .*For Dummies* books came along, normal people never became programmers. (In fact, a good example of an oxymoron may have been "normal person programmer.") If you weren't that special breed of nonverbal geek who loved mind twisters, you'd turn tail at the very first explanations you came to when finding out about programming.

Okay, for example, suppose you started reading about BASIC with the *LotusScript Language Reference* from Lotus Development Corporation (1995). This next quote is practically the first line on page 1-1. (See, programmers even assign page numbers in a scary way.)

> "The statements of a script are composed of lines of text. Each text element is a LotusScript keyword, operator, identifier, literal, or special character."

Yikes! You know what I'm saying? I mean, of course a script is lines of text. Why even bother to point that out? But after that, things get hairy. If you've been around programming before, then I realize that you're just soaking up the information and reading on to the next rule, which, in case you're curious, states,

> "The script can include blank lines without effect."

For most people, though, the crisis hits right away. What if you don't know what a keyword or an operator (or an identifier, literal, or special character) *is?* You may know what the words mean in English, but each word has a highly specialized meaning as it relates to LotusScript. You couldn't know that LotusScript meaning unless you already knew LotusScript. It's a classic Catch-22: If you need the help, you don't know enough to get it — if you know enough, you don't need the help.

Do you go and look up *keywords,* then *operators,* and so on (and you know each word has a cross-reference) and try to remember what you read as you look up the others? Then, laden with all that new information, do you begin writing lines of code?

No, you don't read on. You go buy a cup of cappuccino and a bag of popcorn, you give them to a person wearing bib overalls and wire-rimmed glasses, and you say, "I wonder, please, if you could just help me with a little programming. Please. Please. Please."

Well, I'm not sure that you can find an easier way to start scripting than to get someone else to do it, but sometimes you just want to do it yourself. Maybe you and I can create a little *code* here (as programmers insist on referring to their programs) without even learning a bunch of definitions first. Then, maybe I can slip the definitions past you — introducing each LotusScript element as you meet it in practice — and ease you into scripting without your even realizing anything has happened.

Recording and Running a Script (Without Writing Code)

The easiest way I know to write a script (other than having someone else write it for you) is to *record* it. Then you don't actually write any lines of code yourself. If you don't write the actual code yourself, character-by-character, but let the computer record it, you don't run as much danger of leaving out a parenthesis, a period, or something. And you minimize the risk of putting in a blank space where it doesn't belong or doing one of the million other nit-picking things that you can do wrong when writing a program. (These little errors aren't as big an obstacle as you may think. Everybody makes little typos, even folks in bib overalls and wire rims.)

Recording what you do in a script

You can write the following script in any of the Lotus products that I listed in Chapter 1, but for this example, I'm going to use Word Pro. Not only is choosing Word Pro for my example a natural choice to get you familiar with LotusScript, but I also have another good reason. That is, when I began writing this book, I actually had Word Pro in its latest version with fully functional LotusScript.

Follow these steps to create a script in Word Pro without writing a single character of code yourself:

1. **If you haven't done so yet, click the Word Pro icon to start the program.**

2. **In the Welcome to Lotus Word Pro dialog box, choose Create➪Plain Document. A plain Word Pro screen comes up.**

3. **Choose Edit➪Script & Macros. A submenu appears.**

   To help keep you from getting lost right at the beginning, Figure 2-1 shows you a picture of the menus so far.

4. **From the submenu, choose Record Script.**

   A Record Script dialog box comes up — see Figure 2-2 — with some rather perplexing choices, but you don't have to think about any of them right now.

5. **Click OK.**

   At this moment, you have the power to create elaborate scripts, automating all kinds of activities in LotusScript. Whatever you do (like typing a word, pressing Enter, and so on) until you stop recording, LotusScript records and turns into code. I'm starting with something simple.

6. **Type** `rabbit`**.**

   It doesn't matter what you type, but I just like rabbits.

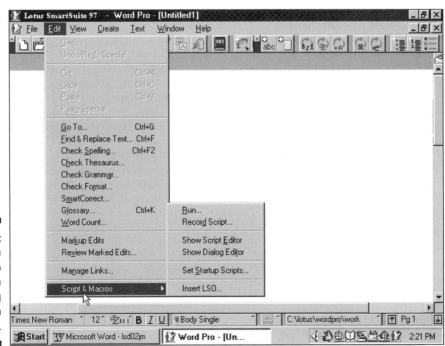

Figure 2-1:
Use these
menus to
reach the
scripting
tools in
Word Pro.

Record Script ×

Welcome to the Script Assistant
Turn on this assistant to record your actions. When you have finished recording, choose Edit Script & Macros Stop Recording. You can use Edit Script & Macros Run to replay your actions.

OK

Cancel

Help

Choose where to store the recorded script:

● Into this file. Enter the name for your script: `Main`

○ Into another file. Enter the filename: `_____`   Browse...

○ Into the script editor at the current location

Figure 2-2:
Just click OK in the Record Script dialog box.

7. **Hold down Shift and press Home to highlight the word(s) you typed on the line.**

8. **Click the B icon at the bottom of the screen.**

   I think you've done enough for this simple introductory script. You've typed a word, selected the text on the line, and made it bold (even though making a rabbit bold is actually pretty hard, because rabbits, by nature, are shy and reclusive).

9. **Choose Edit⇨Script & Macros⇨Stop Recording.**

   The Script Editor comes up with some lines of code in it, as shown in Figure 2-3. Now, admittedly, these lines of code may appear to be nearly indecipherable gibberish as you first embark on scripting. That's all right. The point is that you have it — actual LotusScript code. Get a look and feel for it. Before long, you'll know what `Sub Main` and `.Type` and `!Globals` all mean. You will. But the important thing, for now, is just to be careful not to mess up the code that you see (which is easier to do than you may think).

If you mess up your Script Editor while you're just experimenting around, the easiest way to get a fresh start is just to close the untitled document and the Script Editor and create a new document. The new document will have a new, clean version of the Script Editor along with it. Sometimes knowing how to get a fresh start is important, and doing so is easier with scripts than with, say, marriage.

You can't close just the Script Editor and reopen it, though; your old script will just come back. Each document has its own Script Editor. You have to close the document and start a new one.

At first, the script created by the script recorders seems truly awe-inspiring, as if handed down from the heavens. After I became more comfortable with scripting, though, I noticed that I often improve on the recorder's scripts by putting in my preferred syntax by hand. In this way, I make the scripts easier to follow for myself and more intuitive for someone else who may happen to read

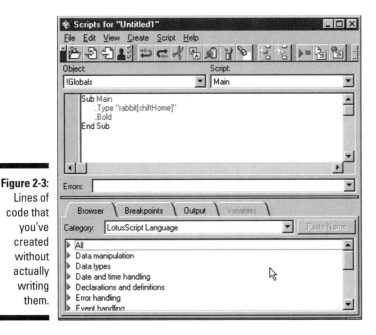

Figure 2-3:
Lines of
code that
you've
created
without
actually
writing
them.

them later. If you wonder how *you're* ever going to improve on these automatic scripts, I'll point out that you come across a number of guidelines for good scripting in the course of this book, and a summary of such principles is in The Part of Tens, in Chapter 26.

Running the script

After you've created a script — cool as it may look, with its *dots* (programmerese for *periods*) and all — it doesn't amount to much until you *run it*. Also, you can't tell if it really works unless you run it. Before doing much more, you can save the file with the name *Rabbit* if you like (and if you want your screens to be identical to those in the book.) Also, if you like, you can press Enter a couple times in the Word Pro document (not in the Script Editor) so that you can see the results on a separate line when you run the script. (To get back and forth between the Script Editor and the document, you can just point and click. Point and click in the document to get there. Point and click back in the Script Editor to get back there. A safe place to click, so as not to change anything by mistake, is on the title bar at the top.)

You can find at least three different ways to run a script; this is an easy way:

1. **With the Script Editor open, click Script to drop down the Script menu, as shown in Figure 2-4.**

   The Script Editor comes up automatically after you record a script; see the previous section for instructions on recording a script.

2. **Click Run Current Sub from the drop-down menu.**

   "What sub?" you may reasonably wonder. "I don't see any submarine." The *sub* refers to the script currently displayed in the Script Editor. Many programs are known throughout the programming world as *subroutines,* or *subs* for short.

If all goes well, LotusScript prints the word **rabbit** in the Word Pro document (and puts it in bold type). It's amazing. You created a script and ran it, and you still may not know what a keyword, operator, or identifier is. And you haven't had to buy any popcorn for anyone, except maybe for yourself to ease you through the anxiety of creating your first piece of LotusScript code.

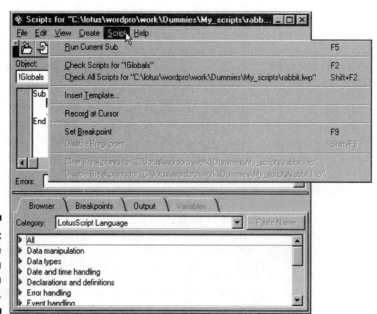

Figure 2-4:
Using the
Script menu
to run
a script.

Scouting out the very basic history of BASIC languages

LotusScript, I hasten to tell you, is a form of the BASIC programming language. You don't have to memorize this for a test tomorrow or anything, but the original BASIC developers were John Kemeny and Thomas Kurtz at Dartmouth College in Hanover, New Hampshire. While much of the '60s generation was indulging in fraternity beer blasts or picketing campus buildings, a few computer zealots were inside one of the buildings developing a computer language.

Previous languages must have been mind-benders indeed, because BASIC was considered a breakthrough in ease of use.

BASIC's biggest contribution was that it used an *interpreter* to follow along as you typed each line, and the interpreter checked each line for accuracy. Before development of the BASIC language, you had to put your whole program together, run it, and then try to find your mistakes.

Also, BASIC replaced arcane and largely indecipherable codes with *English-like* commands like those you see in this book — Call statements, Print statements, If . . . Then, and things like that (which were *user-friendly* in a truly user-hostile time).

I think that the completely unintelligible nature of its predecessors somewhat gave BASIC a sense of complacency. If you are a ten-year-old playing baseball with preschoolers, you can think you're the best player who ever walked. BASIC, likewise, developed an illusion that it was easy and English-like early on when, in fact, it is not truly much of either. To many users, especially those coming to it fresh from using their native language, BASIC is both hard and machine-like. It all depends on your perspective.

In any case, I think that the fact that BASIC's name doesn't mean *simple*, as one might hope, speaks volumes about its essentially academic, scientific, and difficult nature. The name *BASIC* actually stands for something important-sounding — *Beginner's All-purpose Symbolic Instruction Code*.

BASIC caught on because it was, at least, a remotely manageable programming language for someone who wasn't willing to put in years of training. BASIC went through a number of incarnations: BASICA, GW-BASIC, and QBasic, which aren't important any more. You may remember seeing these incarnations (and avoiding them) on IBM PCs that you owned.

In 1991, Microsoft brought out Visual Basic, which was much more important than any of its predecessors. Visual Basic helped programmers prepare user interfaces (dialog boxes, menus, and the various things you see on the screen) by using simple icons and menus instead of having to write elaborate code for them. Visual Basic is now an integral part of the rapidly burgeoning world of Windows programming.

LotusScript, together with its dialog editor (discussed in Chapters 8 and 9), has much in common with Visual Basic. And — for better and for worse — LotusScript descends from the long line of seemingly simple, but actually quite difficult, *symbolic instruction codes* that started out as a major breakthrough at the ivied halls of Dartmouth College.

Creating and Running a Script of Your Own

"Okay, okay," I can hear the skeptics among you grousing. "Well, I don't really write any code when I use the Record Script command. I just record it, and LotusScript makes the code for me automatically. Sure, it *looks* like code, but I could never do that myself. This is a fraud. A cheap trick. I still can't program a single line."

Writing a little actual code

Just wait a second — I have every confidence that you can write code! And I want you to try writing some code from scratch right now. The example in the following steps uses LotusScript along with Word Pro. To get ready, close your current Script Editor and document, if you have any open, and create a new, plain document. Then do these steps:

1. **Choose Edit➪Script & Macros➪Show Script Editor to get yourself into the Script Editor.**

   The Script Editor is really a separate program (that runs inside your Lotus application) where you create your scripts. I mean, you could write scripts inside the document, instead of inside the Script Editor, but they wouldn't run or anything. You could go out and write your scripts in the gravel in the driveway, too, but . . . you know what I'm saying? You have to put your scripts into the Script Editor to have them really be LotusScript code.

   In whatever Lotus program you're using, dragging the Show Script Editor SmartIcon into the icon toolbar at the top is a good idea. With this SmartIcon, you can open the Script Editor with a single click whenever you want it. To find out how to do that, you can go out and buy my book *Word Pro For Windows 95 For Dummies*, also by IDG Books Worldwide, Inc.

   But actually, adding the Show Script Editor SmartIcon to your toolbar is not very hard: In any of the SmartSuite products, choose File➪User Setup➪SmartIcons Setup and drag the SmartIcon you want to the bar at the top.

2. **Click in the blank line between the line that says** Sub Main **and the one that says** End Sub.

   Word Pro puts in the words Sub Main and End Sub for you so that you begin writing a program that is the Main subroutine for the current LotusScript program you're creating. The Main subroutine is not really *sub* (under) anything you can see, because it's actually the top program in the script. And nothing is routine about this if you're writing a script for the first time. It's just a terminology thing. When writing a script, you need a beginning, an ending, and a name for the program, so LotusScript supplies them.

3. Type these words:

```
Print "Good-bye, Cruel World."
```

Figure 2-5 shows the Script Editor with the line typed in it, just as you can type it if you're following along.

Be sure to put in the quotation marks at the beginning and the end.

Many BASIC programming books begin with a "Hello, World," program, except this one, which begins, "Good-bye, Cruel World." It really doesn't matter what short phrase you type (within certain restrictions, such as staying on one line). The word Print is a LotusScript *keyword,* which means that it is a word with a special meaning within LotusScript. And the line, Print "Good-bye, Cruel World", including the keyword, is a LotusScript *statement.* (There, I've slipped two of the definitions that I mentioned at the start of the chapter past you, but now you can see what they mean as you use them. I think that's easier.)

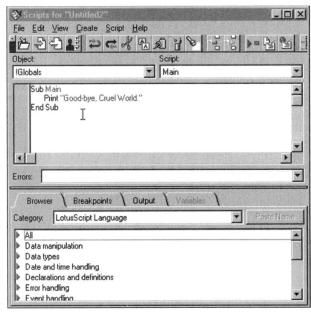

Figure 2-5:
A very simple program, a Main subroutine, as LotusScript calls it.

Paying attention to those picky rules for LotusScript statements

LotusScript's designers actually get pretty picky about what constitutes a statement. I showed you an example here, with the `Print` statement. But I guess that exactly what each item (character, line, space, or whatever) in the statement happens to be matters a lot when something as literal-minded as a computer has to read it. And Lotus must think that statement format is important, because the LotusScript documentation contains eight rules for formatting your statements. If you want to know all the exact ins and outs of a LotusScript statement, I present my paraphrased and summarized version of the Lotus directives here.

✔ You make statements by typing in lines of text. (Here we have the obvious for you — right at the start.) On those lines of text, you put LotusScript keywords, operators, identifiers, literals, or special characters. (I talk about these terms in Chapters 6 and 7.)

✔ You can have blank lines in the script — it's okay. (Having blank lines is nice because you can make things look better by adding a blank line now and then.)

✔ You can indent text, or not. Often, the Script Editor indents for you, so you don't have to worry about it. One of the principles of good programming is to use indents to make the script easy to follow.

✔ You separate elements within a statement with either spaces or tabs. In places where LotusScript allows white space (spaces or tabs), you can put in more than one space or tab.

✔ LotusScript expects you to put one statement per line. If you go to a new line, you have finished the statement you are on. (*Block statements,* statements whose influence reaches past the end of the line and includes all the lines until the end of the statement, are the exception to this rule. The *Sub* statement is an example of a block statement.)

✔ If you want to have multiple statements on a line for some strange reason, LotusScript expects you to put colons (:) between them.

✔ You can put a statement on more than one line by using the line continuation character — known more humbly as an *underscore* (_) — preceded by a white space.

✔ If you are really dying to put something on the same line after the line continuation character, you can put in an apostrophe (') and type in a comment. But that's all you can put there (except blank spaces).

These guidelines, I know, are too much to remember. People learn them by violating them and then finding out that LotusScript won't work unless they play by its restrictive (to say the least) rules.

The many faces of script-running

I show you how to run a script from within the Script Editor in the "Running the script" section, earlier in the chapter, and I mention that you can find at least three ways to run a script. If you're looking for more ways to run scripts, the following sections help you out with a bit more information.

Running "Good-bye, Cruel World" inside the Script Editor

You can run the script for "Good-bye, Cruel World" by selecting from the Script Editor menus, but I'm recommending a shortcut instead. See the instructions in the "Writing a little actual code" section to set up your script (if you haven't already) in the Script Editor. Then do the following:

1. **With the cursor still in the Script Editor (and not, say, in the document, or out in the driveway), press F5.**

    Nothing seems to happen, except that you begin to develop a complex and think, "See, I knew I could never program. Mine didn't work. Everybody else's worked, all over the world. This is *Chapter 2*, for goodness sake. I should be able to do this, but noooo. Mine doesn't work."

    Wait. Hooold on there. Yes, your script does work. You need one more step.

2. **In the lower half of the Script Editor, in what its designers refer to as the *Utilities Panel,* click the Output tab.**

    The phrase "Good-bye, Cruel World" appears on this tab, as shown in Figure 2-6.

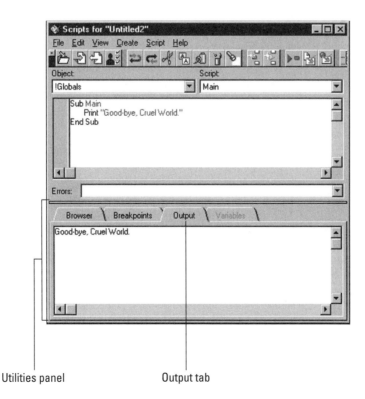

Figure 2-6:
When you use `Print`, your output appears here.

Utilities panel   Output tab

Marketing people always like to turn defects into virtues, as in, "These pants wear out easily in the knees, which keeps you in fashion with modern young people." In this case, you really can (no kidding) see the fact that the `Print` statement puts its results only into the Output panel, not into the document, as a virtue. First of all, the results don't go cluttering up your document. Mainly, though, `Print` is very useful for trying out your lines of code and *debugging them* (fixing mistakes) before substituting a keyword that causes the script results to show up in Word Pro or whichever Lotus program you're using.

Changing the script to show output in the document

As useful as it might be, in a navel-gazing way, to use `Print` and have results appear only inside the Script Editor, having your output appear where others can see it, like in the document, is probably much more useful. And doing that isn't hard; you just use another keyword instead of `Print`.

1. **With the "Good-bye, Cruel World" example still in the Script Editor, double-click on the keyword** `Print` **to highlight it.**

2. **Type the following to replace the keyword** `Print`:

```
.Type
```

This new keyword replaces the previous one. Figure 2-7 shows the changed subroutine.

Figure 2-7:
A subroutine using the .Type method.

When programmers talk about periods (the punctuation mark), they call them *dots*. This is one happy case where programmer-speak is actually less complicated than plain English. Thus, the command you typed in the example is called *dot type*, because it has an unobtrusive-looking but highly important period in front of the keyword.

That little punctuation mark — whatever you choose to call it — is essential. If you put it there in front of `Type`, you use the *dot type method*, and everything is cool. You get the result. If you leave out the dot, you get annoying error messages from LotusScript.

The dot in dot type is carrying a terrible weight, if the truth be known. It tells the program to run the instruction right there in that document. The small piece of script you are typing is actually part of a vast, interconnected universe of code, and the dot helps LotusScript to locate itself in the present moment. This discussion has to do with object-oriented programming (OOP) and dot notation, which I talk about in Chapter 14 (having put it off as long as possible by then).

Please don't feel you should look ahead and go over OOP now. I just wanted to let you know that the dot is important, so I could save you from some of the endless ruminating (over the silly little punctuation point) that I went through while working on my program.

Starting the script from the document

With the `.Type` method in place, you can run the script to see how the output works for this structure. I've shown you two ways to run a subroutine — choosing from the Script menu and pressing F5. Now I'll show you a third way to run a sub; you may choose this approach if you're running a script that another scripter has written:

1. **In the Script Editor, choose File⇨Close Script Editor to (that's right) close the Script Editor.**

   You find yourself faced with a blank document, just as if you were an ordinary user and didn't know you had just written a script.

2. **From the Word Pro main menu, choose Edit⇨Script & Macros⇨Run.**

   A message box comes up and asks whether to run the script from the current file or one from another file; the message box even allows you to choose which script to run. See Figure 2-8 for a look at this message box. This is one instance, though, where the least action is the best.

3. **Click OK.**

   This time, instead of appearing in the Script Editor (where nobody can see them), the words you placed after the `.Type` method appear in a much more useful place — in your Word Pro document.

Figure 2-8:
Just click
OK in the
Run Script
dialog box.

Test your newfound knowledge

The easiest way to run a script is to:

1. Put a leash around its neck and take it to the park.

2. Push it over a cliff, let it land on its feet, and watch it scramble.

3. Press F5 in the Script Editor.

4. Hire Robert Redford or another famous movie director and ask him or her to make something of the script.

When you use the Print statement, the output shows up:

1. In the driveway.

2. In the attic, behind the old stack of Barbie dolls you're saving for your grandchildren.

3. In the Output panel.

4. In outer space, where its behavior closely approximates a black hole.

Chapter 3

Beyond Basics with Your
Basic BASIC Program

*I*f you practiced writing the simple scripts from Chapter 2, you probably found that scripting can be pretty easy. (Although, if you aren't careful, you can go off the deep end and get confused even in simple scripts.) In this chapter, I show you how to experience more of your own power as a programmer. You get to use statements that programmers themselves use most often: the `Messagebox` and `Inputbox` statements.

In this chapter, the main idea is to advance you further into scripting and (with any luck here) to have you experience success doing it. Even at this level, you begin to encounter a couple of sticky things — like funny symbols that you put in to get things to work and variables that LotusScript needs to do its work. If I liken understanding LotusScript to swimming in a pool, then in this chapter, you may get a mouthful of water or two, but you won't drown or anything.

If you're dying for more in-depth discussion, you can always refer to Chapters 12 and 13 for information about such things as subs and functions. Or later you can pause over these things and see what is really going on when you use these LotusScript elements.

Putting in a Message Box

Most of the time when you're scripting, you're not just scripting for yourself. You're creating programs for others to use. (If you come up with something cool, you may use it yourself, but other people will definitely want to use it.) In the previous chapter, I talked about how to use the .Type method in Word Pro to have script results show up in a document. Using .Type is a start toward sending information to users because it's a step beyond having the information just show up in the Output panel of the Script Editor.

Wouldn't it be neat, though, to have a message box pop up and say something to the user? I can picture all kinds of uses for such a feature. "Not now, Buddy," you could say in a box, whenever somebody tried to exit from a particular spreadsheet. Or, you could ask people, "How's the weather today?" to drive them nuts when they click at random moments. But you also find legitimate uses for message boxes. For example, you can have a message box that pops up when users press the wrong key and guides them toward pressing the right key. When a person clicks a Click Here button — in a SmartMaster in Freelance Graphics, for example — the message box could give important information, such as, "Verify all entries in this list in the company reference manual."

Messagebox is a LotusScript statement that displays a message in a box and then just waits until the user does something (such as click OK).

Writing a Messagebox *script*

Try writing some code that creates a message box. The following example uses the Script Editor in Lotus Approach with a sample document based on the Video and Actor SmartMaster:

1. **Create a new document and click on the Show Script Editor SmartIcon to open the Script Editor.**

   You have to place the Show Script Editor SmartIcon on the SmartIcon bar you're using. See Chapter 2 for instructions on how to do this.

2. **Place the cursor on the blank line between** Sub Main **and** End Sub.

   If the words Sub Main and End Sub are not there already, type Sub Main. LotusScript types in the End Sub automatically.

3. **Type this line of code:**

```
Messagebox "Good-bye, Cruel World."
```

Your lines of script now look like this:

```
Sub Main
    Messagebox "Good-bye, Cruel World."
End Sub
```

Scripting is a tricky business. You have to be very exact in what you put into the script. In this case, you have to put the quotation marks around the words in the message, which is called an *expression* in LotusScript. This particular kind of expression, a *string literal,* requires quotation marks. If you don't put in the quotes, LotusScript doesn't know that the phrase is an expression with a beginning and end.

Now, try running just that one line of code to see the neat message box that LotusScript creates for you.

1. **Press F2, which runs the Script checker for the current sub, to make sure that you have no mistakes in the script.**

   If the Script checker finds any mistakes, the line containing the error turns red, and you see an error message in the list box labeled Errors.

2. **If there are no mistakes, press F5 to run the script. The message box comes up, as shown in Figure 3-1.**

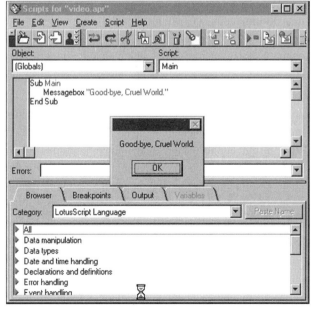

Figure 3-1:
You can make a message box and put any words you want into it.

The `Print` or `.Type` statements aren't nearly as fancy as this, because they only send words to the Output panel or the document. When you use `Messagebox`, this neat message box comes up with an OK button, an X button at the top-right, and everything. Such power at your fingertips!

3. Click OK to get rid of the message box.

Making the most of the online help

Scripting seems to be an endless process of looking up things and finding exactly what you need to do to make a particular LotusScript element work. You can always grab a reference book and look up something. And you can use the Help menu. The best way to look up something fast, though, is to highlight whatever you want to find out about and press F1.

Try using the Help menu with the term *Messagebox,* for example. After you place the cursor on the keyword `Messagebox` in the Script Editor and press F1, help comes in the form of the LotusScript Language Help window, as shown in Figure 3-2.

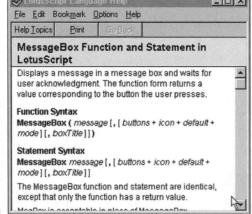

Figure 3-2:
LotusScript
Help
information
for
`Messagebox`.

Actually, when you're looking for a LotusScript command for your script, using the Browser at the bottom of the Script Editor may be even better than using online Help. Click the Browse button, click the item you want from the Browser, and then click the Paste Name button to paste the item into the script you're writing. I talk about the Browser in Chapter 5, but if you're familiar with clicking around in Windows, you may want to start using it right away.

The LotusScript Language Help is aimed mainly at programmers. Unless you're used to working with syntax statements, like the one shown in Figure 3-2, the LotusScript Help may not be that helpful to you. In the section "Reading Descriptions in the Online Reference" near the end of this chapter, I take a . . .*For Dummies* look at those syntax statements. With a few guidelines from this section in mind, you may be able to find what you need in those Help files after all.

Making Your First Input Box Script

You can use another LotusScript statement — Inputbox — to have a box pop up and ask a person to put in some information. When that person puts in information and clicks OK, the statement puts the information back into the program.

Seeing what something like Inputbox does and then explaining it is usually easier than explaining it and then seeing what it does. (Does that make sense?)

Anyway, to try out this other statement, open the Script Editor in a new document or in one with an existing script. (For this example, I'm using the script that I created for the "Writing a Messagebox script" section.) Type in the following statement; I'm using the Sub that contains the Messagebox statement, as shown in Figure 3-3:

```
firstName = Inputbox("What's your name?")
```

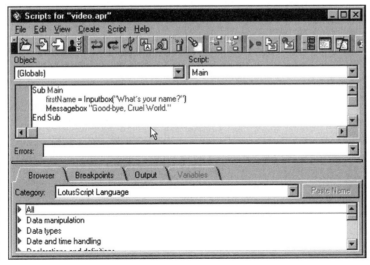

Figure 3-3: Using the Inputbox statement to ask for input.

Your script looks like this, so far:

```
Sub Main
    firstName = Inputbox("What's your name?")
    Messagebox "Good-bye, Cruel World."
End Sub
```

You're going to add another statement before you run the script, though, so don't try running it yet. LotusScript needs more information to work with, and you provide that information with a standard programming device called a *variable*.

Putting in variables to make the script work

You really can't get very far into scripting without running into snags of various sorts. (So now you know the reason that companies pay programmers good money to script for them.) For example, scripts use *variables* to provide places for the script to plug in information. Chapter 6 takes a long look at the whole question of variables that is so basic to BASIC.

In the example that follows, `firstName` and `txtMessage` are variables. In this chapter, just try out using them. I recommend that you resist the temptation to find out about variables now by reading ahead to Chapter 6, but hey, you can if you want to.

After you get used to looking at the code in scripts, telling the variables from the LotusScript keywords is easy. LotusScript keywords begin with a capital letter. Variables often begin with a lowercase letter; they don't have to, but scripters usually get into the habit of starting variables with lowercase letters. Chapter 7 talks more about naming variables.

You find a second difference between keywords and variables: You can highlight keywords and press F1 for Help on them. You won't get any Help, though, if you highlight a variable and press F1.

Type in a middle line, which contains the variables. Don't forget the & in the second line of code, the variable `txtMessage`, and the two commas (`,`) after `txtMessage` in the third line. Your completed script now looks like this:

```
Sub Main
    firstName = Inputbox("What's your name?")
    txtMessage = "This script was written by " & firstName
    Messagebox txtMessage,, "Good-bye, Cruel World."
End Sub
```

Deciphering the variable code

In the code at the end of the preceding section, you notice that I slipped a few *symbolic instruction codes* (or what I like to call *hieroglyphics*) into the document. For example, the second line contains an ampersand (&). And the third line has the two commas (, ,) — not one comma, as you see in English — but two, as you see in LotusScript.

The ampersand in the second line is the *string concatenation operator*. (That's a pretty fancy name for what is actually a twisted-up plus sign.) Using the concatenation operator enables you to put something else after the expression in quotation marks. To you and me, hey, it's a hieroglyphic.

You have to go no further than this simple & symbol to begin to see how scripting can drive an ordinary person nuts. If you leave out the &, LotusScript gives you an error message.

The two commas in the third line, similarly, are just symbolic instruction codes for LotusScript. They don't show up in the input box or the message box; they are *separators* for an invisible code that tells LotusScript what kind of message box to create. You can put in a visible code, such as the number 2, and LotusScript puts up a different message box.

The following script specifies the number 2 in the line that starts with Messagebox, and Figure 3-4 shows the type of message box (with the Abort, Retry, and Ignore buttons) that LotusScript creates when you use this code.

```
firstName = Inputbox("What's your name?")
txtMessage = "This script was written by " & firstName
Messagebox txtMessage,2, "Good-bye, Cruel World."
```

Figure 3-4:
You can use codes to create different message boxes.

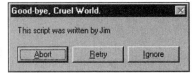

Running the script from another document

Chapter 2 shows you three ways to run scripts — by using the menu inside the Script Editor, by pressing F5, and by running the script from inside the document. You can also run a script while inside *yet another* document. For the previous sections, I used Lotus Approach, which doesn't offer the capability that I want to show here. To run the script from another document, though, I can use one of the other Lotus SmartSuite programs — Word Pro, Freelance, or 1-2-3. If you want to run this example yourself, create the script from this chapter as a script in Word Pro. Then follow these steps:

1. **Click the X in the top-right corner of the Script Editor to close the editor.**

2. **Click File➪Save to save the file.**

3. **In the Save As dialog box, choose a folder and save the file as** Good-bye.

    In Windows 95, you don't have to put a file extension or anything on the filename Good-bye. Just remember which folder you save your script in so that you can find it when you want to run it from another document.

4. **Choose File➪Close to close the document.**

Now, with the document tucked nicely away, you can run the script in it while in another document.

1. **Choose Edit➪Script & Macros➪Run.**

    The Run Script dialog box comes up, as shown in Figure 3-5. Because the program finds no script to run in the current file, Word Pro (or whichever program you chose) defaults to the choice Run script saved in another file.

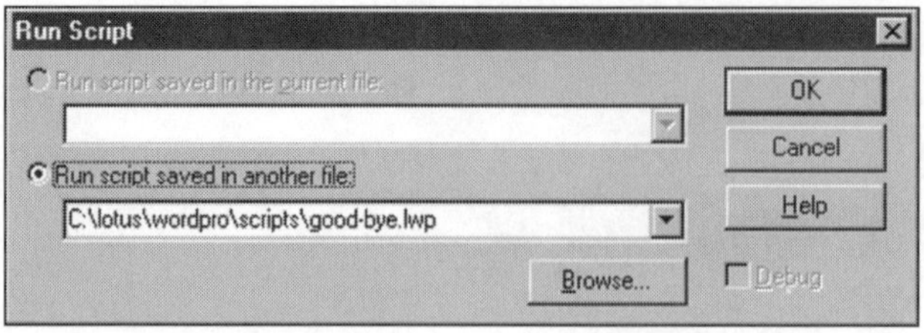

Figure 3-5:
The Run
Script
dialog box.

2. **Click Browse.**

3. **In the resulting browser window, double-click the file named** Good-bye.

4. Click OK to run the script.

An input box comes up and asks, What's your name? See Figure 3-6. That can be a tough one. I filled in my name as Joseph Wiggle, because I'm trying to keep a low profile.

Figure 3-6:
The input box asks you to fill in your name.

5. Type in your name, and press Enter or click OK.

The message box comes up, with your message at the top and the statement of ownership in the box. See Figure 3-7.

6. Click OK to get rid of the box.

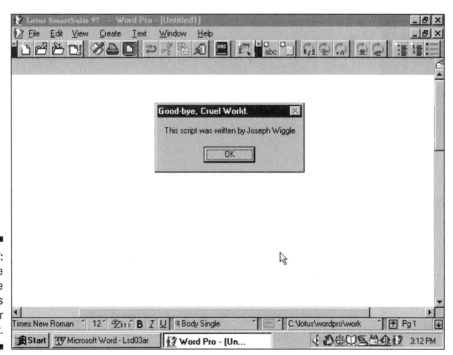

Figure 3-7:
The message box comes up with your name in it.

Making a Function and a Sub

Not a submarine. Not a subterranean. Not a subscription or subhuman or subconscious. A sub*routine*.

If scripts were one, two, or three lines of code like in the previous example, then everybody would be writing them before long, taking away employment opportunities for the truly diligent who are willing to go through the ins and outs of learning to write multiple lines of code. However, scripts generally are not single lines of code. They get broken into parts called *subroutines* or, as it happens, just plain *subs*. You name the sub, and then you can refer to it time and time again within the program. You can also create functions, which are similar to subs. I talk about them in detail in Chapters 12 and 13.

You can write a script with a function and a subroutine that parallels the message box example that I've developed so far in this chapter. In this next example, you first create the Main program, which then calls up information from a function and a subroutine:

1. **In Word Pro, click the Create a New Document SmartIcon and choose Create a Plain Document.**

2. **Click the Show Script Editor SmartIcon.**

   This is the first routine, which is also called a *sub,* even though it is Main and isn't under anything you can see. (Sub Main — it seems like an oxymoron.)

3. **Type these two lines of code:**

   ```
   firstName = GetName
   ShowMsg firstName
   ```

   A translation of the first line is, "This program uses a variable called firstName. The meaning of the variable is whatever comes up in the subroutine GetName."

   A translation of the second line is, "For the function ShowMsg, use the data in firstName."

Now, you can implement a function to provide the information for GetName:

1. **From the Script Editor, choose Create⇨Function.**

   A box comes up asking you to name your new sub. You have to match the name with the name you've given it in the Main subroutine.

2. **To name the sub, type GetName and click OK.**

   LotusScript creates a new, blank sub, where you can type in the lines of code you may want to use over and over again.

This routine has to be a `Function` because a function not only takes in information from the Main subroutine, but also gives information back. (You can find out more about functions in Chapter 13.)

3. Type this line:

```
GetName = Inputbox("What's your name?")
```

And that's it for this function. Now you need a sub.

Creating a subroutine

1. In the Script Editor, choose Create⇨Sub to create a subroutine.

2. In the New Sub box, type the name `ShowMsg` (the same name you set up in the Main sub).

3. Type the line:

```
txtMessage = "This script was written by " & firstName
```

In this case, `txtMessage` is a variable that you're going to use in the next line of the subroutine.

4. Type this line:

```
Messagebox txtMessage,, "Good-bye, Cruel World."
```

The final line of the script calls up a message box and puts in it the `txtMessage` from the previous line and, at the top, puts the message `Good-bye, Cruel World.`

Running the script with subroutines

To see whether you have any errors in the script, press F2. When LotusScript finds errors, it notifies you by changing the color of the code line on-screen and placing a message in the Errors list box. And unless you're different from everybody else, you probably do have errors in your script. Be sure to check spelling, spacing, and punctuation, and you can see Chapter 5 for information on debugging your script. After you press F2 and LotusScript finds no errors, follow these steps to run your program:

1. In the drop-down list box labeled Script in the Script Editor, click Main to return to the Main subroutine.

2. Press F5 to run the script.

An input box comes up and asks for your name.

That programmers are antisocial is not their fault

The extreme literal-mindedness of programming languages (often referred to by programmers as simple *dumbness* on the part of languages) is probably the biggest reason that sane, normal people tend to turn tail at the first prospect of any kind of scripting. The concatenation operator (&), the two commas (, ,), and the variables shown in the section, "Putting in variables to make the script work," are some of the endless examples of literal-mindedness that you encounter while scripting. I mean, although anyone using English would know that the second expression goes with the first; LotusScript needs a concatenation operator to tell it that.

I'm beginning to understand why programmers are almost impossible to converse with in a normal fashion. To converse with whatever computer they work with all day long, they have to be incredibly literal-minded to get any kind of a response back. It's like any other enforced form of not-exactly-normal discourse hour-after-hour, day-after-day — like dog trainers, or kindergarten teachers, or English as a second language teachers, or, I don't know, police officers dealing with very surly gang members.

Your language tends to take on a certain cast forced upon it by circumstance. So, if you say, "Yo," to a programmer, he or she is likely to say, "Unexpected expression; expected 'Hi.'"

Recognizing that the person who said "Yo" wouldn't understand the response in machine speak, maybe the programmer checks himself and doesn't say anything. It's not unfriendliness. It's not nerdiness. (Well, it is, but I'm trying not to say that.) It's just an occupational hazard from having dialog with a computer all day long.

Everyone blames programmers for being antisocial, but it's not their fault. Hey, maybe people persecute them for the way that anyone in their shoes would quite naturally come to treat the English language. Programming forces them into it.

3. Type in your name and press Enter.

I like to use an alias when dealing with my computer, so I typed in the name `Joseph`.

A box comes up on-screen with the message `Good-bye, Cruel World` at the top and the line `This script was written by Joseph`. See Figure 3-8 for a look at my message box.

To run the script with subroutines successfully, you have to be in the Main subroutine (or in the document) when you run the program. If you have the cursor in one of the subroutines of your Main sub, LotusScript attempts to run only the subroutine that you're in. That can be useful if you've designed that sub to work in stand-alone mode. New scripters, though, may get unnecessarily hung up by this LotusScript practice. You'll get an error message unless you're in Main when you run the script.

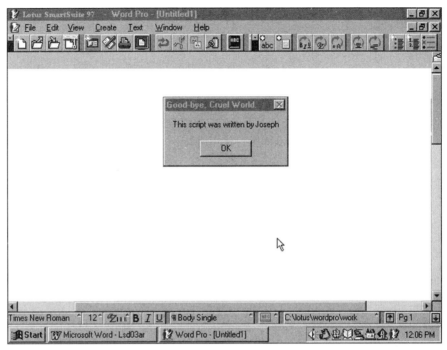

Figure 3-8:
Your
message
box looks
like this (if
your name
is Joseph).

Talking to an Interpreter

Whatever happened to good old nouns, verbs, direct objects, and things? As a former, longtime English teacher, I can tell you: People have enough trouble keeping even those straight.

When you're talking to a BASIC interpreter, though, everything you ever knew about natural language goes straight out the door. You don't say "I want to count marbles." You say `Dim my_Mar as Integer`, and you go on from there. I mean, this is not *language* in any sense you and I ever knew it before. Make no mistake — this is language for talking to a machine (or, as I like to think of it, to a completely left-brained Martian).

By the way, the BASIC *interpreter* is the software that translates the statements you type into the Script Editor into code that the computer understands.

However, because the Martian machine isn't going to change (at least not in the present incarnation as the version of LotusScript covered in this book), you and I have to learn enough about the Martian language to be able to hold up our end of a conversation.

Reading Descriptions in the Online Reference

You have to look up things in the online Help a lot when scripting. And when you do, if you're new to scripting, you can almost wish you hadn't. Suppose, for example, that you want to understand the fascinating little term `Messagebox` that I talked about early in the chapter. When you highlight it and press F1, you get a line of cuneiform . . . almost enough to make you sorry you bothered to ask. I mean, it's that Catch-22 again. If you knew enough to be able to interpret this following statement, you probably wouldn't need help in the first place.

Messagebox(*message*[,[*buttons+icon+default+mode*][,*boxTitle*]]**)**

In any case, you have to press F1 and read statements like this (called *syntax diagrams*) all the time if you expect to have LotusScript explain what it expects from you when you attempt to speak its language. I'm going to help you out by putting an explanation of the symbols and formatting used in a syntax diagram into Table 3-1.

Table 3-1	Deciphering Syntax Statements
Syntax Element	**What It Means**
( )	Whatever is together inside parentheses, goes together. LotusScript reads whatever is inside the parentheses in order, according to its rules of precedence.
Bold	Anything in **bold** has to appear exactly as shown in the diagram. For example, if the word **End** is in the diagram, the script won't work unless you put in **End**.
Italics	Items in *italics* are placeholders for values that you supply. That is, you (or any user) ends up putting something in where you see the item in italics.
,	The comma is a delimiting character that just separates stuff, but doesn't appear in the output.
[]	Items enclosed in square brackets are optional.
|	Items separated by vertical bars are alternatives; choose *one* of these items.
{}	Items enclosed in braces are required alternatives; you have to choose one. The selections are always separated by vertical bars.
. . .	Items followed by an ellipsis can be repeated.

If you aren't in the mood for memorizing all these and you want to know which syntax diagram elements are the most important, I have the following thoughts. (Parentheses) are either very important (because they enclose everything) or not very important at all (because they are as commonplace as highway divider lines), depending on how you look at them. I tend to see them as important. And [square brackets] mean that you can ignore everything inside them anyway. On the other hand, {braces} (which, if you want, you can pull off the keyboard and use to straighten your teeth) tell you that you *have* to choose one of the items inside them. You'll have a problem with your script if you don't look inside them and figure out what's going on.

You'd think that someone could find an easier way to summarize the syntax information, but syntax diagrams have become pretty universal in scripting. I don't know whether you ever actually get used to deciphering them, but you learn to live with them. See Figure 3-9 for a look at how I like to interpret the Messagebox syntax diagram.

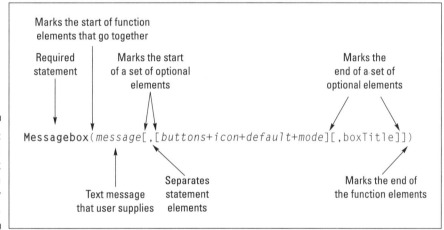

Figure 3-9: What a syntax diagram actually means.

Because syntax diagrams end up seeming like gibberish no matter how much somebody explains them, looking at an example is often the easiest way to understand the statements.

Whereas reading the syntax diagram for the Dim statement may seem confusing:

> {**Dim** | **Static** | **Public** | **Private**} *variableDeclaration* [, *variableDeclaration*]. . .

Reading this line of code from the online LotusScript Help files is almost understandable:

```
Dim x As Single
```

Test your newfound knowledge

A concatenation operator is

1. A person who works for the phone company who is really, really good at what he or she does

2. A fancy, twisted up plus sign (&) used for joining expressions in LotusScript

3. A tricky dance step, used in early jitterbugging

4. None of the above

The most important symbol in a syntax statement is

1. The square bracket ([), because you can ignore what's inside of it if you want to

2. A y, because no one has ever seen one in there, and you're making a big discovery if you find one

3. A ?, because it reaffirms your validity as a human being, telling you that you aren't the only one who is confused

4. A blank space, because if the page were full of them, you wouldn't have to be reading the syntax diagram at all

Chapter 4

The Script Editor: Hey, That IDE Is a Good IDEa!

- -

In This Chapter

▶ Seeing that the Script Editor is a whole lot more than just the Script Editor

▶ Using the Browser for all the Help you'll ever need (besides this book)

▶ Setting and clearing breakpoints with one click of the mouse

▶ Seeing your variables in the Variables panel

▶ Figuring out what, where, and when about the debugger

▶ Checking out what the IDE does to make you an honest scripter in spite of yourself

- -

*Y*ou may get the impression, from using the various Lotus SmartSuite programs, that the little box you work in when you write scripts is the Script Editor. You open the box by choosing Show Script Editor from the Word Pro menu, Show Script Editor from the Freelance menu, Show Script Editor from the Approach menu, or Show Script Editor in 1-2-3. (Notice that only the underlined hot key changes from program to program.)

The highly capable box that you open from the menus *does* have the Script Editor in it, and I find a certain comfort in calling the whole thing that. But this box also has a much grander (even *grandiose*) name. The titles in the Help files don't refer to the modest *Script Editor,* but instead refer to the grandiose name by its initials — the *IDE.* As a matter of fact, a main topic in the LotusScript Help files is "Creating and Debugging Scripts in the IDE."

"The LotusScript *Integrated Development Environment* (IDE)," say the Help files, "is a set of tools you can use to create and debug scripts in Lotus applications." The IDE, as its noble name implies, is much more than just a simple editor. Humble BASIC programs like GW-BASIC and QBasic may have offered *editors* for their users. But I dare say, these programs didn't offer anything like this IDE — a late '90s toolbox of such variety and utility that you can spend hours playing with its possibilities. And you'd be amazed at the trouble you can save yourself by learning a few of IDE's simple tricks early on.

Discovering the IDE's usefulness as you need it is probably better, for the most part, than spending too much time with it up-front. And, so I introduce IDE capabilities as they come up in the book. But because the IDE toolbox contains so much, I do think that an overview is in order.

All Those Panels: "Is This Management by Committee?"

I show you how to start up the Script Editor (which is part of the IDE window) in Chapters 2 and 3. You can click the Show Script Editor SmartIcon or select Show Script Editor from the menus. Although the concept may be confusing, remember that each document in each LotusScript-related application has its own IDE. That is, if you want to work with scripts in some document other than the one you're in, you have to open that document and its own IDE window.

Figure 4-1 shows the IDE window for Lotus 1-2-3 with arrows pointing out its key parts: Script Editor, Browser panel, Breakpoints panel, Output panel, Variables panel, Menu, and Splitter. The IDE, then, is not just a Script Editor. Instead, the IDE is a collection of panels, each of which has special capabilities.

By dragging the splitter that divides the panels of the IDE window, you can display just the Script Editor panel (near the top, see Figure 4-2) or just the panels in the bottom half of the window.

To restore the panels to their previous size, put the mouse pointer on the splitter until it takes the shape of two arrows pointing up and down; then double-click.

Navigating the IDE

The IDE (Integrated Development Environment) consists of a set of panels that appear in a window and guide your trek in the LotusScript scripting realm. As with any other Windows 95 window, you can resize and reposition the IDE by clicking and dragging the title bar or window borders. I want to make sure that you know how to get around the IDE window, so the next few sections tell you some important things to know about this environment.

Menu   Script Editor   Splitter

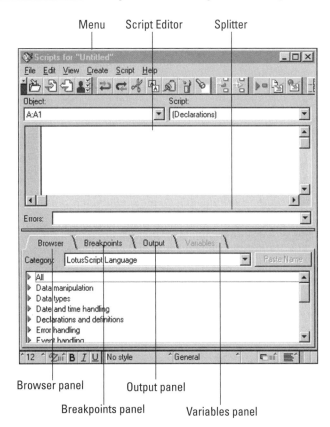

Figure 4-1:
The IDE.

Browser panel   Output panel

Breakpoints panel   Variables panel

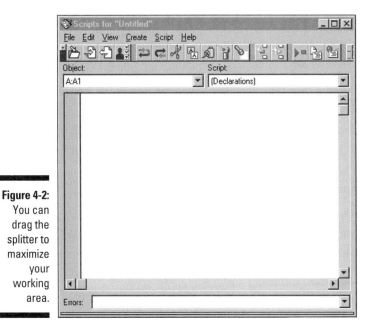

Figure 4-2:
You can
drag the
splitter to
maximize
your
working
area.

Scoping out the menus

As in many other programs, the menus near the top of the IDE window help you figure out how to get just about anything done. Want to create a sub? (See Chapter 12 for more information on this topic.) Click Create to drop down the menu, as shown in Figure 4-3. Then click Sub. You can check out each drop-down menu on your own; these menus are an excellent tactical aid for anyone getting acquainted with scripting.

Figure 4-3:
Use the
Create
menu to
create a
Sub.

This list shows some of what you can do from the IDE menus:

- ✔ Save, import, and export scripts
- ✔ Set your scripting preferences (like what color you want the LotusScript keywords to be)
- ✔ Set up SmartIcons for your favorite scripting commands
- ✔ Print your scripts
- ✔ Perform many standard editing functions — copy, cut, paste, and even undo
- ✔ Change the view in your editing window among various scripts and Panes
- ✔ Create subs and functions
- ✔ Run, check, and record scripts

✔ Get Help

✔ Even get to the Breakpoints, Browser, Output, and Variables panels (though you can just click on them if you want them). You use the Browser to find commands, Breakpoints in debugging your scripts, the Output panel to see results when you use the `Print` command, and the Variables panel during debugging.

You can click the right mouse button with your cursor in any of the IDE panels to get a menu of the tasks most commonly done from that panel. See Figure 4-4.

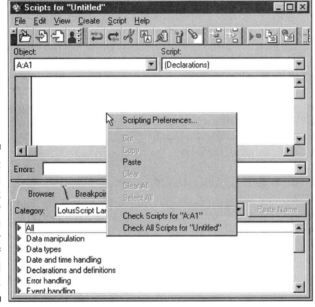

Figure 4-4:
You can
right-click
with your
cursor in the
Script Editor
for a list of
most-used
commands.

Recognizing your "panels of experts"

The Script Editor — the top panel — is of course the most important panel in the IDE window. I mean, you write your scripts in there, and writing scripts is the topic of discussion in this book. Whenever you're writing a script in the Script Editor, you have ready access to the Browser, Output, and Breakpoints panels. Just click the tab for whichever one you want.

Because of its importance, the Script Editor panel gets lots of coverage in all parts of the book. In the sections that follow, I talk about the panels that normally appear in the bottom half of the IDE window, and I point out the expert capabilities of each one.

Investigating the Browser Panel

Without a doubt, debates are still raging as to which is truly the most useful IDE panel (not counting the Script Editor). I tend to favor the Output panel because I'm always trying out scripts with the `Print` command and looking up the results in the Output panel. Lotus has made up its mind on the most useful panel, though, and it seems to favor the Browser. That is, whenever you first open the IDE, you see the Browser panel on the bottom-half of the screen. You have to click the tab for another panel if you want to display that one instead.

The Browser, I do concede, is a great way to look up keywords. You can even look up keywords by logical categories, and you can paste commands from the Browser right into the script that you're creating.

Browsing by category

With the Browser panel, you can browse through LotusScript information in a number of different categories. Click the arrow next to the Category drop-down list box to see the list of categories, as shown in Figure 4-5.

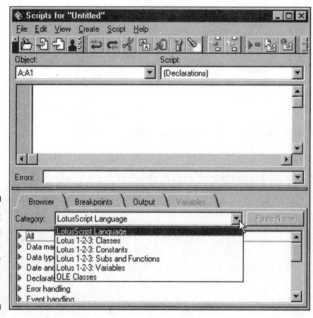

Figure 4-5:
You can browse through any of these categories.

Browsing sounds kind of casual, like what you might do in one of those super bookstores with a cup of cappuccino in your hand. Actually, though, the items in the browser list contain more information than does your average CD-ROM. I mean, this list has everything.

The items that appear in the window under the Category list box change when you choose a different Category.

The list of all items in the outline lists appears in the outline list window (below the Category list box on-screen, as shown in Figure 4-6).

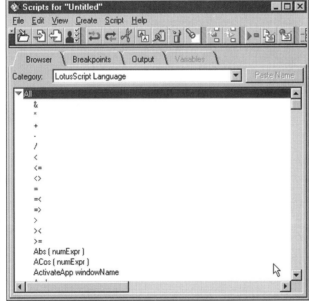

Figure 4-6:
Everything
you ever
want to
know about
LotusScript
is in this list.

Sticking with the LotusScript Language category

LotusScript Language is the category that I use most often when browsing for information. Although you may have occasion to use the other choices in the Category list box, those choices are mostly for seasoned programmers who may be comfortable with object-oriented programming in LotusScript. Novice programmers and those who are *just looking* will no doubt use the LotusScript Language category for their browsing.

Outline lists: "Uh, I don't remember. But I can point to it."

What you can find buried in the Browser panel of the IDE is amazing, to me at least. The LotusScript designers must have known that lots of normal people (who don't remember commands and certainly can't remember syntax) would be writing scripts. Therefore, the designers tried to put everything you need right there in the Browser's outline lists so that you can just point at it. (I suspect that plenty of programmers put the Browser panel to use, too. Much of the information in the outline lists is useful for them as well.)

After you choose the category that you want from the Category drop-down list, use your mouse in these ways to get around in the outline list:

- When the arrow next to the outline topic is pointing to the right (▶), click the arrow to expand the list. That is, click the arrow to see the next level of topics in the outline.

- When a topic in the list is expanded already and the arrow is pointing downward (▼), click the arrow to collapse the list. In other words, click the arrow to hide the topic's lower level.

Table 4-1 gives you a more complete listing of mouse clicks and keystrokes that can help you wade through one of those fancy outline lists in the Browser panel.

Table 4-1 Navigating the Browser Panel's Outline Lists

Action You Want	Symbol or Selection	What You Do
Expand one topic	▶ (expand symbol)	Click the symbol
	Highlight the topic	Press Enter
	Highlight the topic	Press + (plus sign)
Expand all topics		Press Shift++
Collapse one topic	▼ (collapse symbol)	Click the symbol
	Highlight the topic	Press Enter
	Highlight the topic	Press – (minus sign)
Collapse all topics		Press Shift+ –

After you're in a Browser list, you can find a topic quickly by typing the first letter of the item you're looking for. For example, if you're searching for information about the Dim command, type the letter D.

When you're first getting used to LotusScript, you may not know the category to look in to find something. First, expand All and then type the first letter of what you're looking for. Press that letter repeatedly, if necessary, and you get to the item pretty quickly.

Taking advantage of Paste Name

Are you worried that you may copy a command name wrong, even after you find what you're looking for in the Browser? The IDE anticipated that worry and lets you paste the name into the Script Editor from the Browser. Use these steps to try it out, if you like:

1. **Click the arrow symbol next to** All **to expand the list of items in the LotusScript Language category. See Figure 4-6.**

2. **Press the first letter of the command you want, such as** D **for** Dim.

    Press D repeatedly or use the arrow keys to highlight the command you're looking for in the outline list. See Figure 4-7.

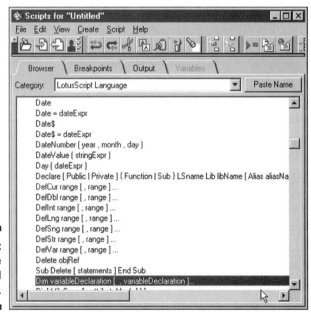

Figure 4-7: Highlight the command you want.

3. **Click the Paste Name button.**

    The command appears in the Script Editor, as shown in Figure 4-8.

Item appears here   Click here to paste

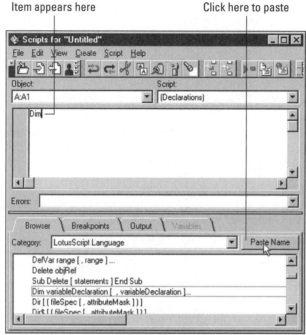

Figure 4-8:
You can
paste items
from the
Browser
into the
Script
Editor.

Those who favor the Browser panel can make a very strong case that no other panel truly has the power that this one does. The Browser panel is a scripting Help file at your fingertips.

Making good use of those mouse shortcuts

On the subject of mouse shortcuts, I may as well mention that you can find many ways to simplify your handling of IDE features by clicking around with your mouse. You can, of course, click with the mouse to move to any part of the IDE window. That is, you can click on panels in the IDE window to make them active.

Within an active IDE panel (depending on which panel it is), you can select (highlight) editable items, expand or collapse outline lists, manage breakpoints, and display right-click menus for that panel of the IDE.

This list shows you some mouse shortcuts that are my personal favorites:

✔ To set a breakpoint on a line in your script, simply put the mouse pointer next to the line at the far left in the area known as the *breakpoint gutter* and click.

✔ To remove a breakpoint, put the mouse pointer on the breakpoint indicator in the gutter next to the script line and click.

✔ To disable or enable a breakpoint, simultaneously press Ctrl and click the breakpoint indicator next to the script line.

✔ To expand or collapse list topics in the Browser panel, click the expand symbol (▶) or the collapse symbol (▼).

Breakpoints Panel

When you get into the nitty-gritty work of debugging your scripts, you work with breakpoints. *Breakpoints* are indicators that you place at critical points in your script to suspend execution of the script and allow you to check for bugs. Chapter 5 talks about breakpoints, how you set them, and what you can do with them.

The Breakpoints panel lists all the breakpoints in your scripts for a particular IDE. With the Breakpoints panel, you can navigate to breakpoint lines in your scripts, and you can clear, enable, and disable your breakpoints. Figure 4-9 shows a sample Breakpoints panel for a sample script.

Breakpoints appear as little red circles in the left margin next to your scripts. When you run your script, execution stops at each one. To clear, enable, or disable breakpoints, you use the <u>D</u>ebug menu (which appears on the menu when you are running a script and have stopped at a breakpoint). You can also use SmartIcons, which appear when you are stopped at a Breakpoint. Try looking under `All` — go ahead, just click the arrow to the left of `All`.

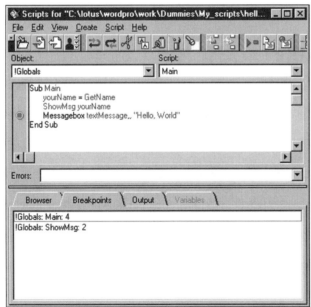

Figure 4-9:
The Breakpoints panel may look like this.

Output Panel

The Output panel displays the output you generate with the `Print` statements in your scripts. Actually, the computer generates the output when you run your scripts. Figure 4-10 shows an example.

Figure 4-10:
You put stuff in the Output panel with the Print statement in your scripts.

Variables Panel

The Variables panel displays information about the variables (that is, the data containers) in the script and lets you change variable values. (See Chapter 6 for more information on using variables.) The Variables panel is available for use only when the Script Debugger is active.

If you're like me, you'll go rushing off to the Variables panel to look at all the variables you declare in your script, and you can't get to them. You can get to the Variables panel, you see, only when you're debugging your script. (Debugging means clearing up all your scripting mistakes so that your script can work. See Chapter 5 for a look at LotusScript's tools for helping you with debugging.)

The Variables panel (shown in Figure 4-11) displays information about variables in a script and lets you change variable values. The following points are good things to know about the Variables panel:

✔ The panel display contains information about variables in the current script (that is, the script for the object and procedure shown in the Calls drop-down list in the Script Debugger).

> ✔ The panel lists variables by name in the order you declare them in the script.

> ✔ The panel also considerately lists each variable's value and current data type.

In special instances (set up by skilled scripters), a variable can be defined as a type with members. I talk about Types and Members in Chapter 14. You can set up categories (types) that group variables; *Members* are the variables that belong to the type. For the variables that have types, the Variable panel goes as far as presenting the variables, with names and types, as expandable entries. You can expand a member-type entry in one of the usual ways (for example, click the associated expansion symbol, or highlight the name and press Enter) to view the variables' members with their values and data types.

Mastering the computer genius style with IDE keyboard shortcuts

I don't know. Keyboards are kind of going out of style. Voice recognition is taking over. And keyboards aren't for dummies anyway. Dummies point. That's just the way it is. Software geniuses memorize keyboard commands and move blithely around using them, thereby totally amazing any dummies who happen to be nearby (because dummies, as I mentioned, only point.) Dummies even sometimes point to such keyboard wizards and say admiringly, "Wow. How did you do that?"

Still, every now and again even the nonexpert user masters a keyboard shortcut or two, usually more by accident than by definite intention. Only the hard-core user masters them all, of course.

I'm sharing my favorite keyboard shortcut (for those who want to learn just one):

To run a script, press F5.

If you are in the mood for just one more, this is my second favorite:

To error-check the current script, Press F2.

The following are other keyboard shortcuts. You can skip these, unless you're reading this book for the fourth time or so and are bored with all the other shortcuts by now.

✔ To display Help for the active area of the IDE or for a script keyword selected in the Script Editor or Browser, press F1. (This is a good one. Maybe I should have listed it as my favorite. Also, you don't have to select the word you want Help on. Just put the cursor on it.)

✔ To switch between the Script Editor or Script Debugger and the panel you used last (Breakpoints, Browser, Output, or Variables), press F6.

✔ To expand or collapse items in an outline list, select the item and press + (plus) or - (minus).

✔ To move between fields in a panel, press Tab to move forward one field or press Shift+Tab to move backward one field.

✔ To move the insertion point in the Script Editor to the previous or next procedure that contains user-defined scripts, press Ctrl+PgDn or Ctrl+PgUp. LotusScript moves the insertion point within an object's scripts first and then from one set of object scripts to the next.

Getting to Know the Debugger

"Debugger? . . . What Debugger?" you may well wonder, because when you first open the IDE, you find no debugger panel. And you'll never find a *panel*. What you get when you use the debugger is a bunch of icons, and these icons appear only when you run a script that contains *breakpoints*. The debugger opens when it encounters the first *enabled* breakpoint during script execution.

The debugger is a great way to look at your script systematically, in small pieces created by the breakpoints, and look for errors in logic or other mistakes that can keep the script from working properly. When a script executes, it stops at each enabled breakpoint — essentially waiting for you to look over everything between the previous breakpoint and the current one. A breakpoint is always enabled at first. The debugger comes up automatically when the script stops at a breakpoint. When you're satisfied with the lines of script up to a certain breakpoint, you can step over or disable the breakpoint and move on to the next one. Chapter 5 talks about debugging in detail.

Figure 4-11 shows the debugger in action with a sample script.

Step icons   Breakpoints icons   Debug menu   Panel icons

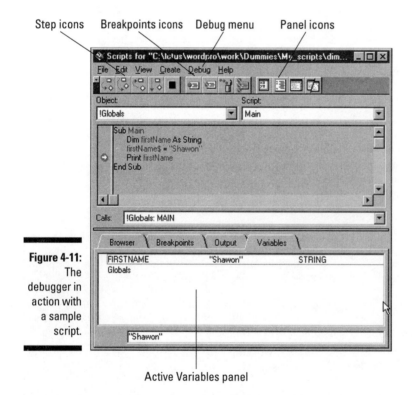

Figure 4-11:
The debugger in action with a sample script.

Active Variables panel

Not Quite Ten Things the IDE Does for You Automatically

The IDE does its utmost to force you into good scripting practice as you work. I don't know whether real programmers find its practices annoying or restrictive. A really smart person might not like so much vigilance from what is, after all, just a working environment and not your boss or something. As a lazy guy who likes things to work smoothly, I love what the IDE does.

The following are my favorite IDE automatic features:

✔ When you're working in the Script Editor, LotusScript puts in the End statement when you create a sub or a function. Because forgetting to tag on the End statement is so easy, you'd have a bug in your program right there if the IDE didn't take care of you.

For those who may want a comprehensive list, the IDE, in fact, completes all these next structures when you close or deactivate the IDE (if you haven't completed them already):

- %Rem blocks
- multiline strings
- object subs
- functions
- property blocks
- user-defined types
- classes blocks

✔ The IDE indents your script lines when you use certain structures — like If statements that you should indent for readability. I don't talk about If until Chapter 10, but you can see examples of the IDE's Smart Indenting in many LotusScript structures.

✔ This wonderful development environment even maintains consistent capitalization in keywords. For example, if you type **dim**, it changes the word to Dim. The script works either way, but the consistent capitalization looks nice and makes the script easier to interpret.

✔ The IDE puts you into a separate scripting block whenever you create a new sub or function. Knowing all about subs and functions (Chapters 12 and 13) isn't required for appreciating this automatic feature.

The general idea is enough: Working with lots of smaller programs, instead of one big one, is a good, responsible programming strategy. And the IDE makes you do just that.

✔ When you exit or deactivate the Script Editor, the IDE automatically saves all scripts for the document.

I could have broken out this preceding list of Technical Stuff things that the IDE closes and put this list into The Part of Tens at the end of this book. That section is pretty well loaded up already, though. I've already included two lists on principles of good scripting, and some of those overlap with things the IDE forces you to do. So, as you can see, I put this list here. I feel pretty good about that.

The IDE, then, really is a good idea. You can fake your way through a lot of things in scripting just by putting the IDE to use. For example, you can find out the name of a LotusScript and its syntax in the Browser panel and then paste it into your script. An ordinary user can end up looking pretty smart just by using a few of the tricks available in the IDE.

Test your newfound knowledge

To display just one panel in the Script Editor, you do the following:

1. Put masking tape over the other parts of the panel. Masking tape comes off from the screen later pretty easily, and it doesn't leave any sticky, gooey stuff on your screen.

2. Drag the splitter between the panels.

3. Get a bigger monitor, then follow the procedure in answer 1.

4. Petition Lotus and insist that they send you a single-panel IDE. Tell them you find the idea of a *splitter* to be unnecessarily divisive. Get lots of signatures on the petition. And threaten a sit-in.

If you want Help with a keyword in one of your scripts, you can

1. Dial 911. Dial it right on your keyboard. It's amazing. Little people come right out of your screen and ask what they can do for you.

2. Put the cursor on the keyword and press F1.

3. Just call out, "Help." Voice recognition software hears your cry and then special software reads your mind to provide what you need.

4. Don't do anything. The deepest levels of intuition work best in an atmosphere of the deepest silence.

Chapter 5

Debugging Your Basic BASIC Program

In This Chapter

▶ Using LotusScript's line-by-line code checking to nip errors in the bud

▶ Recognizing the (small and unimportant) difference between typing mistakes and syntax errors

▶ Using the `Print` statement as your best ally in debugging

▶ Committing a run-time error

▶ Getting into the debugger and using it after you're there

*L*ook. Mistakes happen. Even when you can see no earthly reason why your script won't run, sometimes it won't run. And when that happens, you feel like picking up your monitor by the neck and shaking it until the proper result comes out of your script.

But consider this: I've heard it said (about writing) that good books are not written; they're *re*written (ideally, by their own authors). You can say the same thing about scripts that work. They're not written, either; they're rewritten. To be more precise, scripts aren't written, they're debugged. (Hey, maybe this chapter goes first — first, you see how to debug programs, and then you figure out how to write them!)

Although you can seemingly find an infinite number of ways to mess up a program (and I believe that's literally true), all those infinite errors fall into two main types — simple mistakes in typing and syntax, and mistakes in logic. Mistakes of the first type (typing and syntax) are easier to fix; mistakes of logic (which require thinking and are, therefore, a strain) can be harder to fix.

This chapter covers how to deal with both syntax and logic errors. In looking for simple typing and syntax errors, I talk about LotusScript's built-in, line-by-line checking. In looking for logic errors (where true debugging comes in), I talk about LotusScript's built-in debugger. You can use both tools — the line-by-line checking and the debugger — to look for all your errors. And ultimately, you don't have to remember the various classifications of errors. You just have to find them and fix them.

Checking Line-by-Line for Simple Mistakes

In some ways, seeing how you ever get to the point where you need serious debugging (which I talk about in another part of the chapter) is hard. After all, LotusScript checks every line as you write it. How can you get into too much trouble? What are you going to do — ignore the warnings LotusScript gives you? As you get into long programs, you can quite readily get into trouble despite the line-by-line checking. But it can save you from the nuisance of many small mistakes.

LotusScript warns you of simple errors in your code as you write it by changing the color of your code line when you complete it. Unless you specify otherwise, the color changes to red.

Reviewing the colors of the text and what they signify

LotusScript uses different colors for different text elements on-screen to help you recognize something about that text at a glance. The fastest way to review the colors of text (and what they stand for in LotusScript) is to look over the Script Preferences dialog box where you set up the colors. You have the freedom to change the colors if you like, although leaving them as they are is probably just as well.

1. **In the IDE, choose File➪Script Preferences. The Script Preferences InfoBox comes up, as shown in Figure 5-1.**

   Notice that you can set text colors for several scripting elements: Identifiers, Keywords, Comments, Directives, and Errors. See Table 5-1 for more information about these scripting elements.

2. **If you want to change a scripting element's assigned color, click the arrow next to a color. A palette of possibilities comes up, as shown in Figure 5-2.**

3. **Click outside the color palette to close it.**

Even if you don't want to change a color, the Script Preferences box is a good place to find out what each of the colors stands for.

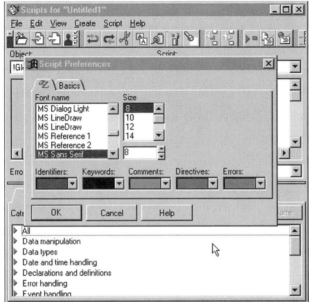

Figure 5-1:
Set your
color
preferences
here or just
review what
the colors
mean.

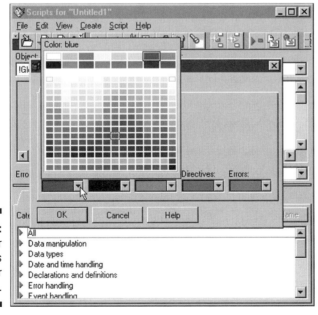

Figure 5-2:
Set a color
from this
color
palette.

Table 5-1   Scripting Elements and Their Default Colors

Element	Example	What It Does	Default Text Color
Identifier	hoursWorked	Names something	Blue
Keyword	Dim	LotusScript built-in command	Black
Comment	'This defines a variable'	Provides commentary; not executed when script runs	Gray
Directive	%Rem	A statement that alters the flow of execution	Green
Error		Shows the script element where the error exists	Red

Speaking Martian 101 — Reading error messages

Did you ever leave a disk in your A drive, reboot the computer, and get the error message, "Nonsystem disk or disk error"? What if the message said, "You have a disk in the A drive, and it's keeping me from getting to the C drive to start up." Wouldn't that message be much nicer? But the computer doesn't communicate that way; it prefers to speak Martian. After seeing the cryptic Martian error message about a million times, you get used to it.

Well, BASIC error messages (like those in LotusScript) are often Martian-like, too. The list in Chapter 26 (in the Part of Tens at the end of this book) looks at some common error messages, and what they mean in plain English. You may find a big difference between the message implied by the splashy sounding words and the actual meaning of the error message.

Often, you can just ignore what the message thinks it wants to tell you and simply check your spelling. For example, if you write **DM x as integer,** you get the message, DIM required on declarations in this scope. You probably don't care anything about scope. You just want to put the *i* into the middle of Dim. Once in awhile, of course, the message is actually right on and tells you exactly what you need. At least after you get used to the way the LotusScript interpreter speaks, you can understand the messages quite readily.

To get details on what an error message means, you can use the same F1 key (the *Help key*) that is so useful when trying to understand keywords. If you click the error message (to select it) and then press F1, the Help window appears, as shown in Figure 5-3.

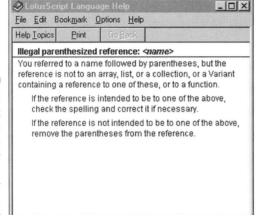

Figure 5-3:
You get
a <u>H</u>elp
window like
this by
pressing F1
in an error
message.

In the Figure 5-3 example, the detailed error message even nicely tells you, "Hey, you probably spelled something wrong."

Typing mistakes

I'm amused by how gleeful we humans can be about typing mistakes. We can read a beautiful, Shakespearean play, find one spelling error somewhere, and say, "Well, that play doesn't measure up. I found a serious mistake in one word."

The LotusScript compiler is even less forgiving, with respect to typing errors, than you or I could ever be. If you make even the tiniest spelling mistake, the compiler (the program that converts your typing into machine code) balks and begins firing out the most impressive-sounding error messages. You may think you'd just committed a capital crime, when really all you did was hit one wrong letter on your keyboard.

Dealing with spelling errors

Suppose you type in a simple line of code like this:

```
yourName = Inputbox("What is your name?")
```

As soon as you press Enter at the end of the line (or move to another line by using the mouse, the arrow keys, or whatever), LotusScript checks the line for any errors it can find. (Predecessors to BASIC programming languages didn't have this line-by-line vigilance. By the way, BASIC languages, like LotusScript, have saved their users millions of hours of misery by nipping mistakes in the bud this way.) If LotusScript finds anything out of order, it lets you know in no uncertain terms.

Suppose your line of code has a typing mistake so that it reads like this (with Inputbox spelled as Inpubox):

```
yourName = Inpubox("What is your name?")
```

Press F2 to check the syntax of your line of code.

F2 is the handy shortcut for syntax checking a script (or a line) that you just wrote. You may as well get into the habit of using F2. It's a fast way to find out that the script you've written still isn't quite right or, to be optimistic, that it is!

When LotusScript detects an error, the line containing the error turns red — or turns to whatever color you have set for Errors in the Script Preferences dialog box. (See the explanation of different text colors in the section "Reviewing the colors of the text and what they signify").

You can get an error message like this one when you make a typing error:

```
!Globals: Main: 2: Illegal parenthesized reference: INPUBOX
```

Although you made a simple typing mistake, the message that you see doesn't really say that. Instead, the error message gives you some specific, technical information about the error detected. Notice that the error message begins by telling the location of the error — which object (!Globals:), which script (Main:), and which line number (2:). Then it tells you which phrase it doesn't like (INPUBOX).

I've now shown you the most common error condition — you make a small mistake in spelling or syntax, the line changes color, and an error message appears. Because this situation is at the heart of all line-by-line checking, pausing a bit to review what happens is worthwhile. You see this common error condition often as you script.

Dealing with syntax errors

"Syntax errors . . . spelling errors . . . what's the difference?" you may wonder. You don't find much difference because both types of errors can result from inadvertent slips of the finger on the keyboard. A spelling error happens when you put a wrong letter into a word, leave out a letter, put in extra letters, and so on. The term *syntax error* is a fancy way of saying that you left off a punctuation mark or, in some other way, mishandled one of those pesky little commas, colons, quotation marks, and such.

The following is a correct line of code in a script:

```
yourName = Inputbox("What is your name?")
```

Suppose that you make a syntax error by leaving off the parentheses at the end, like this:

```
yourName = Inputbox("What is your name?"
```

When LotusScript checks your script, you get an error message that's completely different from the message caused by the typing mistake in the example from the preceding section (where Inputbox was spelled as Inpubox). This time the message says this:

```
!Globals:Main:2:Unexpected:End-of-line;Expected:Operator; ,;)
```

If you click on the message and press F1, you get the Help message shown in Figure 5-4. The message never quite comes right out and tells you to put in the missing parenthesis (though, in fairness, it does say it was expecting an operator such as parentheses). LotusScript's syntax checker leaves the line colored red, though, until you figure out that you have forgotten the simple punctuation mark.

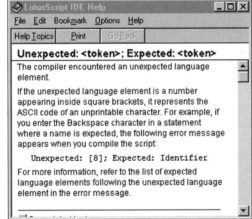

Figure 5-4:
The Help
message for
the omitted
parenthesis
syntax error.

Often, debugging scripts amounts to little more than finding the mistakes in spelling and syntax. Life is not always so simple, though. In dealing with more complex script errors, the debugger comes into play.

Why bugs are *bugs* and not something else

In a world of elevated phraseology, like that of computer programming, it's perhaps a bit surprising that errors in programs have earned the simple, quaint, and nearly universal name *bugs*. Nevertheless, a mistake in a program is a *bug*.

And I appreciate the legend behind the name *bugs*. The earliest computers, you see, used mechanical relays that actually opened and closed instead of using modern electronics. Once, when a computer malfunctioned, an engineer found a moth blocking one of the relays. The problem in the computer was, literally, a bug. The name stuck, and it does a favor for all future generations by giving us a name we can readily relate to, instead of something like "conceivable error condition or other malfunction."

Debugging with the Print *Statement*

The Print statement doesn't send output to your document, but only to the Output panel of the IDE (Integrated Development Environment, see Chapter 4). But using the Print statement is an invaluable way to find out what your script is doing at any given point.

Suppose, for example, that you had a script like this:

```
Dim a As Integer
Dim b As Integer
Dim c As Integer
a% = 5
b% = 4
c% = a*b
```

When you press F2 to check your script line-by-line, you don't get any error messages. When you press F5 to run the script, you don't get any error messages either. But how can you tell if the program is doing what you want? Use the Print statement, like this:

```
Dim a As Integer
Dim b As Integer
Dim c As Integer
a% = 5
b% = 4
c% = a*b
Print c          'Output is 20
```

"Compiling" a program

Unlike its fellow technical term *bug*, the word for getting your program ready to run has retained a highly technical moniker — *compiling*. Doesn't that sound like a fancy possibility? As if you'd have to go to a highly technical college for a long time before you'd ever be able to compile something. Really, though, you don't have to do a whole lot to compile your script. You just press F2 or choose the Check Scripts command from the menu to check it. Or you can run the script, using one of the methods explained in Chapters 2 and 3. The script *compiles* at that time and, if it doesn't come together properly for some reason, LotusScript lets you know with an error message.

The results of the script show up in the Output panel, and you can evaluate those results that you can now see. You can use the Print statement in many similar situations, simply to see what results your program is creating and decide whether such results are, indeed, what you are looking for.

Catching Run-time Mistakes

Some mistakes don't show up when you check your scripts for spelling and syntax errors (by pressing F2 or choosing Script⇨Check Scripts for . . . from the Script Editor's menu), but wait until you actually run the program. Then, the LotusScript Debugger comes into play to help you locate your pesky bugs and get rid of them. When you run your script for the first time, you cross your fingers and hope for zero mistakes. The odds are against you, though, as the relentless LotusScript error-checking looks for anything that might possibly be amiss.

Looking at a sample run-time error

I'll present a sample run-time error situation by using a simple program with two subs. (I explain subs in detail in Chapter 12.) The scripts look like the following:

```
Sub Main
    'Define two subs and then invoke them with the Call
        statement
    Call PrintResult(30, 10) 'Prints product of two arguments
    Call PrintTotal(30, 10) 'Prints sum of two arguments
End Sub
```

(continued)

(continued)

```
Sub PrintResult(a As Integer, b As Integer)
Print a% + b%
End Sub
Sub PrintTotal (a As Integer, b As Integer)
Print a% + b%
End Sub
```

When your script gets data that it doesn't quite know how to handle correctly, the script gets a run-time error. Just image that you went up to a mail carrier, tossed a stick, and said, "Fetch." The mail carrier's reaction may indicate that your request, as the popular saying now goes, "does not compute." Use the following steps to change the script so that it doesn't compute:

1. **Change the** `PrintResult` **sub so that it performs division by substituting this line:**

```
Print a% / b%
```

2. **Change the statement that calls the** `PrintResult` **sub so that it looks like this:**

```
Call PrintResult(30, 0) 'Prints quotient of two
arguments
```

   If you press F2 to check the program line-by-line, no error shows up. That is, the line color doesn't change to indicate an error condition, because (if you typed the line in exactly as you see it here) you've made no errors in spelling or syntax. When you run the program, though, a problem does show up.

3. **When you press F5 to run the program, the program turns gray, and an error message says** ! `Division by Zero`, **as shown in Figure 5-5.**

Often, error messages show up in the Errors drop-down list box, although in this example, the error message appears in a special box. An arrow appears next to the first line where an error occurs. This example shows you one of the many error conditions that don't show up until you run your script but that, nevertheless, are errors.

Of course, you can readily fix this !`Division by Zero` error by changing the second argument after `PrintResult` to something other than zero, or by changing the operator in the `PrintResult` sub from division to multiplication. However, finding your run-time errors isn't always so easy. That's why you use the debugger and step through the program, breaking the script at various points as it runs to find the error. The next section explains all about using the LotusScript Debugger.

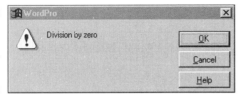

Figure 5-5:
A run-
time error
message.

Gak! The box turned gray and won't work

When LotusScript encounters certain errors during run-time, it stops running the program (or, in its terminology, *terminates execution*). It's great for somebody on death row to have an execution terminated. For your average person somewhat new to scripting, though, it can be disheartening to have your program suddenly freeze up and the screen turn color.

You can point and click madly, but most of the things you do don't help. You can't even fix the error, even if you know what it is. Some people have been known to give up, close the document, and retype the script in a fresh window just to get another go at it.

Actually, many of the icons in the Script Debugger (explained later in this chapter) are for working in just these gray conditions. You use the icons to step through the script. However, the easiest way to get the gray out and be able to try the script again is to follow these steps:

1. Click on the Debug menu.

The menu appears, shown in Figure 5-6.

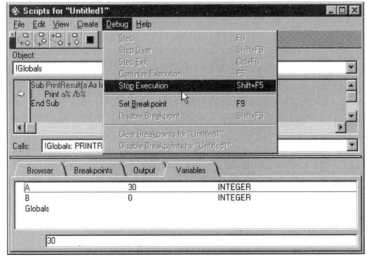

Figure 5-6:
The Debug
menu.

2. Click on Stop Execution.

The Script Editor turns white again, and you can try running scripts again. (Of course, if you don't fix the error, the box will turn gray again.)

Debugging with the Script Debugger

Debugging, as near as I can tell, is the process of painstakingly stepping through a script, piece-by-tiny-piece, trying to figure out what is wrong, not finding anything, begging people to help you (but they're too busy), giving up, and finally exclaiming the next day, "This simple thing is all that's wrong? That's nothing . . . how could I have missed that?"

Working with breakpoints

Breakpoints are points in your script where an indicator (that you set) tells LotusScript to stop running the script so that you see what's happening at that point. With the IDE Script Debugger, you can set, clear, enable, and disable breakpoints, and you use those breakpoints to step through a script to locate bugs.

You don't choose to activate the Script Debugger from a menu or something; the Debugger takes over when it encounters the first enabled breakpoint while executing a script. When you have either a breakpoint or a bug in a script, LotusScript stops execution of the script at the point where it encounters the breakpoint or the bug.

To run a script, make sure that you're in the Main sub, then choose Script⇨Run, or press F5.

Putting in breakpoints

Putting in breakpoints is easy. In the Script Editor, place the cursor pointer in the left column next to the line where you want to place a breakpoint and click the mouse. Figure 5-7 shows a sample breakpoint next to line 2 in the sub named PrintResult.

You can also set breakpoints with the menus; although, setting them with the mouse is so easy that I recommend that method over the menus. But so that you know, you can follow these steps to set a breakpoint by using the menus:

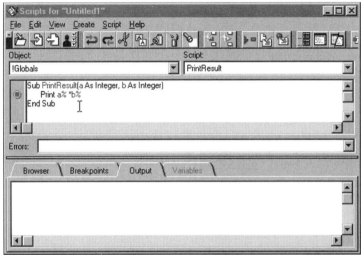

Figure 5-7:
Click the
mouse to
put in a
breakpoint.

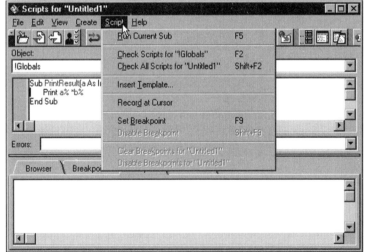

Figure 5-8:
You can
use this
menu
to set
breakpoints.

1. **Place the cursor in the script line where you want the breakpoint.**

2. **Click the Script menu.**

   The menu that opens appears in Figure 5-8.

3. **Click Set Breakpoint.**

Taking out breakpoints

You can take out breakpoints by using your mouse as easily as you can put in breakpoints:

1. With your mouse, point to the breakpoint icon.

You can tell which script lines have breakpoints by the little icon that appears in the gutter next to the line at the far left of the Script Editor window.

2. Click.

The breakpoint disappears.

To remove a breakpoint with the menu, click in the script line that has the breakpoint, click the <u>D</u>ebug menu, then choose <u>C</u>lear Breakpoint. See Figure 5-9.

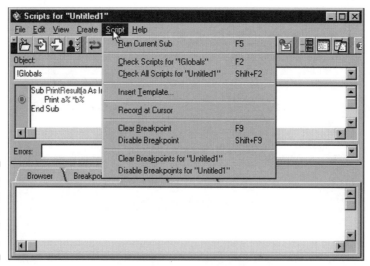

Figure 5-9:
Use this menu to clear breakpoints.

Looking at all available options in the Script Debugger

A complete new set of options, in the Script Debugger, opens automatically when LotusScript stops running the script at a breakpoint. When the Script Debugger is open, the following things are true:

✔ The Debug menu appears in the main menu.

✔ The Browser, Output, Breakpoints, and Variables panels are all accessible (including, especially, the Variables panel, which isn't available at other times). Figure 5-10 shows an active Variables panel, listing variables by name, value, and type.

✔ The script containing the breakpoint is, of course, the one displayed in the Debugger, and the current line is the one with the active breakpoint.

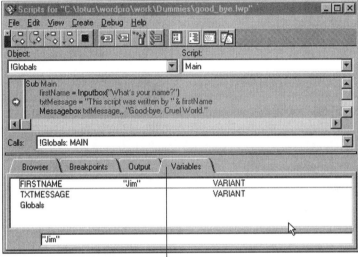

Figure 5-10: When the debugger is active (and only then), you can see your variables in the Variables panel.

Variables panel is active

You may want to experiment with the options available in the Debugger. Point to each of the icon buttons and read the helpful information that pops up in the *bubble* to see what the button does. With these icon buttons, or with the Debug menu, you can do these things:

✔ Set, clear, enable, and disable breakpoints for debugging

✔ Step through a script and stop script execution

For example, if you click on the left-most button icon on the Debugger toolbar, the arrow that points to the active script line moves on to the next line, and you can step through the script. You also find icons for Step Over, Step Exit, Continue, and Stop — icons for working with breakpoints and panels; see Figure 5-11.

Figure 5-11:
The
debugger
icons.

High-stepping through breakpoints

You find fine shades of difference between the Debugger's choices — Step, Step Over, Step Exit, Continue, and Stop — for moving around through a script. Although the differences don't matter much in short scripts, they may become important as you find yourself spending all day debugging large programs. The following is a discussion of the various ways to step around in the Debugger:

- ✔ **Step:** You use this one for working one statement at a time. Lotus puts it first on the menu, and it does seem like a handy one to use a lot. When executing stops at a line, you can choose Debug⇨Step from the menu or click the appropriate icon (shown in Figure 5-11). LotusScript then executes the script statement and, if the statement calls a subroutine, executes the called sub, too.

- ✔ **Step Over:** Suppose that you don't really want to run the sub that's called from a script line where you set a breakpoint. You don't have to. Use this command. When executing stops at the line containing the Call statement, choose Debug⇨Step Over from the menu. LotusScript does execute the line with the Call statement, but doesn't execute the called sub. Then it steps to the line after the breakpoint line.

- ✔ **Step Exit:** You use Step Exit to get out of a called sub. When execution of the subroutine stops (that is, when the screen turns gray and nothing else happens), choose Debug⇨Step Exit from the menu to exit from the called sub.

  When you exit from a called sub, the script starts executing again with the line after the Call statement in the calling procedure.

- ✔ **Continue Execution:** This one seems an awful lot like Step when you read about it. The difference is that it doesn't stop at the next statement the way Step does. Use Continue Execution if you want to execute the current statement and then keep on going until the script finishes or runs into another breakpoint.

- ✔ **Stop Execution:** (or, as I like to think of it, *Stay of Execution*) This one just bails you out of the whole mess you've gotten into. LotusScript stops trying to execute anything (and, if your screen has turned gray, it goes back to white again).

Making and finding mistakes, then, is a way of life in scripting. As you script, you may find yourself more like a *de*programmer (or, at least, a de*bugger*) than a programmer. LotusScript has some powerful tools in its debugger to help you through the nerve-wracking, frustrating, maddening process of finding mistakes in your scripts. In the final analysis, if your program still won't work, these debugging tools — no matter how nicely designed — may not be all that much consolation.

Test your newfound knowledge

To find out the meaning of an error message:

1. Read it backwards.

2. Click on the error message and press F1.

3. Close your eyes and think about someplace quiet and beautiful.

4. Yell at it. An error message is easily intimidated and will yield up its inner meaning.

The debugger opens when:

1. It encounters the first enabled breakpoint while executing a script.

2. It feels like it, depending on the time of year.

3. You have asked it not to.

4. You pour motor oil into your computer.

Part II

Getting Your Equipment in Order for the Trek

The 5th Wave   By Rich Tennant

"Please, if we can show some respect here, Ken has offered to point out his handy techniques for working with the IDE".

In this part . . .

$\mathcal{P}$art I looks at maps, compasses, and so on — basic
stuff you need to have before you leave scripting base
camp. Part II shows you the real stuff — ropes, climbing
gear, weapons. In scripting terms, you find out about the
fundamental fundamental in scripting — variables. You find
out about other ingredients that you use to help make your
variables into a scripting language: expressions, operators,
keywords, and comments. And you find out about dialog
boxes, those tools that you use to communicate with your
scripting public.

Chapter 6

Variables: I'd Rather Call Them Unknowns

*U*sually, when I come across the term *variable* in programming books, help files, and the like, the term is simply another definition in some big list. That kind of coverage just doesn't give variables enough importance. (It's like having somebody tell a joke and then deliver the punch line in a monotone — you could miss it.) Let me tell you the way I see variables: Variables are the *big thing*. And many other programming elements — like identifiers, data types, constants, and so on — have definitions that somehow relate to variables. Variables aren't just another thing in a long list; they're *the* thing.

Variables are at the heart of everything you do in scripting. To me, variables are like the monthly paycheck that you receive, hidden among the stacks of other pieces of mail. That check isn't just another piece of mail; it's what keeps your household going. Likewise, variables give your scripts what they need to keep going — a way to come up with and handle results.

I took a while to figure out the importance of variables, and I want to save you the same difficulty. *Variables* are containers for the data in your script, and they effect all parts of your scripting. That is, variables hold the data that your script uses to do its work, and often, the purpose of a script is to determine a previously unknown value for a variable. Knowing the importance of variables to scripting distinguishes the term *variables* as not just one of hundreds of confusing, programmerese terms to master, but *the king and ruler* of all confusing, programmerese terms.

All Right, What Is a Variable Then?

All right. You could just go ahead and use variables and gradually have their importance dawn on you. But I think that understanding the essence of variables at the outset makes everything else about scripting easier.

Defining variables in a formal way

Reading formal definitions is just a start toward understanding variables, but I'll share a couple of definitions with you anyway. The *LotusScript Programmer's Guide* (from Lotus Development Corporation) says the following: "**Constants** and **variables** are identifiers that name locations in memory that hold (or can hold) data of one or another of the types that LotusScript recognizes." And the booklet, *Using LotusScript in Approach* (also from Lotus Development Corporation), has a somewhat more understandable definition: "A variable is a uniquely named container for storing a piece of data."

But unless you're already familiar with using variables in programming, neither definition helps that much. A *variable,* in a program, isn't anything until something else makes it something — like those men who only get an identity from the woman they are with (Tom Arnold with Roseanne, some may maintain, though I, of course, would not so that he can't sue me, even though he's a public figure and it's okay to make remarks about him).

Similarly, mathematics describes variables as *having no fixed quantitative value* because they derive their values from the mathematical processes in which they're involved. This mathematical description helps you understand variables in programming — variables derive their values through the processes in a program.

But a rose is always a rose

When you design scripts, you essentially ask yourself, "What do I want to find out?" After you decide that, you name variables for those things that you want to find out. To establish variables for your script, you need to *declare* them. When you declare a variable, you give it a name (so that you can refer to it later) and a data type (such as Integer or Currency).

A variable's name and type *don't change!* (That is, those characteristics of the variable don't vary.) A variable named student_ID is always named student_ID.

However, the data value that the script establishes for the variable *does* change as the script executes. For example, the value of student_ID changes along with each different student that has an ID. (And that's what the mathematicians who first designed the BASIC programming language must have thought about when they used the term *variable*.)

Using Variables: A Scripting Example

The following example shows a script that works with the variable firstName:

```
Sub Main
    Dim firstName As String
    firstName$ = "Shawon"
    Print firstName
End Sub
```

Following is a line-by-line explanation of the script:

- ✔ **Line one:** Uses the Dim statement to declare the variable, give it the name firstName, and identify its data type As String (that is, a bunch of letters).

- ✔ **Line two:** Assigns the value to firstName (with the $ to identify that the variable has a String data type).

- ✔ **Line three:** Tells LotusScript to print the variable firstName in the Output panel of the IDE.

  When you run the preceding Sub Main, you see the following name in the Output panel:

  ```
  Shawon
  ```

Suppose that you were writing a script to take prospective customers' first names and put them into a list for salespeople. The script would probably use the variable firstName and lots of different first names would come out on the list. Because variables can identify what you want to find out in your program (like the first names of prospective customers), variables really make scripting worth doing.

Because variables are integral parts of your script, they're very helpful for documenting a script. That is, you can read back through the variables to see what you wanted to find out. Most scripters find that listing their variables right at the start of the script is a good idea. With this up-front listing, scripters can readily see the names and types of the data used in the program. Also, finding all the variables in one place is helpful when the inevitable time comes for *debugging* (that is, finding and fixing errors in) the script. Chapter 5 has more information on debugging.

Although you can name a variable anything you want, most experienced scripters believe that giving your variables names that represent the data that they hold is a good idea. For example, if you're creating a variable that holds the name of a new car manufacturer, naming the variable carMaker or auto_Mfg makes sense. Naming this variable movie_Star or something impossible to remember, like lkfk_44ty, *doesn't* make much sense.

However, LotusScript could care less what you name your variables. The following script works perfectly well and returns the word Shawon in the Output panel, even though the variable name lkfk_44ty doesn't make sense to you or me.

```
Sub Main
    Dim lkfk_44ty As String
    lkfk_44ty$ = "Shawon"
    Print lkfk_44ty
End Sub
```

Declaring Variables: Dim *What?*

You declare variables in your scripts with the Dim statement. Dim is short for *Dimension,* which, in my opinion, seems odd. Using Dec for *Declare,* Cre for *Create,* or even Def for *Define* would make more sense because I don't commonly think of *Dimension* as a verb. Besides, variables don't have dimensions such as 3-inches x 5-inches. However, variables do take up a certain amount of memory in your computer. In the mind of the early BASIC designers, naming the statement Dim (to stand for dimensioning an area of memory) probably made perfect sense.

The syntax of the Dim statement looks like this:

```
{Dim|Static|Public|Private} variableDeclaration1
        [ , variableDeclaration2 ]...
```

Aside from the Static|Public|Private stuff at the beginning, the statement essentially says that you declare a variable with the Dim keyword and that, by separating the variable declarations with commas, you can declare as many variables as you want with the one keyword.

The main thing, actually, is that you create the variable in the first place, because you need it to work with information in your program.

You can also declare a variable *dynamically,* or *implicitly,* within a script, instead of using the Dim statement at the beginning. This on-the-fly method of declaring a variable looks like this in your script:

```
hoursWorked% = 0
' This is a dynamic declaration of hoursWorked
```

The preceding statement names the variable (hoursWorked), sets the variable data type to Integer (%), and initializes the variable value to 0. Even when you declare a variable with a Dim statement, you *assign* a value to the variable by using a statement like hoursWorked% = 0.

Initializing Variables: Much Ado about Nothing

Initializing is one of those many terms in BASIC that seems to me like much ado about nothing. That is, initializing isn't even something that you have to do yourself. You can initialize a variable if you want, but LotusScript assigns a default value if you don't.

LotusScript assigns a variable's default value based on the variable's data type. Table 6-1 shows the default initial values for different data types.

Table 6-1	Variable Default Values by Data Type
Data Type	*Initial Value Assigned*
Numeric (includes Integer, Long, Single, Double, Currency)	0
Variant	EMPTY
String (fixed length)	A string filled with the null character *Chr(0)*
String (variable length)	The empty string (" ")

Variables are data containers. When you initialize a variable in your script, you assign a starting value for that variable to contain. For example, you can give the variable named firstName an initial data value such as Shawon by using a statement like the following:

```
firstName$ = "Shawon"
```

Although you initialize a variable only once, the script may change the value of the variable any number of times as the script executes.

Setting Variable Data Types

You can assign data types (such as Currency or String) to each variable that you create in your script. Then when you execute your script, LotusScript expects to fill this data container (the variable, that is) with data of that type. If a variable expects *currency,* for example, and the script delivers a bunch of letters (a *string*), LotusScript gets all huffy and issues an error message.

The advantage, from a programmer's point of view, is that LotusScript screens the variable values delivered during script execution and makes sure that these values make sense. If your script is looking for a salesperson's name (like *Wanda*) to fill the variable firstName and, instead, receives an amount of currency (like *$50.00*), LotusScript tosses you a type mismatch error message so that you can go back and make the program work right.

Seeing data type error messages is a good thing for serious scripters. If you go to the trouble of writing scripts, you no doubt want your scripts to give you the right output. After all, a script that runs but isn't accurate doesn't really work.

You can assign a data type by using As in the Dim statement, like this:

```
Dim money_Amounts As Currency
```

You can also assign a data type by using a data suffix character, like this:

```
Dim money_Amounts@
```

These two statements mean the same thing: Declare the variable money_Amounts and allow it to hold values of Currency only.

Recognizing data types and suffix characters

BASIC languages throw around codes (Symbolic Instruction Codes, that is) like confetti. Such codes seem as normal as *a, an,* and *the* in English, after you get used to seeing them. But when you're just getting started in scripting, you can wonder about those perplexing codes at the end of words. An identifier may look like this: my_Dog%, which means, "The variable my_Dog has the data type Integer" or, to you and me, "my_Dog is a whole number."

Table 6-2 has a summary of LotusScript's data types and the corresponding data suffix characters.

Table 6-2	LotusScript Numeric and String Data Types	
Data Type	**Value**	**Data Suffix Character**
Integer	A whole number in the range -32,768 to 32,767	% (percent)
Long	A whole number in the range -2,147,483,648 to 2,147,483,647	& (ampersand)
Single	A *floating-point* value — that is, a really large number (10 or 15 digits), or a really small number (10 or 15 digits to the right of a decimal point)	! (exclamation point, or *bang* to programmers)
Double	Like a Single, but twice as much	# (pound sign)
Currency	A number representing a monetary value, calculated to four decimal places. (Accounting folks like this data type because it keeps their scripts from rounding off their numbers.)	@ (at sign)
String	A series of letters, numbers, even punctuation marks. For example, Rag is a string; so is rage#*,ty.	$ (dollar sign)
Variant	Any value	No suffix character

Why these BASIC languages don't use the symbol $ for Currency is beyond me, except, of course, that the first BASIC language did it that way. And why use % (the percent sign) for whole numbers (integers)? I might think that someone were intentionally trying to confuse people. But more likely, the BASIC pioneers assigned the symbols knowing that the compiler wouldn't be confused by them.

At any rate, the data suffix characters you're most likely to use as a beginning programmer are %, @, and $.

Working with string data types

Strings are series of characters that most of us would be tempted to call *words* or *sentences*. These series can be fixed or variable in length. That is, a variable (like firstName) with a variable length can accept the values *Dave, David,* or *Davidson*. However, if firstName has a fixed in length of 5, the variable can accept the values *Dave, David,* or any value shorter than 6 characters.

If you don't declare a string with a fixed length, then LotusScript leaves it with a variable length. These examples show how to declare fixed or variable length string variables:

```
'variable length
DIM employee_Loc As String
  'fixed length
DIM emp_Title As String *10
```

LotusScript recognizes any characters enclosed in double quotes (" "), vertical bars (| |), or curly braces ({ }) as a string. Vertical bars and curly braces, in fact, are completely interchangeable.

The vertical bars and curly braces have one advantage over quotation marks that may matter to you as you script. LotusScript does not allow strings within quotes to span multiple lines, but you can put very long strings (like long messages, sentences, and so on) within vertical bars or curly braces.

The following example shows how you can have a multiline message by using vertical bars:

```
Sub Main
    Dim trial_Balloon As String
    trial_Balloon = |This is the information
    you've been expecting
    for a long time.|
    Print trial_Balloon
End Sub
```

If you try to use quotation marks, as in the following script lines, you get an error message:

```
Sub Main
    Dim trial_Balloon As String
    trial_Balloon = "This is the information
    you've been expecting
    for a long time."
    Print trial_Balloon
End Sub
```

Using (or not) the Variant data type

Although the term *Variant* sounds much like the word *variable,* Variant is actually a data type that you can assign to a variable. The following conversation, for example, makes perfect sense:

"What kind of a variable did you declare?"

"I declared a Variant variable."

To me, the term *Variant* suggests *something that I don't know what to do with, so I throw it in there undefined*. I see the Variant data type as kind of like the Miscellaneous folder you keep on your computer (or in your file drawer) — each becomes more and more useless as you cram more things into it.

If you don't assign any data type to a variable, LotusScript assigns the Variant data type. And when you use a Variant data type, LotusScript determines the value of the Variant variable when the script executes. Sloppy scripters may like to have all variables be Variants. Serious scripters, though, assign other data types to their variables so that LotusScript can verify that their variables contain appropriate values when their scripts execute.

An Oxymoron: Variables as Constants

You'd think that constants would be the opposite of variables, as if variables would change all the time and constants would stay the same. But that's not exactly right, because constants actually are variables (go figure!).

The definition of a constant as being a variable is actually more confusing than the reality. Constants *are* variables — identifiers that you use to reference a data value. You can even initialize constants, that is, assign an initial value (like you do for any other variable), but after you do, the *initial value never changes while the script is executing*.

You use the `Const` statement to declare a constant when you want a value that won't change as the script executes. LotusScript looks over the statements that the script executes and, if any statement attempts to change the constant's value, won't allow the change.

For example, suppose that you don't want the interest rate used to calculate a loan payment to change. You can create a script like the following, where the loan payer's name and the amount of the loan are variables, but the loan interest is a constant:

```
Sub Main
     'Define a variable, of String data type
   firstName$ = "Eileen"
     'Define a constant, of Single data type
   Const Interest! = 0.125
     'Define a variable, of Currency data type
   Loan@ = 4350.20

     'Display a message telling interest owed
   Messagebox firstName$ & " owes " _
   & Format(Loan@ * Interest!, "Currency")
End Sub
```

This script generates a message box like the one in Figure 6-1. When you script, remember to use a constant whenever you encounter a situation where you want to ensure that a value (interest rate, sick days allowed, minimum wage, and so on) doesn't change.

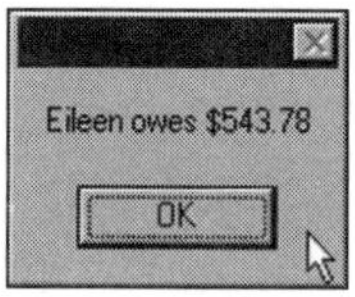

Figure 6-1:
A message box showing an amount figured by using a constant.

Eileen owes $543.78

OK

Test your newfound knowledge

A variable is

1. The weather in Iowa.

2. The emotional commitment of an extremely fickle person.

3. A uniquely named container for storing a piece of data.

4. All of the above.

To *initialize* a variable, you do the following:

1. Carve the first letters of your name into it.

2. Assign it a value.

3. Berate it savagely and sentence it to a lifetime of hard labor.

4. Make it stand up straight and tall and put a coat on it.

How do you make a variable a constant?

1. Declare it by using the `Const` keyword.

2. Put it in a straight jacket.

3. Put it through a 12-step program and then send it to rehab.

4. It's kind of a poetic thing, the coexistence of opposite values — Yin/Yang, Man/Woman, Cubs/Cardinals — like the mysterious nature of our universe.

Chapter 7

Naming Stuff: LotusScript Lexical Elements

- -

In This Chapter

▶ Recognizing one important rule for names: Don't put in spaces

▶ Figuring out what an expression is

▶ Relating expressions to identifiers

▶ Determining which is more powerful, an asterisk (*) or a plus sign (+)

▶ Getting to know LotusScript keywords

▶ Using comments to get relief from the ever-critical compiler

- -

*A*s you work along in LotusScript, you sometimes have to name stuff. That is, you have to identify the various elements of the language that you're using. In LotusScript, the words for all the names that you give these elements are *identifiers.* When I first heard the term *identifiers,* I thought that they were another class of LotusScript elements — like variables. But instead of a separate group of things like that, identifiers are, you know, like *names.* (And wouldn't *names* be easier to say and less confusing?)

Almost all the time, the LotusScript elements that you name are variables. (You can refer to Chapter 6 for a great discussion on variables.) The only people who name anything else — for example, properties, classes, and types — are more advanced in their LotusScript knowledge.

But besides naming stuff yourself, you sometimes need to use the identifiers that LotusScript has assigned to its *keywords* (you know, those words that have special meaning in LotusScript). Of course, LotusScript has some rules that you need to know and follow when you assign and use names, so this chapter's discussion on naming things covers that information, too.

Identifiers: That Means Names of Stuff

In LotusScript, *identifiers* are the names you give to . . . what? — to anything in a script that you can assign a name to. Most of the time, you name variables, and you can also name subroutines, which I talk about in Chapter 12. You can name constants, but constants are just variables that don't vary that much.

You can find a few other things to name. You can name a data type, which you assign to variables. That's getting pretty advanced, though, and you have to have read Chapter 14 on object-oriented programming, *OOP*, before you even know where to begin with that. You can name a class, but you also need to read the chapter on OOP to do that. And you can name a property, which is a special form of a variable (also used in OOP).

This list shows some sample identifiers:

- ✔ calc_Emp_Pay
- ✔ emp_ID
- ✔ emp_ID_Number

And the following are a few keywords:

- ✔ Currency
- ✔ Integer
- ✔ Print
- ✔ TRUE

In the preceding lists, you may notice that none of these identifiers contains any spaces. No spaces is one of LotusScript's requirements for the names that you create. Reference manuals usually set forth the rules for languages in stern terms, using the phrase "You MUST" over and over again, as if all the responsibility is on *you* for doing everything. I think that the rules should be phrased more apologetically, in words like, "I'm sorry, but to get this to work, I'm afraid we require you to . . . ."

Regardless of the presentation, you need to follow these rules for naming identifiers:

1. Identifiers can consist of uppercase or lowercase letters and begin with uppercase or lowercase letters (so that, basically, this is a nonrequirement). LotusScript ignores case. That is, it reads Mydog the same as mydog or MYDOg.

2. The first character of the identifier has to be a letter (such as *a*). LotusScript won't let you start an identifier with a number (such as *2*), as much as you might want to do it. So, forget about it.

3. The rest of the characters in the identifier can be more letters, digits (now you can use numbers!), or the quite unnatural-looking underscores. That's the hardest part to get used to — putting in underscores when you would use a space in English. For example, you type my_dog, not my dog. LotusScript can't *read* the spaces in an identifier and gives you an error message if it sees one.

4. Identifiers can be no longer than 40 characters (and yes, those underscores count as characters). I don't think you'd want a name much longer than 40 characters anyway.

LotusScript begins its keywords with a capital letter. You can quickly differentiate between LotusScript's own keywords and the elements you create yourself by starting your identifiers, especially variable names, with a lowercase letter.

You can't give a variable the same name as a LotusScript keyword. That would be understandably confusing to LotusScript, so the program doesn't allow it.

You can easily get carried away with identifier names and make them sound really highfalutin'. Most of the time, though, simple is best. You can name a variable calc_emp_Pay or even spell it out and say calculated_employee_Pay. Unless you're doing something really important with calculated, though, you may as well leave it off and just call your variable emp_Pay. And unless you're contrasting employees with owners or something, possibly even the name pay would do. Why not? The important thing, as I discuss in Chapter 6, is to have identifier names that are understandable.

Looking at Expressions, Operands, and Operators

You and I put words into sentences. LotusScript puts variables and other things, like numbers, into expressions. That's about the size of it. When LotusScript puts variables into expressions, it uses *operators* as more or less the verbs of those sentences.

Breaking down expressions

In BASIC talk, the term *expression* is much closer to the meaning of the same word in English than are many other terms in this chapter. In English, an expression is a particular word or phrase. In mathematics, the meaning of *expression* is almost exactly what you see in LotusScript: According to my American Heritage Dictionary, an expression is "a designation of any symbolic mathematical form, such as an equation."

You may think, then, that variables qualify as expressions. And in fact, you're right! A variable is an expression; so is, of course, a constant (because a constant is a form of variable anyway). Furthermore, any identifier is an expression as well. Then why, when all identifiers are also expressions, don't we simply use the term *identifier* and be satisfied with that?

Well, the term *expression* is a bit looser and more general than identifier. All identifiers are expressions, but not all expressions are identifiers. Many non-identifier types of expressions also exist. For example, this set of terms is an expression:

```
my_Monthly_Salary = my_Yearly_Salary / 12
```

Variables inside the expression, like `my_Monthly_Salary`, are identifiers as well as expressions. The elements like the equal sign (=) and the division sign (/) are part of the expression, but are not identifiers.

When referring to expressions, you refer to two parts:

- **Operands:** That which gets operated on. If surgeons spoke BASIC talk, a person undergoing open-heart surgery, for example, might be called an *operand*. ("Hey, Doc, we're ready for surgery here. Bring in the operand.")

- **Operators:** That which performs various operations on the operands. (In our surgery example, the surgeon, the anesthesiologist, and their tools are all *operators*.)

In the next sections, I talk a little more about operands and operators and give some examples.

Working with operators

Operators, the surgeons of LotusScript, perform the actual work in the script. The operators tell the compiler what to do to a particular operand — for example, *multiply* it. You do lots of things in LotusScript by using operators. Suppose that you want to calculate monthly payments when you know that yearly payments are $14,460.24. You can divide by 12, like this:

```
Print 14460.24/12
```

And you get this output:

```
1205.02
```

LotusScript has three groups of operators. As operators, *parentheses* stand in a class by themselves. LotusScript also has numeric operators for working with numbers, string operators for working with words, and logical operators, too.

Recognizing operator order of precedence

LotusScript definitely has a pecking order among operators. You may remember some rules of this order from expressions in high school math. For example, in a mathematical expression, you multiply before you add stuff.

Parentheses

The most powerful operators are parentheses ( ). Who would have ever thought that these simple curved lines would one day rule? In LotusScript, they do. Operators have an order of precedence in LotusScript, and parentheses have the highest precedence. (Try saying the last part of that sentence three times, really fast!) Whatever is inside parentheses gets done first.

For example, from this expression

```
Print 2+4*6+3
```

you get this result:

```
29
```

If you put in parentheses, like this

```
Print 2+4*(6+3)
```

you get this result:

```
38
```

The other operators (besides parentheses)

When operators (like * and /) with the same precedence appear in the same expression, LotusScript evaluates the expression from left to right. Table 7-1 lists the other operators (besides parentheses) in their order of precedence.

Table 7-1	Operators in Order of Precedence
Operator	*What It Does When It Operates*
Mathematical operators (in order of precedence)	
^	Exponentiation
- (*unary)	Negation
*	Multiplication
/	Division (same precedent as multiplication)
\	Integer division (no remainder)
Mod	Modulo division (remainder)
-	Subtraction
+	Addition (same precedent as subtraction)
& or +	String concatenation
Numeric or string comparison operators (all have equal precedence)	
=	Equal to
<> or ><	Not equal to
<	Less than
<= or =<	Less than or equal to
>	Greater than
>= or =>	Greater than or equal to
Logical operators (same precedence as all comparison operators)	
Like	Pattern matching
Not (unary)	Logical negation (*bit-wise)
And	Logical and (bit-wise)
Or	Logical or (bit-wise)
Xor	Logical exclusive-or (bit-wise)
Eqv	Logical equivalence (bit-wise)
Imp	***Logical implication
Is	Object reference comparison

* *unary*:   one operator.

** *bit-wise*:   Compares bits from the identical position in two numeric expressions and sets the bit in the corresponding place in the result. (This is *literally* getting down to bits and bytes here. I apologize; I'm not sure how this happened.)

*** *Logical*   Logical operators use a table and apply standard logic. When combining implication expressions, if expression *1* is TRUE and expression *2* is TRUE, then the expression *1 and 2* is TRUE.

If your operand is a *Variant* — a variable without a defined data type — then LotusScript can mistakenly interpret + as addition (adding numeric values) instead of concatenation (joining strings of characters). To be safe, use & for concatenation all the time. Trust me on this one, even if you don't yet have any idea what I'm talking about when I say Variants and defined data types. (See Chapter 6 for an explanation.)

Keywords

LotusScript reserves a whole set of *keywords* for itself. These keywords are a bunch of identifiers (names for stuff, like the ones I talked about in this chapter), but they are LotusScript's special names for its own statements, built-in functions, built-in constants, and data types. The following are some more examples to add to those I show early in the chapter:

- ✔ If
- ✔ Dim
- ✔ Integer
- ✔ TRUE
- ✔ Kill

You can't use keywords for the names of your own variables. Doing so, after all, is confusing to the LotusScript compiler because, when it sees the term used as both a keyword and a variable, the compiler has to decide which way *you* intended to use it. The compiler has enough other stuff to worry about, and so it throws up its hands and refuses to proceed when you use a keyword as a variable.

Using Comments

I like comments because you can put them wherever you want and they have no effect on the script. Writing comments is like writing in good-old English, because you actually are writing in English (or whatever your current tongue may be).

Using comments is easy as long as your comment takes up a single line or less in your script. Things get a little tricky if you want your comment to take up more than one line.

Following are two examples of one-line comments; each example shows you a different way to tell LotusScript that you're including a comment. The first example uses the Rem (short for remark) statement. The second uses an apostrophe (') to indicate that the line is a comment:

```
Rem This comment can say whatever I want.
```

```
'This comment, too, can be pretty free-flowing.
```

LotusScript doesn't allow you to use the *line continuation character* — an underscore preceded by white space — with comments. If you want to write a comment of more than one line, use the %Rem directive. Look at the use of this structure in the next example:

```
%Rem
I want this comment to fill up more than one line, so I
          really have no choice but to use this approach.
%End Rem
```

The compiler ignores everything between %Rem and %End Rem, which, for you, means complete freedom to put whatever you want in there without causing your script to break.

Comments are a great tool for ordinary people who happen to be programming. Thanks to the freedom of comment that LotusScript allows, you can tell yourself — or anybody else who happens to read your code — what you really mean to do in your script.

For example, you may be confused later when you come back to a script statement like this:

```
Dim sum_Camp As String
```

You create helpful documentation for yourself if you add plain English comments like this:

```
'Variable to use for names of summer camps
Dim sum_Camp As String
```

You can use comments to explain your variables, to explain a logical sequence of steps in a process, to remind yourself of the purpose of a subroutine, to tell people why you think an If statement is a good idea in a particular instance, or about anything else you can think of.

I hope that you haven't gotten the impression from this chapter that I consider identifiers anywhere near as important as variables. Identifiers are just names for variables. Expressions can be important at times, when you want to create a formula that does something. And knowing something about all these elements can help you understand and get going in LotusScript so much the better.

Test your newfound knowledge

The one most important rule to remember when naming stuff is "Don't put in any . . . ."

1. Kitchen sinks

2. Rabbits, dogs, mosquito wings, or used cars

3. Spaces

4. All of the above

If you want to drone on and on in your script without having LotusScript throw in error messages all along, do this:

1. Speak into the microphone on your computer.

2. Write a letter to LotusScript and get formal, written permission to say whatever you want without getting error messages.

3. Use a Comment.

4. None of the above.

Chapter 8

Taking Over the Controls: Making Your Own Dialog Boxes

* *

* *

*G*etting people to do what you want, anybody knows, can be pretty tricky. People have things other than what you want on their minds, or they don't understand what you want, or they're outright stubborn and resist you. Many times in a script, you want the user to enter information or express a preference. But how do you get the user (a person) to comply when their inclination may be not to?

In the world of software, you can use dialog boxes to help contend with this recalcitrant nature of human behavior. That is, you use dialog boxes to try to deal with the fact that getting people to do what is best for them can be hard.

LotusScript gives you the ability to create dialog boxes to go along with your scripts. You can have quite a field day creating dialog boxes with buttons, check boxes, and other kinds of controls. This chapter presents the goods on how to use the Dialog Editor to create dialog boxes. To put your dialog box master-pieces to work, of course, you attach scripts to them. Chapter 9 tells you how to do that.

Looking Over Some Real Dialog Boxes

If you're like me, you may never have pictured yourself creating dialog boxes for others to use. I thought that using the dialog boxes that some *real* programmer puts in front of me was enough.

Microsoft Windows and Lotus programs are forever putting dialog boxes in front of you as you work. For example, if you're using Lotus 1-2-3 and want to open a new worksheet, a dialog box like the one shown in Figure 8-1 comes up, asking you to identify which worksheet you want to open.

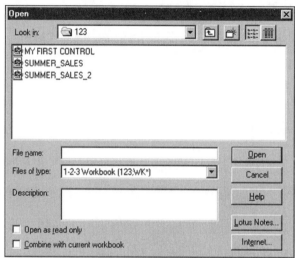

Figure 8-1:
You see dialog boxes like this all the time as you use Windows programs.

Or, suppose you click the Edit menu in Word Pro and then choose Paste Special. You get the dialog box shown in Figure 8-2.

When you script, though, you can create your own dialog boxes. You don't *have* to create dialog boxes to create scripts that work. When you want to get input from the user (that is, have a dialog with him or her), a dialog box is a good way to go.

And fancy dialog box buttons and boxes are not just neat devices that you see as you use software; they're useful — like traffic lights that guide you as you cross the street. In the LotusScript Dialog Editor, you can create your own traffic lights (that is, dialog box elements) to guide users and help them get the most out of the scripts that you write. That's a pretty good deal!

Radio buttons   List box   Check box   Command buttons

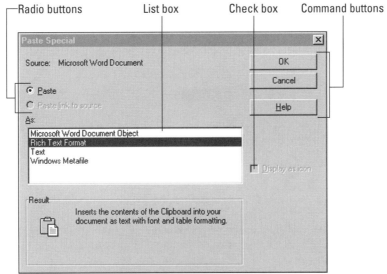

Figure 8-2:
A simple
dialog box
from
Word Pro.

Starting the Dialog Editor: Vrooom

The Dialog Editor used to be a separate program, and sometimes it was a little bit hard to find. Now the Dialog Editor is integrated, along with LotusScript, into the Lotus program that you're using. And it's easy to find. To locate the Dialog Editor in Word Pro, try these steps:

1. **From the Word Pro main menu, choose Edit⇨Script & Macros.**

   A submenu, as shown in Figure 8-3, appears.

2. **From the submenu, choose Show Dialog Editor.**

   And the dialog editor, as shown in Figure 8-4, appears.

If you use the dialog editor a lot, why not put a SmartIcon for it on your Universal SmartIcon bar. The SmartIcon for the Dialog Editor is shown in the margin. You can add this icon to your SmartIcon bar through the File⇨User Setup⇨ SmartIcons Setup menu choice. (See Chapter 2 for more discussion of putting SmartIcons where you want them.)

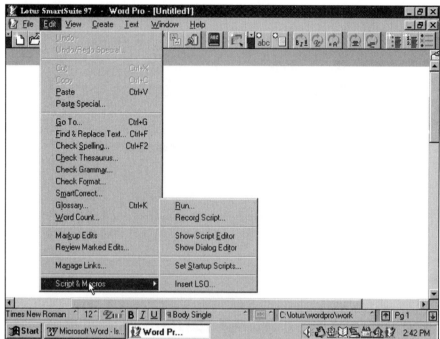

Figure 8-3:
Start the
Dialog Editor
here.

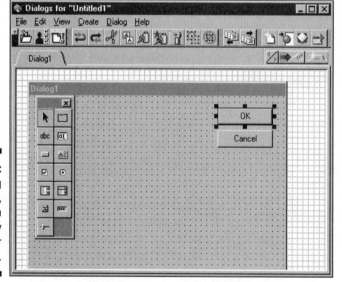

Figure 8-4:
The Dialog
Editor,
before you
add any
buttons or
anything.

Turning Over Control of Your Dialog Box

In the Dialog Editor, you can create the controls that help users interact with the scripts that you write. That is, by including controls, like buttons, check boxes, and text boxes in your dialogs, you let the script users participate in controlling their interaction with the script.

The OK button

You can always offer people an OK button. Unless you change the setting in the Dialog Editor (and you may confuse your user if you do), the OK button is the *default* button for the dialog box you're creating. The default button works like this: If users look at the dialog box and press Enter, they activate the (default) OK button (just as if they'd clicked OK).

The Cancel button

You may frequently offer a Cancel button, too. For a dialog box, clicking the Cancel button is the same as pressing the Escape key.

Looking over other controls

You can create quite a few different kinds of controls as you work. Chances are, you'll start out by using just two or three that you like — the OK button, the Cancel button, and perhaps text boxes, list boxes, and radio buttons.

The toolbar that appears on the left when you start the Dialog Editor contains the icons for the tools that LotusScript thinks you may use most often. The callouts on Figure 8-5 label each of the tools in the toolbar.

Remember that you can use Lotus bubble help to get a description of any icon. Just place the mouse pointer over the icon, and you can read the description.

Creating a control: Kind of a drag . . .

Creating controls in your dialog box is much like using drawing icons in Lotus Freelance Graphics or other graphics programs. You just click and drag. Suppose, for example, that you wanted to create a Lotus Label.

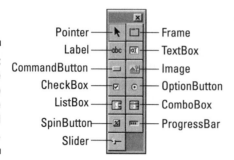

Figure 8-5:
Use these
icons to
create the
most-used
controls.

Pointer — Frame
Label — TextBox
CommandButton — Image
CheckBox — OptionButton
ListBox — ComboBox
SpinButton — ProgressBar
Slider

Follow these steps:

1. Click the Lotus Label icon.

The mouse pointer changes into a crosshair.

**2. Click and drag in the Dialog Editor window where you want the label to
appear; then release the mouse button.**

Figure 8-6 shows a sample Lotus Label, Label 1.

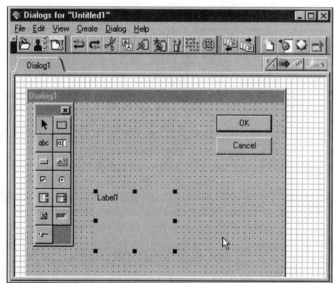

Figure 8-6:
Click and
drag to
create a
control.

You can, of course, use the menus instead of the toolbar to create your controls.
In fact, if you prefer reading the names of the controls to see what an icon
stands for, you may definitely want to use the menus. Figure 8-7 shows the
selections that you see if you choose Create⇨Control from the Dialog Editor menu.

Whether you use the icons or the menus, you have several options for elements and controls to use in your dialog boxes. Table 8-1 gives a brief description of dialog box elements.

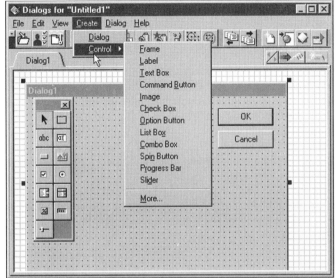

Figure 8-7:
If you like choosing from words instead of pictures, use this menu.

Table 8-1	LotusScript Dialog Box Elements
Control	*Description*
Frame	Container for other controls
Label	Text the user can't change
Text Box	Text the user *can* change
Command Button	The user clicks on it to begin or end a process
Image	Displays a bitmap, an icon, or a metafile as a graphic
Check Box	Allows the user to choose or not choose a single option
Option Button	Usually comes as part of a group of option buttons and allows the user to choose only one (kind of like the "Test your newfound knowledge" sections in this book)
List Box	Displays a list, from which the user can select one or more items
Combo Box	Lets the user select by typing text into a text box or by selecting an item from a list

(continued)

Table 8-1 *(continued)*

Control	Description
Spin Button	User clicks on arrows to change a setting
Progress Bar	Shows progress as an activity is being completed
Slider	User drags the slider to change a setting

You can create dialog boxes with more than one kind of control. If you want to create a dialog box with a text box, a check box, and a combo box, you simply click and drag to place each element. Figure 8-8 shows a sample dialog box with a text box, a check box, and a combo box.

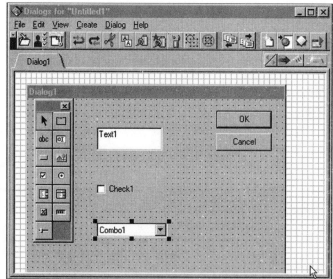

Figure 8-8: A sample dialog box with three popular controls.

Arranging the controls in your dialog box

You don't have to use just your eyesight to size and place controls properly on the form. You can get the Dialog Editor to arrange the controls for you. The trick is to select all controls first. Suppose that you wanted to realign the boxes shown in Figure 8-8. You can follow these steps:

1. From the Dialog Editor menu, choose Edit⇨Select All.

LotusScript selects all the controls, including the common OK and Cancel buttons.

2. Then choose <u>D</u>ialog⟹<u>A</u>lign, Dialog⟹Equal <u>S</u>pacing, or Dialog⟹Equal Si<u>z</u>ing.

You see some alignment or sizing options, as shown in Figure 8-9.

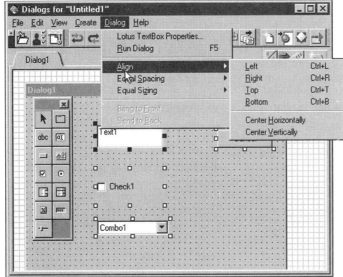

Figure 8-9:
Use this menu to help you size and place your controls.

Figure 8-10 shows the arrangement in the sample dialog box that you're creating when you choose <u>D</u>ialog⟹<u>E</u>qual Spacing⟹<u>H</u>orizontal.

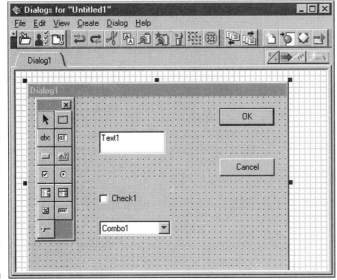

Figure 8-10:
The dialog editor can set up equal spacing better than you can by eyeballing it.

What if you really hate your new control element alignment after you get it? Well, never forget the good old Undo choice (on the Edit menu). If you choose Undo right after you align your controls, they go back to the way they were before your new alignment. You even have a keyboard shortcut for Undo: Ctrl+Z.

Naming and Saving Your Dialog Box

You can also change the names of dialog boxes to more useful appellations than *Dialog1;* I show you how in Chapter 9. To name the dialog box, you first select the dialog box, right-click it, and then type in a new name in the resulting Lotus InfoBox.

You can save a dialog box in the same way you save a script in the Script Editor — namely, you save the whole document that the Dialog Editor is in. If you're working in Word Pro, you save a document. If you're working in 1-2-3, you save a worksheet, and so on. From your program's main menu, choose File⇨Save and then name the document in the usual way. If you want to get back to your Dialog Box later, just open the document.

Setting Properties: When You Need a Name Change

Buttons come with default properties — properties like their names, the fonts they use, their positions on the page, and their border styles. You don't have to go through and set all those things up yourself, if you like the defaults.

However, sometimes you definitely want to make changes to the default properties. I mean, a label that says Label1 doesn't really tell the user anything meaningful. Unless you're going to change the text displayed on the label, you may as well not create the label in the first place.

To change the properties of a control, you use the Lotus InfoBox, a tool that you probably recognize from various Lotus programs. For example, you can use the following steps to change a label so that it displays a meaningful message.

1. **Click the label to select it.**

2. **From the Dialog Editor's main menu, choose Dialog⇨Lotus TextBox properties.**

    The Lotus InfoBox comes up, as shown in Figure 8-11.

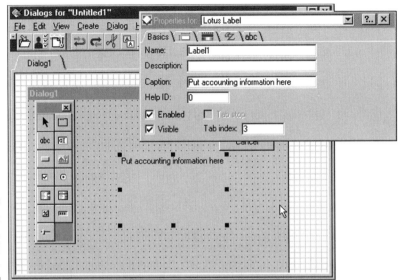

Figure 8-11:
The revised, meaningful label.

As is so often the case in Windows 95, you can use the right mouse button for a shortcut. To show the InfoBox, right-click the object — like the label or other control — and then click Properties from the shortcut menu.

3. In the Caption text box, delete the word *Label1* and type in a meaningful caption.

In Figure 8-11, you can see the caption Put accounting information here. The caption appears as the new text in the label box — a meaningful message in real English!

This advice for making changes to a control is deceptively simple, but it isn't necessarily intuitive. Unless you read this, or figure it out on your own, you may try to put text in a label by clicking inside the text box (or using similar techniques that you may be accustomed to using in other programs). When you're working with dialog boxes and controls through the Dialog Editor, however, you face more restrictions than in those other, familiar programs. In the Dialog Editor, you can't just click and type to add words to a control, but must use the Properties InfoBox instead. I could see people getting frustrated and saying, "Okay, I give up, how do I get this text box to have *text* in it?"

Test your newfound knowledge

A dialog box is

1. Kind of like a cardboard box, but usually smaller.

2. The way that scripters contend with this basic truth of human nature: It's hard to get people to do what you want.

3. More useful than a dialog circle, because it's square and stays solidly in place on its base.

4. A place where people go to talk, a lot like a Chat room on the Internet.

To create a control in a dialog box, you

1. Take on your most authoritative air and just act like you're in charge. You'll get all the controls you need.

2. Just do it. Hey, nothing's stopping you. Just go ahead and put the control in there.

3. Draft your control on a drafting table. Spend all day doing it and be sure to use a ruler. Then stick it on your computer screen.

4. Click on the control you want in the Dialog Editor toolbar; then click and drag to position it in your dialog box.

Chapter 9

The Dialog Box Redux: Scripting the Box and Its Controls

● ●

In This Chapter

▶ Creating dialog boxes and controls, again

▶ Attaching a neat script to a dialog box control

▶ Running the dialog box with neat scripts attached

▶ Scripting not a control, but a whole dialog box

● ●

*I*n Chapter 8, I talk about how to splash fancy controls, like buttons or drop-down lists, all over a dialog box that you create. Using LotusScript's Dialog Editor to create dialog boxes can give you quite a feeling of power. And you can take charge of the dialog box controls by changing their properties — like giving them meaningful names.

For a taste of real power, though, you can do more than change the properties of your dialog box controls. You can script controls; in fact, you can script the whole dialog box. In this chapter, I talk about how to attach scripts to dialog boxes and their controls.

Starting the Dialog Editor (Again)

You must create a dialog box with controls before you can attach scripts. And to create a dialog box, you use the LotusScript Dialog Editor. These steps show you how to get a new, blank dialog box:

1. **Start one of the Lotus programs that contains the Dialog Editor: Word Pro, 1-2-3, or Freelance Graphics. Create a new document.**

   The example that I picture in the chapter uses Word Pro and saves the sample document with the name *Dialog*.

**2. Click the Dialog Editor SmartIcon or choose Edit⊅Script &
Macros⊅Show Dialog Editor from the program's main menu.**

A new dialog box, as shown in Figure 9-1, appears.

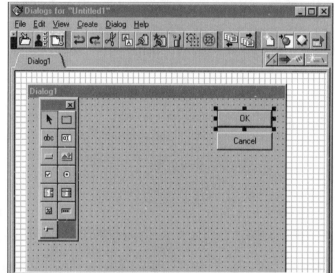

Figure 9-1:
A new
dialog box.

Scripting a Control

Controls in a dialog box are elements like buttons, list boxes, and check boxes
that make up the user interface. That is, users click buttons, view lists, select
options, and so on through these dialog box controls. In turn, the user interaction with these controls gives information to the relevant program — your
attached scripts.

When you change the properties for a control, you can give information to the
users and also get the control to act in certain ways. When you *script* the
control (attach a script to the control), however, you can get the control to do
anything — that is, anything you can write a script to do.

Setting up your control

Use these steps to create a dialog box control and set the properties for it:

1. **With the Dialog Editor open and a new dialog box showing, click the icon for the control that you want to create in the Dialog Editor's toolbar.**

   The mouse pointer becomes a crosshair to guide you as you draw and place your control in the dialog box. To follow this example, click the Lotus CommandButton icon, shown in the margin, in the toolbar.

2. **Click and drag in the dialog box until the control is the shape and size that you want. Then release the mouse button.**

   Figure 9-2 shows the dialog box with the new command button.

   Controls are easier to work with when they have names that mean something to users. As a scripter, you can create command buttons and attach frequently used commands to them.

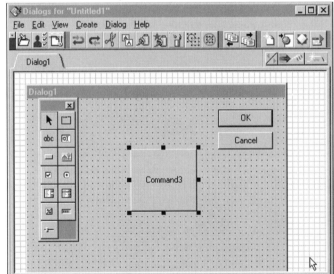

Figure 9-2: A sample dialog box with a sample command button.

For this example, suppose that you often want to display the date, and so you decide to create a control that lets you display the date with just a mouse click. You can name the command button accordingly.

3. **With the control selected (that is, with the square black handles showing on its border), choose Dialog⇨Lotus CommandButton Properties from the Dialog Editor main menu.**

   The Lotus Properties InfoBox, as shown in Figure 9-3, appears.

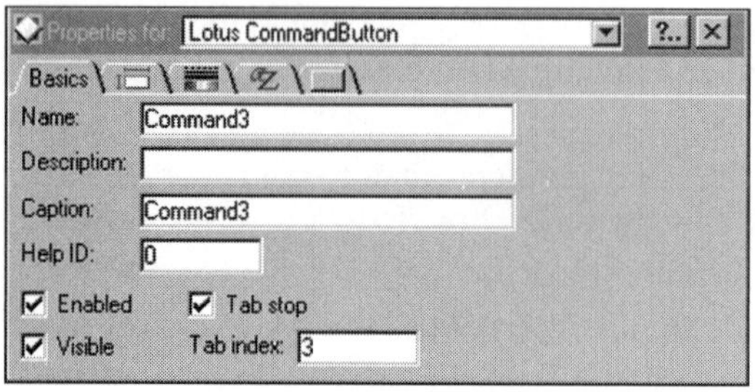

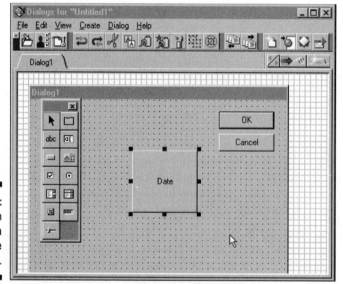

Figure 9-3:
Change
properties in
this InfoBox.

4. In the Basic tab of the InfoBox, change the text in the Caption text box to Date.

You can change other characteristics of your control if you want, like its size, location, and the font used for the caption. You find these options on the various tabs of the Properties InfoBox.

5. Click the close button (X) to close the InfoBox.

Figure 9-4 shows the command button with its new, meaningful name.

Figure 9-4:
The button
now has a
recognizable
name.

Creating a script for your control

After you create a dialog box with a meaningful control, you're ready to get down to the real business of this chapter — scripting the control.

1. **In the Dialog Editor, select the control that you want to attach a script to. (That is, click the control.)**

   For the example, select the Date command button.

2. **Choose View⇨Show Scripts.**

   The Script Editor opens, ready to help you write the script for the control that you're working with. Figure 9-5 shows the Script Editor window. Notice that the Script Editor opens to the right place, with the right associations for scripting your control. That is, the name of the control is already in the Object list box, and a blank sub for the selected control is ready for you to enter your script lines.

Name of control   Associated event

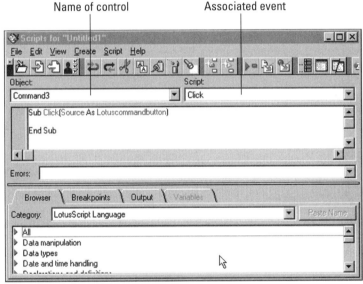

Figure 9-5:
The Script
Editor, for
scripting the
control.

Because the example uses a command *button* as the selected control, the script is automatically associated with the *event* of a mouse click. (You know, users click buttons on-screen.) This association explains the name Click in the Script drop-down list box. You can see Chapter 15 for more information on attaching scripts to objects and events.

A shortcut to bringing up the Script Editor for a control is to double-click the control — like the button in the example in this chapter. Double-clicking is nice and mindless, and you don't even have to remember which menu commands to use.

3. Type in the LotusScript statements for what you want the script to do.

For this example, type this script line:

```
Print Date$
```

4. Click the close or minimize button at the top right of the Script Editor window and go back to the Dialog Editor.

When you complete these steps, you've scripted the control. In the next section, you can see how to try out your scripted control.

Running the Scripts Attached to Controls

When you have scripts attached to your dialog boxes or controls, you don't have to close the Dialog Editor to check them out. That is, you can run your scripts from the Dialog Editor.

You can't just click on the button (or other dialog box control) to find out whether an attached script works. (I can picture almost everybody trying that the first time: Click. Click. Click. "Oh, man, this doesn't work. How do I get it to work?") But when you're creating a dialog box (or a control in the dialog box), that dialog box or control isn't yet functional. You have to do something special to your creation to tell it to stop being created and start performing.

Use these steps to try out your dialog box script from the Dialog Editor:

1. From the menu, choose Dialog⇨Run Dialog, or just press F5.

A dialog box with the control you added comes up. The example with the Date command button is shown in Figure 9-6.

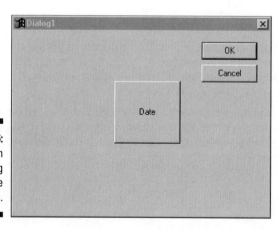

Figure 9-6:
You can run the dialog box you're building.

2. **In the dialog box, activate the control that has the script attached.**

   How you activate the control depends on the control itself, you click a button, select an option, check the check box, and so on.

   In this example, click the Date button. The date prints in the Output panel of the Script Editor.

3. **Click the close button (X) in the top-right corner of the sample dialog box to close it.**

Controls become powerful when you script them. You can use all the scripting techniques that I talk about in this book (and others that I don't talk about) to build really creative dialog boxes. And dialog boxes are great for communicating with users that interface with your scripts.

Scripting a Whole Dialog Box

The steps for scripting a dialog box are the same as those for scripting a control (except, of course, that they're for a dialog box instead of a control). You can give the dialog box a meaningful name, and you can run the dialog box from the Dialog menu.

Naming a dialog box

To name the dialog box, you change the property in the Lotus InfoBox as follows:

1. **Click on the dialog box to select it.**

   Be sure that the handles show on the dialog box, not on a control.

2. **From the Dialog Editor menu, choose Dialog⇨Dialog Properties.**

   The Lotus Properties InfoBox for the Dialog box, as shown in Figure 9-7, comes up.

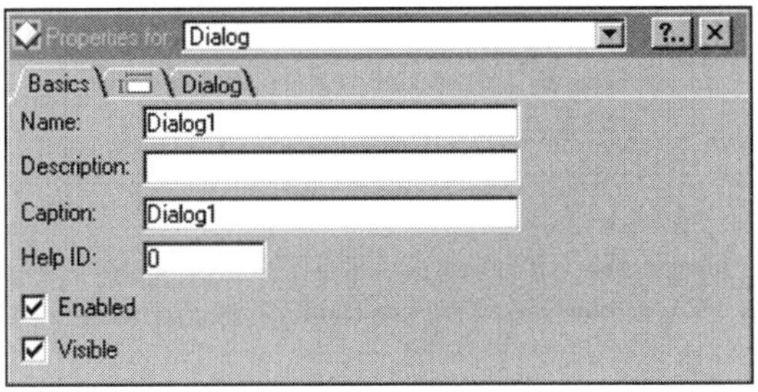

Figure 9-7:
The Lotus
InfoBox for
Dialog
properties.

Properties for | Dialog

Basics \ 🔲 \ Dialog \
Name: | Dialog1
Description: |
Caption: | Dialog1
Help ID: | 0
☑ Enabled
☑ Visible

3. Fill in the Name and Caption text boxes.

The example changes both the name (which you use to refer to the dialog box in your scripts) and the Caption (which appears on the tab for the dialog box) to the name `Date_box`.

Figure 9-8 shows the completed InfoBox and the changed name on the dialog box.

The changed name shows up here

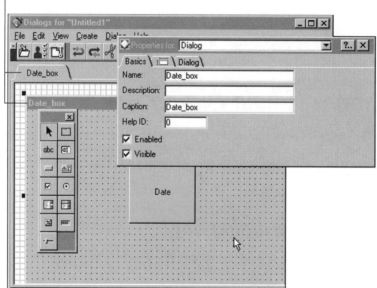

Figure 9-8:
The renamed dialog box.

4. Click the X in the upper-right corner to close the Properties InfoBox.

Renaming dialog boxes with meaningful names is a good idea because they're more intuitive to work with. You don't *have* to change their names or anything.

Scripting a dialog box

To script the dialog box, go to the Script Editor and write the script for it, just as you do with a control.

1. With the Dialog box selected (that is, with the black handles showing on it), choose View➪Show Scripts. Or just double-clicking the dialog box is easier.

The Script Editor comes up for the dialog box, ready for you to type in your script. It has the name of the dialog box in the Object list box and everything.

2. Type in your script.

The example uses this simple message box:

```
Messagebox "This is a good way to get the date."
```

Running the dialog

You can run the script for the whole dialog box in the same way that you run the script for a control: From the Dialog Editor main menu, choose Dialog⇔Run Dialog. The script for the dialog box runs, and after you click OK in the message box, the sample dialog box comes up with the Date command button.

Calling a dialog box

You may want to use a dialog box by calling it from the middle of some other script that you're writing. To call a dialog box, you call it by name, as in the following code where Date_box is the dialog box name.

```
Sub Main
    Date_box.show
End Sub
```

Test your newfound knowledge

How do you script a control?

1. Very, very carefully, because controls don't like being scripted.

2. Double-click the control, then type in the script.

3. You can't do it. Controls are rebellious and resist any kind of supervision.

4. Use a felt pen and write all over your computer monitor.

How do you run a script in a dialog box?

1. Keep it on its leash. Otherwise, it will run into the wall of the dialog box.

2. I don't know. That's too hard.

3. From the Dialog menu, choose Run Dialog.

4. Yell "Run" really loud at the Dialog box. If it doesn't work the first time, keep yelling.

Part III
Lost in the Wilderness: Loops, Ifs, Subs, and So On

"Larry, do you remember when I suggested removing the Print statement from the loop in your script?"

In this part . . .

You know that you're really launched on your expedition when you see no one around but you, the trees, a guide . . . and when you hear the sound of wild animals in the distance. In scripting, a time comes when you have to get down to the real work. And when you do the real work, you'll use the structures described in this part — loops, If statements, subs, and functions. Oh, you'll probably get lost at times, but that goes with the territory.

Chapter 10

If Statements: To Be, or Not to Be . . .

In This Chapter
- Writing an If statement, and why you want to
- Working with alternatives by using ElseIf
- Deciding to select Select Case instead of If
- Nesting your Ifs

*I*n Chapters 6 and 7, I talk about variables, expressions, and operators — various pieces in the language of LotusScript. Of course, individual language elements don't do much by themselves — in English, Martian, BASIC, or any other language. In the case of LotusScript, putting these language elements together helps you build scripts that accomplish the work you intend. For example, you can use a script to keep from repeating work — by moving time sheet data from Notes into Word Pro automatically.

To put variables, keywords, operators, and all those elements to work in LotusScript, you use statements. Probably the most widely used programming statement is the If Statement. If you had minimal time to practice with LotusScript and then had to write a complex program for your company (something, I believe, that has happened often in the past), you would almost definitely make use of the If statement.

The Syntax of the If...Then...Else Statement

According to its formal definition, the LotusScript If...Then...Else statement conditionally executes a statement (or statements) in a script's code depending on its evaluation of an expression. The syntax for the complete statement looks like this:

```
If condition Then [ statements1 ] [ Else [ statements2 ]]
```

In the syntax of the `If` statement, the script writer supplies the `condition`, `statements1`, and `statements2`. In English, the `If...Then...Else` syntax statement means this: If a certain `condition` is true, then put one or more other statements (`statements1`) into effect. Otherwise (else), if the `condition` is not true, put another set of one or more statements (`statements2`) into effect.

If...Then

The following script shows a simple example of an `If...Then...Else` statement:

```
Sub Main

'Create a variable to return a grade
    Dim grade As Integer
    'Put in an input box to get a sample value for the
            variable
    grade = Inputbox("What is your grade?")
    'Put in the "if" portion of the statement
    If grade < 75 Then
        'Use the Print statement, sending results to Output
            panel
        Print "Your grade is unsatisfactory."
'Put in the Else statement and what to print for it
    Else
        Print "Your grade is GREAT!"
    End If

End Sub
```

The preceding script accepts the `grade` as input, `Inputbox("What is your grade?")`, and executes the `If...Then...Else` statement based on the value of the `grade`. If you run the preceding script and put a value less than 75 into the input box, the script evaluates the condition (`grade < 75`) as true and executes the script's first `Print` line. If you enter a value of 75 or greater, the script sees the condition (`grade < 75`) as false and executes the `Print` line that follows the `Else`.

For example, when you type in **65** for the grade in the input box, you see this result in the Output panel:

```
Your grade is unsatisfactory.
```

When you use the `Print` statement in your scripts, the resulting output appears in the Output panel of the IDE. See Chapter 4 for more information on the IDE (Integrated Development Environment).

. . .Else

When you run the preceding sub and change the grade that you type in to **80**, you see the following result in the Output panel:

```
Your grade is GREAT!
```

One reason that `If` statements are so popular with scripters is that they enable the scripter to skip code in the script that doesn't always need to be executed. By providing conditions for evaluation, the `If` statement helps the script to ascertain right at the outset whether to go ahead with what can be a complex series of instructions.

Start with this example as a base:

```
Sub Main
'Create a variable to hold a person's net worth
   Dim net_Worth As Currency
   'Ask for a value for the variable
   net_Worth = Inputbox("What is your net worth?")
   'Put in the "if" portion of the statement
   If net_Worth < 100 Then
   'Use the Print statement, sending results to Output panel
      Print "Please come back tomorrow."
   'Put in the Else statement and what to print for it
   Else
      Print "Yes, please come in."
   End If

End Sub
```

If a person enters **85** in the input box, this message comes up:

```
Please come back tomorrow.
```

And the program stops executing.

If the person enters **105** in the input box, this message comes up:

```
Yes, please come in.
```

The script could go on to execute a whole series of statements and subroutines — like asking for the detailed information needed for filling in a loan application. This series of statements and subroutines executes only when the If decides that the right conditions are met.

To me, this use of the If...Then...Else statement explains the rather abrupt habit (shared by many scripters) of saying "Wrong!" most emphatically in the midst of otherwise free-flowing conversations. In a world where so little is truly black and white, scripters sometimes see things with an almost gleeful simplicity.

Looking on to If...Then... ElseIf...

The simple If...Then...Else statement is essentially an either/or proposition. If the conditions are met, one result comes up. If they are not, the other result comes up. End of story.

But adding another statement to your script — ElseIf — allows you to handle more than one alternative for the If statement. If the first conditions are not met, but these other conditions are, or these, or these . . . then your script can execute a set of one or more statements based on those other conditions instead.

For example:

```
Sub Main
    'Create a variable to return a grade
    Dim grade As Integer
    'Put in an input box to get a sample grade
    grade = Inputbox("What is your grade?")

    'Put in the "if" portion of the statement
    If grade < 75 Then
    'Use the Print statement, sending results to Output panel
        Print "Your grade is unsatisfactory."
    'Put in the ElseIf statement
    ElseIf grade < 85 Then
        Print "Hey, that's pretty good."
'Put in the Else statement and what to print for it
```

```
    Else
        Print "You did GREAT!"
    End If

End Sub
```

When you run the preceding script with the `ElseIf` statement, you now have
the possibility of seeing three different results in the Output panel. If you type in
70 as a grade in the input box, you see the following:

```
Your grade is unsatisfactory.
```

If you type in **82** as your grade in the input box, you see this line in the Output
panel:

```
Hey, that's pretty good.
```

And finally, if you type in **85** (or any greater value), you see this line:

```
You did GREAT!
```

Working with Alternatives — Select Case

I don't know. . . . I think I'd be satisfied to write even a real long script using
`If...Then...Else` and `If...Then...ElseIf` structures. I've never been one
to scurry after all the memory saving secrets, shortcuts, tricks, and hints that a
certain breed of computer user goes after. If I can get this one to work, then go
out and watch some good television or have a cool drink by the pool, I'm happy.

However, LotusScript provides a second kind of statement that does the same
kind of work (that is, selectively executing statements based on criteria) as do
the `If` statements. This second statement is the `Select Case` statement.

The `Select Case` statement syntax looks like this:

```
Select Case selectExpression
    [ Case condtionList1
        [ statements1 ] ]
    [ Case condtionList2
        [ statements2 ] ]
    ...
    [ Case Else
        [ statementsx ] ]
End Select
```

The following is an example of the Select Case statement in practice. Imagine that each candidate for a position has a certain number. In the example script, I just assign the number in the line that says candidate = 14. (Some other elaborate function or subroutine could provide the number crunching to come up with the candidate's number, but I don't show that in this example.)

The Select Case statement looks at the value of an expression (the value for candidate is 14, in the example) and attempts to match the value with the value of each Case. After finding a match for the value, the Select Case statement executes whatever statements are associated with that value. (The example script prints a message to the match *winner* in the Output panel.) If Select Case doesn't find a match, it executes the statements called for by the Case Else part of the structure. After executing the statements for a successful Case match or for the Case Else condition, the Select Case statement is done.

```
Sub Main
    Dim candidate As Integer
    candidate = 14
    Select Case candidate
    Case 14
        Print "Jolene comes through!"
    Case 2
        Print "It's your day, Harvey!"
    Case 18
        Print "Frank's a winner!"
    Case Else
        Print "No worthy candidate today."
    End Select
End Sub
```

When this example script runs, it prints the output "Jolene comes through!" in the Output panel. You can try other values for candidate and see what output each one creates.

The advantage that some programmers see to the Select Case statement over the If...Then...Else statement is that the Select Case structure is a little easier to read. These programmers can easily look back through their scripts and see what was going on. And this structure avoids repeating the variable name on every ElseIf. I can see that avoiding repetition may cut down on typing mistakes, too.

Nesting with If*s and* Select Cases

In the past, I've been a bit, oh, sardonic with the way BASIC languages use the familiar English tongue — like calling an *ampersand* (&) the *concatenation character,* referring to *names* as *identifiers,* and so on. In all fairness, I must point out that, in at least one occasion, BASIC uses a perfectly simple, normal, unpretentious, everyday word for one of its elements. And that word is *nest.*

To *nest,* according to my dictionary, is "to put snugly together or inside one another." When computer languages nest their Ifs, they put one If statement snugly inside another If statement. In this case, the formal computer term *nest* is easy, descriptive, a little quaint, and readily understandable.

You and I may rarely nest our own ifs, in English, exactly the way LotusScript does in scripting. But you or I may say, "If my cold is gone, and if it's not raining, I'll go out running today." But LotusScript puts *complete* If...Then expressions inside each other, as if to say: "If my cold is gone, then I'll look outside, and if it's not raining, then I'll go out running today."

In code, these statements would look as follows:

```
If my cold is gone Then
    I'll look outside
    If it's not raining Then
        I'll go out running today
    End If
End If
```

The following is a real scripting example of a nested If structure:

```
Sub Main
'Create a variable to hold a grade
    Dim grade As Integer
    'Put in an input box to ask for a variable value
    grade = Inputbox("What is your grade?")
    'Put in the "if" portion of the statement
    If grade < 75 Then
        'Put in the "nested if"
        If grade >= 70 Then
            Print "Come in for a make-up test."
        End If
        'Use Print to send results to Output panel
        Print "Your grade is unsatisfactory."
    'Put in the Else statement and what to print for it
```

(continued)

(continued)

```
    Else
        Print "You did GREAT!"
    End If

End Sub
```

When you run the preceding sub and put in a grade of **71**, the nested If executes, and you see this result:

```
Come in for a make-up test.
Your grade is unsatisfactory.
```

You can include any number of ElseIf expressions in the block of If statements, too. When you include an If statement within an If statement (that is, nest your Ifs), you must terminate each If block (set of code lines) with an End If. But LotusScript helps you remember this by supplying the End If each time you type in an If.

Programmers refer to a *block* of code as a set of code lines that go together to make up some larger, logical structure. For example, the multiple script lines of an If...Then...ElseIf... statement can be called an If block.

Although, as far as the compiler is concerned, you can nest Ifs inside Ifs to your heart's content, you may find that trying to come back later and figure out what you have done is confusing. Experienced scripters tend to use subs instead of nested Ifs, because they're easier to read, easier for the human mind to keep straight, and easier to debug. Chapter 12 talks about subs.

Test your newfound knowledge

When does an If statement execute something?

1. When that something is definitely guilty of a capital crime.

2. Anytime. If is completely out of control and is running amok.

3. When If finds the expression in its *condition* to be *true*.

4. When no one is looking.

Under what circumstances is it useful to nest an If statement?

1. If you want to breed your Ifs and you want them to live comfortably and happily.

2. When you want to set up a second set of If conditions for the first set of If conditions.

3. If you want to hide an If so that no one but you knows it's there.

4. None of the above.

Chapter 11

Loops: Run That One by Me Again

. . . .

In This Chapter

▶ Counting with `For` loops (Why `For` loops are great if you want the loop to go off an exact number of times.)

▶ Stopping your `For` loop (Why you don't want your `For` going off `For`ever.)

▶ Working with nested loops

▶ Conditioning your loops to respect the truth (How `While` loops can last as long as a condition is true.)

▶ Recognizing that false conditions can run your loops, too (How `Do` loops can last as long as a condition is false.)

. . . .

*G*oing up to a programmer and saying, "Why would I want to use a loop anyway?" (as, I must confess, I did) is about like saying to a surgeon, "I can't really see the value of scalpels," or, to a law enforcement official, "What would anybody want a squad car for?"

Loops are a stock tool-of-the-trade for a programmer. Programmers use loops to save themselves time and trouble when programming. That is, because the structure of a loop is such that a program statement or series of statements repeats itself, the programmers don't have to repeat the statements or series of statements in their code. When an instruction has to repeat many times, an effective programmer puts that instruction in the program only once, within a looping structure, so that it repeats over and over again.

But programming without loops would make for a long and tedious journey — like being a one-person water brigade and having to walk back-and-forth to the well to put out a fire. Setting up a complete brigade (in a loop, that is) and letting it run on its own is much more efficient.

Recognizing the Value of Loops

Suppose that a program's purpose is to go over to a database of customers and pull out data — you know, something confidential and juicy — like salary information for Employee 2052. Then, the program goes back to go get salary information for Employee 2053 . . . then Employee 2054 . . . and Employee 2055; you get the idea.

The program goes to the database, again and again, to pull out the confidential salary information for each employee. But the program instructions that actually search the database and return the salary information need to appear in the program code only once. When you write these instructions into a loop, the program can repeat them as often as needed to accomplish its task.

I believe that loops are as intrinsic to scripting as variables — almost. They may not be quite as essential. You may get the result that you want from your script without using loops, but you often can't get results at all without defining a variable at the outset.

LotusScript has three main looping structures for the LotusScript programmer — For, While, and Do loops. Each type of loop has certain advantages and uses. So without any more aDo, I introduce the For loop.

Counting It Out with For *Loops*

The simplest of the looping statements in LotusScript is For, also known as For...Next. The syntax statement looks like this:

```
For countVar1 = firstnum To lastnum [ Step increment ]
  [ statements ]
Next [ countVar1 ]
```

This For statement, roughly translated into English, means that you loop through the For structure governed by a variable (countVar1) for counting the repetitions. The expression firstnum is the initial value of the loop counter and lastnum is the final value. You follow the For line with one or more statements to be repeated in the loop. Then, you finish the For structure with a Next statement.

You can tell by the brackets [ ] that the [Step increment] part of the For syntax statement is optional, and therefore, you may not need to think about that element right now. But if you're curious, just know that you can change how you count your way through the For loop by using this optional element. And you can read the sidebar "The two-step and other fancy maneuvers" in this chapter for more information.

Looking at a sample For *loop*

Of course, seeing a specific example of a statement in use is always easier than imagining what the statement does by looking at its syntax diagram. The following simple script uses a For loop (and actually works; I just ran the script and then copied it over from the IDE).

```
Sub Main
    For count = 1 To 4
        Print "The current count is " count
    Next
End Sub
```

You can try this script in the LotusScript IDE yourself, if you like. If all goes well, the output you get in the Output panel looks like this:

```
The current count is = 1
The current count is = 2
The current count is = 3
The current count is = 4
```

The For block of the script, line-by-line, means this:

- **Line 1:** Create the variable count, set its value to 1 to start out, and keep going in the loop until count reaches 4.

- **Line 2:** Print (in the Output panel) the words The current count is followed by the value of the variable count at that point.

- **Line 3:** (Next) Add 1 to the value of count and go back to the first line of the For block.

Of course, real programmers don't just print lines like The current count is 1, and so on, or write scripts to mark time by repeating beeping sounds. No, with those loop statements in between the For and Next script lines, they can search databases, compute salaries, print reports, or do all kinds of other neat things. (At least, that's what my programmer friends helped me realize.)

Deciding whether For *is for you*

After you decide to do a little looping in your script, you still have another choice to make. You can choose among For loops, While loops, and Do loops.

When you use the `For` statement, you set up your loop to go off a certain number of times by assigning first and last values to the variable that counts the loop, as in the expression `count = 1 To 5`. Programmers turn to the `For` loop, in fact, when they need to specify a set number of repetitions for the loop to execute. (Neither the `While` nor the `Do` loop, also discussed in this chapter, has nearly the same inherent ability to be so specific — to count to an exact number, that is.)

The two-step and other fancy maneuvers

What won't these BASIC originators think of? Unless you (as the scripter) specify otherwise, LotusScript counts by . . . as you may expect . . . *ones,* as in 1, 2, 3, 4, 5, and so on, when counting its way through a loop.

However, with the `Step increment` expression, you can have LotusScript count by, say, twos (or tens, or thirteens, or whatever). Now, this great flexibility is of little concern to most of us. But the feature is there, so I'll mention it for those curious enough to be reading these "Technical stuff" notes.

Suppose that you ran the following example, using the `Step increment` option, like this:

```
For count = 1 To 6 Step 2
   Print "The current count is "
   count
Next
```

And the output in the Output panel looks like this:

```
The current count is 1

The current count is 3

The current count is 5
```

Notice how the script counts by twos? That's because the script contains the optional element `Step 2` in the first line.

You can even have it count backwards. Your script may look something like this:

```
For count = 6 To 1 Step -2
   Print "The current count is "
   count
Next
```

The output then looks like this:

```
The current count is 6

The current count is 4

The current count is 2
```

That's pretty cool, in a literal-minded, programming sort of way. At least, the `Step increment` element is pretty flexible. Now, I don't have a lot of occasions when I would want to count backward or by something other than ones. But some people have such occasions, I dare say, and I think the fact that LotusScript has that capability, thanks to `Step`, is nice for them.

Warning: Endless For loops (or For Forever)

Creating endless loops with the other loop statements that I discuss in this chapter — While and Do — is actually easier than creating endless loops with For. Nevertheless, you can do it, so beware. An endless loop is a loop in a program that goes on, and on, and on . . . like the Energizer bunny.

Endless loops are kind of funny, but they're disconcerting to new scripters, who don't realize that everybody who programs eventually (and inadvertently) creates an endless loop.

I want to tell you, before we go any further, how to get out of an endless loop when you find yourself in one (because, inevitably, you'll one day find yourself in one). When you're running your script and find yourself caught in an endless loop, press the Esc key (top left of the keyboard) to stop the script.

With a For statement, you can cause an endless loop if you somehow changed the value of the counting variable inside the loop, like this: (Remember, don't do this. This is an example of something not to do, as in, "Don't pull open the emergency door when you're flying on an airplane.").

```
Sub Main
   For count = 1 To 6
      Print "The current count is " count
      count = 3
   Next
End Sub
```

Following is a summary of what these derelict, undesirable script lines say to do:

- ✔ **Line 1:** Create a variable called count and set its starting value to 1.

- ✔ **Line 2:** Print the words The current count is followed by the value of the variable count.

- ✔ **Line 3:** Assign the value 3 to the variable count.

- ✔ **Line 4:** Add 1 to the value of count. (Because count is always equal to 3 at this point, 3+1 makes count equal to 4.) Go back to line 1.

After the first time through the loop (where the Print statement shows count with an initial value of 1), count will always equal 4, and the Output panel will fill up with lines that say current count = 4. Your computer will dutifully reach the same conclusion over, and over, and over again. Endlessly. And you can see that such results are not good, so don't go changing the value of the counting variable inside the loop.

Nesting your For loops

Whereas nesting sentence after sentence isn't that desirable in English (and the human mind quickly loses the thread of what's going on), nesting your script statements can be quite practical for computers (which don't lose the thread, no matter how long it is).

You can include a For loop within a For loop, as in the following example:

```
Sub Main
Dim a As Integer
Dim b As Integer
For a% = 1 To 5
    For b% = 1 To 2
        Print a% ;
    Next        'Next b
Next            'Next a
End Sub
```

The script lines in this example mean the following:

- ✔ **Line 1:** Declare the variable a as an integer.
- ✔ **Line 2:** Declare the variable b as an integer.
- ✔ **Line 3:** When the variable a is equal to a number from 1 to 5
- ✔ **Line 4:** Then, for each a when the variable b is equal to from 1 to 2
- ✔ **Line 5:** Print the value of a at that time.
- ✔ **Line 6:** Then add 1 to the value of b and go to the next b (line 4).
- ✔ **Line 7:** Then add 1 to the value of a and go to the next a (line 3).

If you run a script with this code, you see the following values in the Output panel:

```
1 1 2 2 3 3 4 4 5 5
```

Conditioning Your Loops with While

Whereas you set up the For statement to loop for a specific number of times, you set up the While statement to go off as long as (that is, *while*) a certain condition is true.

Look at this example of the `While` statement:

```
Dim count As Integer
count = 1
While count < 5
    Print "The current count is " count
    count = count + 1
Wend
```

The output for this example looks like this in the Output panel:

```
The current count is 1
The current count is 2
The current count is 3
The current count is 4
```

A *while* can be a very long time if the condition in the `While` statement always is met. In fact, a while can be forever. Almost nobody wants a program to go on forever, caught in another of those endless loops. (A virus-maker or some other pesky troublemaker might want it, but most people don't.)

To keep your `While` loop from going on forever, make sure that you have at least one instruction inside the loop that makes the condition expression of the `While` statement become false. That way, the `While` condition can no longer be true, and the loop stops.

If you ran the following script, you'd be caught in an endless loop (and that wouldn't be good). Notice that the line in the loop statements that adjusts the counting variable `count` has been commented-out — that is, the single quote mark (`'`) has been placed at the beginning of the script line, as if the line were a comment:

```
Dim count As Integer
count = 1
While count < 5
    Print "The current count is" count
    'Comment out the line that changes
            the value of the condition
    'count = count + 1
Wend
```

The line that saves the day, to keep the endless loop from occurring, is the line `count=count+1`. This line increases the value of the variable `count` by 1 and eventually changes the condition (`count < 5`) from true to false (once the `count` reaches 6).

Doing It with Do Loops

Do loops are really my favorite of the three kinds of loops in this chapter, just because *do loop* is neat to say. It kind of rolls around on the tongue. And I like the internal rhyme of *do* and *loop*. As for whether Do is any more useful than For or While, well no, I can't say that it is.

Both Do and While repeat the loop statements as long as the initial condition remains in effect. A While loop continues until the While condition becomes false. But I can't make the same blanket statement for the Do loop because it has two forms — the Do While and the Do Until. And like so much else in scripting, these loop statements can get confusing: The Do While form of the Do loop (which is an awful lot like the While loop) continues to repeat the loop statements until the While condition becomes false. The Do Until form of the Do loop repeats the loop statements until the Until condition becomes true.

The syntax for the Do statement looks like this:

```
Do [ While | Until condition ]
    [ loop statements ]
Loop
```

Alternatively, the syntax can look like this:

```
Do
    [ loop statements ]
Loop [ While | Until condition ]
```

Do While

This is an example of a Do While loop:

```
Dim var1 As Integer
var1% = 1
'Test var1's value before executing loop.
Do While var1% < 5
    var1% = var1% + 1
    Print var1% ;
Loop
```

These are the values that appear in the Output panel when you run a script with the preceding code lines:

```
2  3  4  5
```

Do Until

Programmers are fond of saying that the loop can be either entrance controlled or exit controlled. You exercise entrance control when you put the control statement (the While or Until condition) before the instruction that changes the value (on the Do line). If you want exit control, you put the While or Until condition after the instruction that changes the value (on the Loop line).

You can put the control statement after the instruction that changes the value, and say Loop Until, like I show in this example:

```
Dim var2 As Integer
var2% = 1
Do
    var2% = var2% + 1
    Print var2% ;
' Test var2's value after executing loop.
Loop Until var2% >= 5
```

For this loop, the values in the Output panel look like this:

```
2  3  4  5
```

Understanding the high esteem with which experienced programmers hold their loops may be hard for the novice scripter. Although looping structures can seem confusing, what with While and Do While and Loop Until and so on, remember that the computer has a very logical, black-and-white approach. Go back through your loops, substituting in the values that you've specified and checking the conditions that you've set. A little double-checking up front may save you the frustration of dealing with endless loops.

Test your newfound knowledge

When are programmers most likely to use a For loop?

1. When putting on a magic show and tying knots in a tricky piece of rope.

2. When looking for an excuse to say "What is a For for?"

3. When they want to specify a specific number of times for the loop to continue.

4. When a three loop is too small and a five loop is too big.

What is an endless loop?

1. A really, really big lasso

2. The Chicago loop during rush hour

3. A Zen concept which, when fully grokked, leads to enlightenment

4. A programming loop that goes on, and on, and on

Chapter 12

Subs: I'll Take Meatball on White

· ·

In This Chapter

▶ Looking at procedures — named sections of a script — in LotusScript

▶ Ordering a sub — you know, from the menu

▶ Calling a sub — by name or with the `Call` statement

▶ Having arguments with your subs

▶ What properties are (a type of procedure), and why they don't get their own chapter

· ·

*I*f you write even the simplest script, you use a sub. Even the basic BASIC program in Chapter 2 uses a sub for its structure. When you open the IDE to start a new script, the statements needed to start a sub are already put in place for you. So the question is, "If you're already living in the house, do you need someone to tell you that a house is a building used as a dwelling?" Perhaps not, but looking over the walls, windows, front porch, and (especially) the roof of the house can help you find out about the intricacies of the house.

The same detailed inspection is in order for subs. Understanding subs and how they work can help you increase your scripting confidence.

I Certainly Know What a Procedure Is

Subs are one form of procedure, and *procedure* is one of my favorite bits of terminology from BASIC languages. After all, isn't just about anything you do over and over again a procedure? When you tie your shoes, that's a procedure. When you type a statement into a script, name a variable, delete an argument, debug your script, or whatever . . . isn't every one of those things, you know, a procedure?

You can think of a procedure, generally, as a way of performing or affecting something. Many times, a procedure is thought of as composed of steps, and maybe that definition is the basis for the use of the term *procedure* in BASIC languages.

Throughout the programming world in general, procedures are programs. In LotusScript, therefore, a procedure is a script. The BASIC language has messed with my mind, again, by taking a term that can apply to just about anything and applying it to something very specific. (Why not take the word *characters* and have it mean *left-facing quotation marks?*) In any case, just remember that LotusScript uses the term *procedure* to refer to specific script structures.

Procedures, by formal definition, are "named sections of a script that you can invoke by name." In other words, procedures are little programs with names. (They don't have to be little, but many times they are, so I like to think of them that way.) A sub (the topic of this chapter) is one form of procedure; a function is another form (see Chapter 13 for more information on functions). The third and final form of procedure in LotusScript is a property (which I discuss in the section, "Properties — Procedures of the Third Kind").

Although subs and functions are both procedures, these structures have a distinctive difference. That is, a sub doesn't return a value back to the script that calls it, whereas a function does have that highly admirable reciprocity.

Next is the syntax for the Sub statement, followed with an explanation:

```
[Static] [Public|Private] Sub aSubName [([arguments])]
    [statements]
End Sub
```

If you're like me (but chances are, you're a lot less lazy), you look at the syntax to see what's inside the brackets first (in case you know that you don't really need what's there). With the Sub statement, everything, other than the statement itself and the sub's name, is inside brackets. So, the essential syntax of the Sub statement looks like this:

```
Sub aSubName
End Sub
```

Defining a sub with the Sub statement, then, is just a way of naming some lines of code that you want to group together and refer to later. All that Static, Public, and Private stuff in brackets is a technical discussion for another time.

Creating A Sub (And Why You Would Want To)

The one main reason to create a sub is to record script lines that you plan to use over and over again — instead of rewriting the code line-by-line each time, you just put in the name of the sub that contains the reusable code. You can see the efficiency to that, after all, especially if the sub contains quite a few lines of code.

You also may want to create a sub for code that you use just once, but that performs a smaller role in a larger program (like performing a single calculation in a multistep equation). Using a sub is a neat way to group lines of code. And when you want to debug your script, you can more readily debug separate subs than single, long scripts.

Names for subs follow the rules for naming anything else in LotusScript (see Chapter 7 for more information). These next four items are the basic naming rules for subs:

- ✔ The sub name must begin with a letter.
- ✔ The remaining characters (after the first letter) in the sub name can be letters, digits, or underscores.
- ✔ Sub names can contain 40 characters or less.
- ✔ Sub names can't be LotusScript keywords.

Making a sub from scratch

Suppose that you want to create a sub that displays a message box with the words "Stand back, baby!" (Maybe you're writing a game, and you want to have that message pop up frequently.)

1. **Click on the Script Editor SmartIcon to open the Script Editor.**

   Or use whatever method you like in your Lotus program to open the Script Editor.

2. **Choose <u>C</u>reate⇨<u>S</u>ub from the Script Editor menu or press F3.**

   The Create Sub dialog box comes up.

3. **Type a name for the sub —** stand_Back**, for example. Then click OK.**

   LotusScript places the cursor in an empty Sub statement block. The statement elements Sub and End Sub should already be there; you don't have to type them. But if they aren't, type Sub, and LotusScript puts in End Sub automatically. In Figure 12-1, notice that the name you entered for the Sub appears in the Script text box.

Name of sub appears here

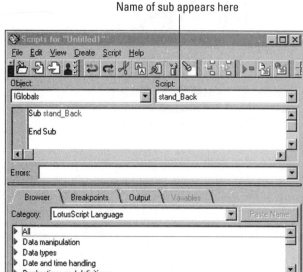

Figure 12-1:
When you
type a name
for a sub,
LotusScript
opens to an
empty Sub
statement
block.

4. Type in the statement(s) to make up your sub.

For example, you can type in a Messagebox statement so that your sub looks like this:

```
Sub stand_back
    Messagebox "Stand back, baby!"
End Sub
```

5. Press F5 or choose Script⇨Run Current Sub to run your sub.

Figure 12-2 shows the message box that you see when you run the stand_Back sub. Notice that I've slipped in an extra step on the sly. That is, I've actually run stand_Back by referencing the sub's name in the Main sub. See the section "Calling a Sub: Earth to Sub . . ." in this chapter for more information about referencing subs.

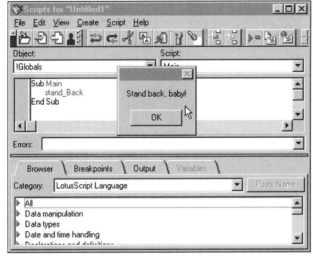

Figure 12-2:
The
stand_Back
sub creates
this
message
box.

Making a sub by copying and pasting

You can also create a new sub by pasting a valid sub (or a function or property) into the script area. The LotusScript IDE then formats a new statement block and puts the appropriate End statement on it. You have a new Sub and can type in additional statements for it if you want.

Calling a sub later

LotusScript's documentation sets requirements like the following for using a sub over and over: "If you create your procedure in (Globals), and you have not deleted the Option Public statement that the IDE puts in (Globals) (Options), your new procedure is public by default."

The translation of this requirement goes something like this: After you create a sub, you can call it from any other sub you create for the document.

Also, if you create the procedure (sub) for an object, you can call the procedure from the object's Initialize or Terminate Sub, from object event subs, and from other procedures that you create for the object.

Calling a Sub: Earth to Sub . . .

You have two ways to reference, or call, subs in LotusScript. I like to call subs by name — because calling by name requires less typing and looks a little better on-screen. However, calling subs in the second way — with the `Call` statement — is also great. But LotusScript doesn't care which sub calling method you use because the computer can work with either one.

Calling subs the easy way — by name

After you create a sub for a document, you can reuse that code in any other sub in the document by simply *calling*. To call one sub from another sub, just put in the name of the sub to call like this:

```
Sub Main
    stand_Back
End Sub
```

The preceding `Main` sub calls the sub named `stand_Back`.

Using the `Call` statement

You can also call a sub by using the `Call` statement, like this:

```
Sub Main
    Call stand_Back
End Sub
```

"What," you may wonder, "is the advantage of using the `Call` statement in my script?" Actually, using `Call` has a certain appeal to the novice scripter. After you've created a bunch of subs and have a pretty complex program, you can go back and readily find your subs by looking for `Call` statements. And referencing subs with `Call` statements helps to distinguish your subs from functions (because you can reference functions by name only).

Of course, you have a really easy way to identify your subs anyway, without looking line-by-line through all of your scripts. Click on the arrow for the drop-down list box labeled Scripts, and you see your subs names listed there. Figure 12-3 shows a listing of sub names. Still, if you use the `Call` statement to reference subs in your scripts, you find your code easier to decipher later on (when your script fills up with all kinds of things besides calls to subs).

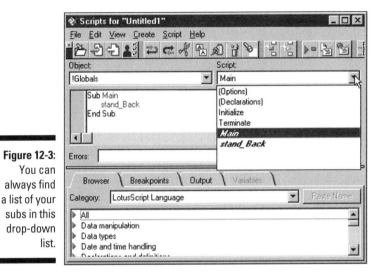

Figure 12-3:
You can
always find
a list of your
subs in this
drop-down
list.

Deleting a Sub

I had to figure out how to delete a sub on my own. LotusScript has no Delete Sub command on the menu. And I couldn't find a way to highlight the name of a sub on the Scripts menu and then press the delete key. But this is what I found out: To delete a sub, go to the sub that you want to delete (so that the code lines for the sub appear in the Script Editor) and delete all the code, even the Sub and End Sub statements. Then the name of the sub disappears from the Scripts drop-down list as well.

Passing Arguments (And Why You Would Want To)

Personally, I was raised to avoid arguments as much as possible. And *passing* arguments sounds about like passing a kidney stone or something. However, in the arcane world of programming, passing *arguments* (bits of information) between programs is a common practice. In LotusScript, you can pass arguments between subs and functions.

The meaning of *argument* in scripting obviously has little to do with what you or I ordinarily think of as an argument. In the discipline of logic, an argument is the minor premise in a syllogism. In logic, when you have a major premise that says, "If A, then B," the minor premise is *A*. This logic construction indicates that you need to know *A* before you can know *B*. Similarly, an argument in LotusScript is the *A* — that is, the little piece of information that enables a sub (the major premise) to do its work.

I found a partial explanation of arguments in the *Using LotusScript in Approach* booklet (published by Lotus Development Corporation, 1995): "Arguments are the information in parentheses next to the name of the Sub. An argument is the information that is supplied to the Sub so that it can perform its tasks."

The following example may help to clarify, too. First, you have a `Main` sub that looks like this:

```
Sub Main
    Dim x As Integer
    Dim y As Integer
    x% = 1
    y% = 2
    Sum x%, y%
End Sub
```

The word `Sum` is the name of a subroutine that the `Main` sub calls, and `x%` and `y%` are variables of the data type Integer. The variables `x%` and `y%` are the arguments passed to the `Sum` sub.

The following is the code for the `Sum` sub, with the arguments `x%` and `y%` in parentheses after the name of the sub:

```
Sub Sum(x%, y%)
    Dim z as Integer
    z% = x% + y%
    Print z%
End Sub
```

This script consists of two subs, `Main` and `Sum`. You run the script by pressing F5 or by choosing Script⇨Run Current Sub from the Script Editor menu.

You must make sure that your sub that passes the arguments (in this example, the `Main` sub) is showing in the Script Editor when you run the script. If you try to run the script with the called sub (in this case, the `Sum` sub) showing, you get an error message that says something like, "Cannot run procedure." The called sub cannot run on its own because it needs the arguments supplied by the calling sub in order to do its work.

When you run the script that consists of the Main and Sum subs, you see the following in the Output panel:

```
3
```

When you pass arguments in LotusScript, the called sub looks to these arguments (in the parentheses) for information that it needs — in this example, Sum uses the values of x% and y% to calculate the value of z%, which is then displayed in the Output panel.

Properties: Procedures of the Third Kind

The third type of procedure is a property, which I probably ought to talk about somewhere along with the discussion of subs and functions in Chapters 12 and 13. A property is a special type of procedure whose purpose is to allow the indirect manipulation of variables. And from what I understand, properties do their work on the sly — that is, to the script as a whole, the property looks like just another variable, but is actually much more.

You define a property with a Property Get statement and a Property Set statement. The property (like a variable and about everything else in LotusScript) has a name and a data type. It has no parameters and takes no arguments (a good attitude in a property, and also in a teacher or a baseball umpire).

The syntax statement for Property Get or Property Set is as follows:

```
[Static] [Public|Private] Property {Get|Set} propertyName
         [As data type]
   [ statements ]
End Property
```

Basically, the syntax statement means that you have to use Get or Set with Property, and you have to give the property a name. So a Property statement block may start like this:

```
Property Get new_Info%
```

In the preceding line, the property name is new_Info and the data type is Integer (%).

This example shows a `Property Get` statement used in the `Main` sub:

```
Property Get pInt As Integer
    pInt% = 3
End Property
Sub Main
    Dim saveInt As Integer
    saveInt = pInt%
    Print saveInt
End Sub
```

When you run the `Main` sub, it gets the value for `saveInt` from the property `pInt` and displays the result in the Output panel as follows:

```
3
```

I think of Property as kind of like the fourth Marx brother. That is, three of the Marx brothers — Groucho, Harpo, and Chico — are the obvious, funny ones. And then this unfunny, good-looking other guy — Zeppo — hangs around in some of the movies. He's different, somehow, and doesn't seem to be around all the time. Property is like Zeppo. Subs and functions (like Groucho, Harpo, and Chico) are well known and used all the time. Properties aren't, but they exist, so I need to talk about them.

I'll put it this way — subs and functions each get a separate chapter. All properties get is this lousy Technical Stuff section.

Test your newfound knowledge

The difference between a sub and a function is:

1. You can ride in a sub, but a function is something your body does on its own.

2. A sub doesn't return a value back to the program that calls it, whereas a function does have that reciprocity.

3. Sub starts with *S;* function starts with *F.*

4. All of the above.

How do you find a sub you've created before?

1. Yell really loud, "Sub. Sub. Sub." Eventually, it gets sick of hearing your voice and just pops out of the computer.

2. Radar works.

3. Get a specially trained police dog.

4. Click on the arrow for the drop-down list box labeled Scripts, and you see your subs listed there.

Chapter 13

They Call Them *Functions,* but Do They Really Do Anything?

- -

- -

A *function,* as you and I probably think of it, is what our employers describe as an assigned duty or activity. If you check badges at the door of your office building all day long, badge-checking is your function. If you sit in the corner office and sign everybody's paycheck, then you must be the top banana, and check-signing is your function.

When you're trying to understand the specialized, programmerese meaning of BASIC terms, seeing what the term means in mathematics is helpful. In math, a function is a variable related to another so that for each value assumed by one variable, a value is determined for the other.

The meaning from mathematics is, indeed, close to the meaning in LotusScript. All right, it *is* the meaning. In LotusScript, *functions* are procedures (blocks of related code) that return a value to the calling program. Subs, which I describe in Chapter 12, are procedures, too, but aren't required to return a value when called from another program. So really, a function is quite a privileged and influential procedure.

As for subs, you always create them yourself. In the case of functions, though, you can create them yourself, or you can draw on a whole library of predefined functions in LotusScript. (I mention the predefined functions because you can get confused between the functions you make and the ones already available.)

Looking Over the Syntax for a Function

The syntax for defining a function looks a lot like that for defining a sub. But because of its special job of returning a value to the calling program, a function has another optional element at the end of the statement.

```
[Static] [Public|Private] Function afunctionName
          [([paramList])] [As areturnType]
    [ statements ]
End Function
```

Any syntax statement elements that appear in straight brackets [ ] are optional. If you disregard all the optional stuff in brackets, the syntax for a function in its simplest form looks like this:

```
Function afunctionName
    [ statements ]
End Function
```

If you include the important options for passing parameters and setting return data types, you see the syntax that is familiar to many functions:

```
Function afunctionName ([paramList]) [As areturnType]
    [ statements ]
End Function
```

Scripting with Functions

You can use functions in a script to do repetitive activities, like calculations that must be performed for a number of changing variables. Instead of repeating the code to do the calculations over and over again, you simply reference (call) the function by name from your script. Suppose that you write a Main sub that calls a function named Sum. Your Main sub looks like this:

```
Sub Main
    Dim x As Integer
    Dim y As Integer
    Dim z As Integer
    x%=1
    y%=4
    z%=Sum(x%, y%)
    Print "The Sum function returns the value " z%
End Sub
```

The preceding script passes the arguments x% and y% to the function Sum and assigns the value returned from the function Sum to the variable z%. Then, the Print statement shows z% in the Output panel of the IDE.

Creating a function

As is characteristic of functions, Sum returns a value to its calling program. In this example, Main is the calling sub. You can follow these next steps to create the Sum function:

1. **With the Script Editor open, choose Create⊃Function from the Script Editor menu.**

   The Create Function dialog box appears, as shown in Figure 13-1.

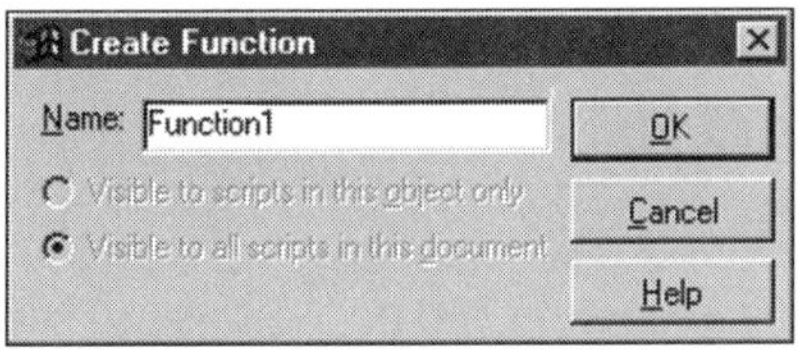

Figure 13-1: Name your function in the Create Function dialog box.

2. **Type in a name for your function. Then click OK.**

   In the example shown in Figure 13-2, the function name is Sum. A blank script block appears in the Script Editor, with the Function and End Function script lines in place.

3. **Type in the optional elements and statements for your function, including passed arguments, the data type for the function's return value, and any statements needed to determine the returned value.**

   For this example, the passed arguments are x% and y%, the data type for the function's return value is As Integer, and the statement to calculate the return value (between the Function and End Function script lines) is Sum=x%+y%. Your function now looks like this:

```
Function Sum(x%, y%) As Integer
    Sum = x% + y%
End Function
```

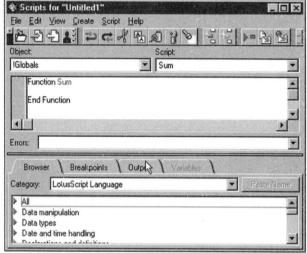

Interpreting a function

The function Sum receives input values (the arguments x% and y%) from the calling sub Main and (because it's a function and not just a sub) sends back the calculated value (the *sum*) to Main as an Integer data type.

Following is the line-by-line translation of the Sum function:

✔ **Line 1:** Define the function Sum with its arguments x and y as integers (%), and with the return value data type As Integer.

```
Function Sum(x%, y%) As Integer
```

✔ **Line 2:** Add the values of x and y and set the result equal to the return value of Sum.

```
Sum = x% + y%
```

✔ **Line 3:** End the function Sum.

```
End Function
```

Running a sub with a function

Running a sub with a function is as easy as running a sub without one. You can press F5 or use the Script Editor menus to run your script. Refer to Chapter 2 for more information about how to run a script. When I ran the example `Main` sub that calls the function `Sum`, I saw the following line in the Output panel of the IDE:

```
The Sum function returns the value 5
```

After you create a function, you must return to the calling program before pressing F5 or using another method to run the script. For the preceding example, you can click the arrow at the right side of the Script scroll box to see the drop-down list of your subs and functions; then click `Main`, the calling sub, so that `Main` appears in the Script Editor. Then you can press F5 to run the script. If you press F5 to run the script while the `Sum` function is showing in the Script Editor, you get an error message like, "Cannot run procedure." You see this error message because the function is expecting input arguments from the `Main` sub and doesn't get them when you don't run the script from `Main`.

However, you can press F2 (with the `Sum` function open in the Script Editor) to check just the syntax of your function. If the syntax checker finds no errors, you won't get an error message. But sometimes you do, if you've made an error in spelling or left out some syntax element. See Chapter 5 for more information about checking and debugging your scripts.

Calling a Function

You don't use the `Call` statement with functions as you do with subs (see Chapter 12 for the lowdown on calling subs). You can call a function only by name. By eliminating a choice here, LotusScript keeps life simple.

Following is a simple example where I use the name `Multiple` in the `Print` statement to call the function:

```
Sub Main
    Dim x As Integer
    Dim y As Integer
    x%=2
    y%=4
    Print "The product of x and y is " Multiple(x%,y%)
End Sub
```

The script lines for the function Multiple look like this:

```
Function Multiple (x As Integer, y As Integer) As Integer
    Multiple = x * y
End Function
```

In the `Print` statement in the `Main` sub, you reference the name of the function `Multiple`. That is, you *call* the function by stating its name. When you execute the script, the `Main` sub (through the `Print` statement) calls the `Multiple` function (with the arguments x% and y%), receives the return value (the product of x and y), and displays its message in the Output panel.

```
The product of x and y is 8
```

User-Defined Functions

When you write your own LotusScript function, you create a *user-defined* function. You are free to create as many as you want and use them over and over again. And you can readily use your user-defined function many times within the same document. Suppose, however, that you create a really useful function and you want to use it with a script for a different document.

Although you can refer to subs and functions that you created in one document from the scripts in another document, the methodology is quite advanced. The predefined functions that come with LotusScript are already set up to be accessible from many documents. The chapter on OOP (that is, object-oriented programming, Chapter 14) gives you some idea of the concepts involved in sharing your scripts within the broader universe — like with other Lotus products or other Windows applications.

I know a simple way to reuse your user-defined functions, though. Use the Edit menu of the Script Editor to Copy the function you like from one document and Paste it into a blank function block in the Script Editor for another document. You can see Chapter 12 for more information on copying and pasting. This method may not be as elegant as simply calling the functions by name (as you do to reuse the predefined functions that come with LotusScript). But this method works, and hey, for a beginning scripter, having scripting practices that work is good! Elegance can come later.

Some Famous Predefined Functions

If you look over the LotusScript language reference in the Help files for your Lotus product, you see that many entries are either statements or functions. For example, out of seven entries beginning with *A*, six are functions (Abs, ACos, Asc, ASin, ATn, ATn2), and one is a statement (ActivateApp).

Functions certainly seem to outnumber statements (at least under _A_). In general, LotusScript has an awful lot of functions already available for you to use. However, you don't need to see these functions in separate blocks of code, the way you see any user-defined functions that you create. (See the section "Scripting with Functions" in this chapter for information about creating user-defined functions.)

You can use predefined functions in the same way that you use LotusScript statements. When you reference the function name in your script, some hidden, unchangeable block of code somewhere executes for you.

You never know what's going to be in a sub and you don't get anything back when you use one, so I don't really know any famous subs. Functions, though, are a different story. LotusScript's predefined functions perform certain tasks and return expected results. They are often useful within scripts, and many have gained a certain widespread recognition among computer users.

As is the case with certain LotusScript statements, some predefined functions are more useful to programmers than to businesspeople, golfers, or other kinds of real-world people. But using some LotusScript predefined functions can help you do routine tasks. Using a conversion function, like CCur to convert a number to currency format, is a good example.

LotusScript predefined functions fall into categories. The following sections tell you about these categories and give some sample functions for each one.

Mathematical functions

Mathematicians, as you may expect, love functions in all kinds of forms. Spreadsheet programs are bursting with mathematical functions — to what extent, I could only begin to imagine. (Don't tell anyone I did this, but I started counting functions in 1-2-3 and quit when I got to 50.)

Mathematical functions are mostly useful to people doing math — statisticians, ordinary scientists, and of course, rocket scientists. These next functions are examples of mathematical functions:

- ✔ Abs — Returns absolute value of a number
- ✔ Round — Rounds a number to a certain number of decimal places
- ✔ Sqr — Returns the square root of a number

The following script shows the Sqr function in action:

```
Sub Main
    Dim sqRoot As Double
    sqRoot# = Sqr(225)
    Print sqRoot#                   '  Prints 15
End Sub
```

The line-by-line explanation of the script lines within the Main sub is as follows:

- **Line 1:** Declare the variable sqRoot with the data type Double

- **Line 2:** Initialize the variable sqRoot# to the value of the square root of 225 by using the Sqr function to return the desired value

- **Line 3:** Print the value assigned to sqRoot in the Output panel of the IDE. (The comment ' Prints 15 indicates what the printed value should be.)

Conversion Functions

When you're working with variables in LotusScript, data types are very important. The most frequent scripting errors arise from what LotusScript perceives (no doubt accurately, in its narrow universe) as a misuse of data types.

Very helpful to scripters are functions that accept one value and convert that value to another specific data type. The following are examples of conversion functions:

- CInt — Converts a value to an integer
- CCur — Converts a value to currency
- CStr — Converts a value to a string

And a script that uses CCur looks like this:

```
Sub Main
    Dim eachPrice As Double
    Dim numSold As Integer
    Dim amountDue As Currency
    eachPrice# = 13.390625
    numSold% = 34
    amountDue@ = CCur(eachPrice# * numSold%)
    Print amountDue@                    ' Prints 455.2813
End Sub
```

The script lines inside the `Main` sub translate as follows:

- ✔ **Line 1:** Declares the variable `eachPrice` with the data type `Double`
- ✔ **Line 2:** Declares the variable `numSold` with the data type `Integer`
- ✔ **Line 3:** Declares the variable `amountDue` with the data type `Currency`
- ✔ **Line 4:** Initializes the variable `eachPrice#`
- ✔ **Line 5:** Initializes the variable `numSold%`
- ✔ **Line 6:** Multiplies `eachPrice#` by `numSold%` to get the total cost, uses `CCur` to convert the cost to `Currency` data type, and assigns the result to `amountDue@`
- ✔ **Line 7:** Displays the `amountDue` (calculated in line 6) in the Output panel of the IDE. (The comment shows what the amount should be.)

Date and time functions

I keep a list of movies that I have on tape in a Lotus 1-2-3 spreadsheet. Periodically, I like to print out this list to keep near my VCR. So that I'll know how current my list is, a date field near the top of the spreadsheet uses a function to pull in the current date. Then whenever I print out the spreadsheet listing, I see the current date at the time I printed it. Having the date on my movie listing is very useful because the information on the list changes a lot.

Date and time functions are useful in many such ways. Examples of LotusScript date and time functions are as follows:

- ✔ `Date` — Returns the current date
- ✔ `Day` — Returns the day (an integer from 1 to 31) of a valid date expression supplied as an argument
- ✔ `Today` — Returns today's date
- ✔ `Now` — Returns the current date and time

The date and time functions in the preceding list (with the exception of the Day function) return values based on the computer's system date.

For example:

```
Sub Main
    Print Date        'Prints the current system date
End Sub
```

String functions

String functions perform various activities on *strings* (which, to the rest of us, are a series of characters). You can see how word processing programs use types of string functions when performing certain formatting — for example, converting from uppercase to lowercase.

Examples of string functions in LotusScript are as follows:

- ✔ String — Returns a string consisting of a particular character that the scripter supplies as a parameter

- ✔ Space — Returns a string filled with the number of spaces specified by the scripter

- ✔ Ucase — Converts all characters in the supplied string to uppercase

- ✔ Lcase — Converts all characters in the supplied string to lowercase

- ✔ Len — Returns the length of the supplied string — that is, the number of characters that make up the string

Many functions need input that is supplied by the scripter, and string functions are no exception. Before you can use any predefined function in your script, you must find out what kind of input the function requires. You can look up the functions in the Browser panel of the IDE, or you can refer to the LotusScript help files to find out exactly what data you need to supply to the functions that you use.

The following script shows the String function in action:

```
Sub Main
    Dim lbSign As String
    lbSign$ = String(5, "#")
    Print lbSign$              ' Prints #####
End Sub
```

The line-by-line description of the script lines inside the Main sub is as follows:

- ✔ **Line 1:** Declares the variable lbSign and sets its data type to String

- ✔ **Line 2:** Assigns the value of the variable lbSign$ by using the String function. Input parameters for the function tell how many characters to return, 5, and what ASCII character to use, "#".

- ✔ **Line 3:** Shows the resulting string in the Output panel of the IDE.

Examining I/O functions

Two functions — `Messagebox` and `Inputbox` — are so frequently used by scripters that I actually slipped them into early chapters of the book. I used these functions to help create some example scripts that make common sense. Using `Inputbox` allows you to get input from the user, and using `Messagebox` helps you return output to the user.

Scripters formally call functions like `Messagebox` and `Inputbox` *I/O functions,* which is short for input/output functions.

Using `Messagebox`

`Messagebox` has quite a range of capabilities. You can use this handy function to give information to users whenever you want. If someone clicks a field on a questionnaire, you can have a message box come up with a reminder. If a person puts in wrong information, you can have the message box politely tell the person that they've made a mistake. Or you can have the message box say things just for fun. See Chapter 3 for more talk about message boxes. The syntax of the `Messagebox` function looks like this:

```
Messagebox ( message [ , [ buttons + icon + default + mode ]
             [ , boxTitle ] ] )
```

The `buttons + icon + default + mode` elements of the `Messagebox` syntax statement help you to control the appearance and interaction of the message box that you create. That is, supplying a value for `buttons` determines whether your message box displays one button that says `OK`, two buttons (one each for `Yes` and `No`), and so on. LotusScript has graciously predetermined some values for these function elements, which lets you easily customize your message boxes. See Table 3-1 for a description of these `Messagebox` elements and their values. (Don't try to make any sense out of LotusScript's predetermined values; just accept that they do what the table descriptions indicate.)

Table 13-1	Optional Messagebox Elements	
Element	*Value*	*Description*
buttons	0	Display one button that says OK
	1	Display two buttons: OK and Cancel
	2	Display three buttons: Abort, Retry, and Ignore
	3	Display three buttons: Yes, No, and Cancel
	4	Display two buttons: Yes and No
	5	Display two buttons: Retry and Cancel

(continued)

Table 13-1 *(continued)*

Element	Value	Description
icon	16	Display an icon that looks like a stop sign
	32	Display an icon that looks like a question mark
	48	Display an icon that looks like an exclamation point
	64	Display an icon that says Information
default	0	Make the first button the default
	256	Make the second button the default
	512	Make the third button the default
mode	0	Stop the current application until the user responds to the message box
	4096	Stop all applications that are currently running until the user responds to the message box

Messagebox can be either a statement or a function, depending on whether it returns a value to the program. The following sample script uses the Messagebox function:

```
Sub Main
    ' Display a message to the user
    ' in a message box labeled "Proceed?"
    ' Put in Yes and No buttons for the user's response.
    ' Assign the value returned by Messagebox
    ' to the variable yesOrNo
    ' and display yesOrNo in the Output panel
    Dim yesOrNo As Integer
    yesOrNo%=Messagebox("Yo. Do you want to go on?", _
        4+32+0+0,"Proceed?")
    Print yesOrNo
End Sub
```

When you execute the Main sub, you see a message box like the one shown in Figure 13-4.

You can use comment lines (that begin with a single quote mark, ') to document what you're trying to do with your script. Notice, for example, the comment lines at the beginning of the preceding script. When you go back to look over your scripts, you can read (in English) what you intend for the script to do. Hurray for comments! No more trying to quickly decipher lines of code.

JIM'S GEMS

"But I already have functions in 1-2-3 . . .

Lotus 1-2-3 already includes hundreds of pre-defined functions. 1-2-3 has the famous @Sum function, which is the only one that a lot of us use very much. It has @Round, @Sum, @Today — many functions that you find in LotusScript as well. (LotusScript doesn't have a Sum function for some reason. Go figure.)

Well then, if you're using 1-2-3 and want to do one of the things a function does, which kind do you use — the 1-2-3 function or the LotusScript function?

If you are using @functions in the cells of your worksheet, just use them the same way you always did.

Now, you can use @functions in your scripts as well. The distinction between the two kinds of functions — predefined 1-2-3 functions and new ones that you write — is the same as the distinction between predefined functions and user-defined functions. The @functions in 1-2-3, though probably more famous than predefined functions in any other Lotus product, are just the functions that are already available for use.

You can use the existing @functions inside the scripts you write in 1-2-3. And you can create new @functions by writing them inside the Script Editor. I talk about that in Chapter 17. So, in the modern world of 1-2-3, @functions (called *at functions*) are just functions, that's all. Use them like other functions.

Figure 13-3:
Giving the user a choice with the Messagebox function.

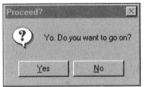

Using Inputbox

The Inputbox function displays a prompt and waits for the user to enter something. Often, your scripts have to interact with the outside world. They don't just give messages, but also ask people to put in the information that the script is going to use — their name, their age, their phone number, their blood pressure — all kinds of things.

The syntax for this function is as follows:

```
InputBox[$] ( aprompt [ , [ atitle ] [ , [ adefault ] [ ,
  anxpos , aypos ] ] ] )
```

The following script shows an example of using `Inputbox`:

```
Sub Main
    'Ask your user for an integer, then convert the number
    'from a string to an integer.
    Dim quant As Integer
    quant% = CInt(Inputbox$("How many do you want?"))
End Sub
```

Test your newfound knowledge

What can a function do that a sub can't do?

1. Nothing, really. It's all in the sub's head. If the sub would just try a little harder, it could be just as good as any function.

2. Perform high-wire acrobatics.

3. Return a value to the calling program.

4. Time travel.

How do you use a predefined function?

1. With a predefined function executor, available over the counter at Wal-Mart.

2. You can use predefined functions in the same way that you use statements. When you use the name of the function, some hidden, unchangeable block of code somewhere executes for you.

3. Very, very carefully, because, if it breaks, you'll be sorry.

4. You don't. Reading and contemplating predefined functions is okay, but don't put them into programs. (It's an existentialist thing.)

Part IV

Claiming New Territories: Scripting Lotus Products

The 5th Wave   By Rich Tennant

...And we feel so lucky to have him. He's the best debugger in the business.

In this part . . .

Have you ever been climbing all morning, only to discover (as you look upward at the mountain) that you'd just been moving through the foothills? You may feel the same way after you work through some simple scripts and then come upon object-oriented programming (OOP). The OOP structures in the LotusScript design are what make the scripting language so appealing to advanced programmers. This books is not for advanced programmers, so you won't need to climb that OOP mountain. You find out a little about OOP, though, and maybe you can climb up a little way.

Also in Part IV, I show you what's distinctive about scripting in Word Pro and Approach. And you get a small indication of what you can do with those programs later, if you get serious about OOP.

Chapter 14

They Call This *OOPs.*
It Must Be for Me!

* *

In This Chapter

▶ Broadening your view with object-oriented programming (OOP)

▶ Seeing how types get you ready to look at classes

▶ Identifying classes and other OOP elements

▶ Setting up classes in your scripts — variables, subs, and functions

▶ Changing what you think of as objects — from stones to *whatever*

▶ How OOP lets you plagiarize like crazy (legally) and save yourself a ton of work

* *

L otusScript belongs to the form of programming known as object-oriented programming (or OOP), which, in the plural, is *oops* — a popular word among the uncoordinated. In object-oriented programming, you form programs by having self-contained collections of data structures and program routines (*objects*) interact with other self-contained collections (other objects).

A person can use LotusScript as a self-contained programming language for a long time without ever understanding OOP. But using OOP elements provides the means to connect with other layers of the Lotus program you are in, with other Lotus products, with the operating environment, and with other programs.

Consider this example: You are riding a train (or an airplane) to Chicago. Either way, you sit in a seat and play a video game on your laptop during your journey. And you get to Chicago (most of the time, except occasionally on some of the small commuter flights). You can get up and walk along the aisles in the train or plane, and you don't think much about your broader environment.

However, if you're the engineer of the locomotive or the pilot of the plane, you must be able to interact at levels other than just *going along for the ride.* You must be aware of the outside environment, its characteristics and rules, and its effect on your vehicle. Knowing that your hurtling means of transportation is in the air rather than on tracks is useful. An airline pilot who steps into the cockpit and says, "We're going to keep this baby on the tracks the whole way!" doesn't inspire much confidence.

The brief introduction to OOP in this chapter sets you up for working, not with just a few lines of code in a single LotusScript script, but with scripts that have influence throughout a single Lotus product, throughout the Lotus SmartSuite, and throughout Windows.

Types: The Still-Living Ancestors of Classes

Before you do object-oriented programming, understanding basic terminology and concepts is important. What does the OOP programming world mean by *classes* and, of course, *objects?* A good way to start understanding the terms, like classes, is to meet the ancestor — types. Types aren't specifically OOP elements, so why do I begin this chapter with something that isn't OOP? Because understanding types is simpler, and this helps you understand classes, which *are* important OOP elements.

Chapter 7 tells you that variables have certain established data types — Integer, Currency, Single, Double, and so on. But you can create other data types, called *user-defined* types, and have variables with those types, too. Gosh, you and I may not be in any rush to go out and do such a thing, unless we wake up tomorrow and find we've miraculously become die-hard programmers. Existing data types can create enough headaches and error messages as it is.

The point is that LotusScript allows you to create user-defined data types. And defining types allows you to group variables together and to work with them as a unit. When you define a type, you declare at least one variable to belong to, or be a *member* of, that type's group. This grouping feature is where the similarity between *types* and *classes* takes off.

Constructing a type from variables

You use the LotusScript Type statement to create your user-defined data type; its syntax is as follows:

```
[ Public | Private ] Type atypeName
    member declaration statements
End Type
```

If you're a glutton for punishment (or a serious scripter) you may want to refer to the LotusScript Help system under *Type Statement* for a technical explanation. In this case, as in most others, an example is worth a thousand syntax statements. The comment lines in the following example code tell you about the user-defined data type, custRecord.

```
' Define the custRecord type with members to hold
' the customer's name, age, phone #, city, and zip code
'
Type custRecord              'Begin the type definition
   custName As String
   custAge As Integer
   custPhone As String * 12
   custCity As String
   custZip As String * 10
End Type                     'Now the type is defined
```

After you define the `custRecord` type, you can declare a variable with the type `custRecord` and set initial values for the member variables. To refer to each member, use dot notation (in the form `variableName.memberName`), as follows:

```
' Define the variable oneCust
' as type custRecord and
' initialize each member
Dim oneCust As custRecord
oneCust.custName$ = "Mary"
oneCust.custAge% = 22
oneCust.custPhone$ = "111-222-3333"
oneCust.custCity$ = "Anytown"
oneCust.custZip = "99999-9999"
Print "Your customer is " & TRIM$(oneCust.custName$) _
   & " from " & TRIM$(oneCust.custCity$) _
   & ". You can reach him/her at " _
   & TRIM$(oneCust.custPhone$) & "."
```

If you run a sub that includes the preceding data type definition and variable declaration, you see the following in the Output panel of the IDE.

```
Your customer is Mary from Anytown. You can reach him/her at
          111-222-3333.
```

In this example, you create a new data type — one called `custRecord`. You can then assign that data type to variables that you use in your script. The `Type` statement allows you to group variables together as members of an entity. Likewise, the closely related (but much more powerful) OOP _classes_ allow you to create member groupings.

Naming your type and its elements

To refer to the members of a type as you script, you use a technique called *dot notation*. Now, dot notation is not the same thing as a *dot-to-dot,* a technique that you used as a little kid to convince yourself that you were drawing a picture by connecting dots. *Dots,* as in the dot notation you use in scripting, are periods. You use periods to separate the variable name from the member name, as in these lines of code from the example in the preceding section, "Constructing a type from variables":

```
Dim oneCust As custRecord
oneCust.custName$ = "Mary"
oneCust.custAge% = 22
```

In the second and third lines of code, the term `oneCust` is a variable name, `custName` is a member of the type `custRecprd`, and the period between them is the dot referred to in the phrase *dot notation* (which, as I mentioned, has almost nothing to do with a dot-to-dot).

Classes: What Objects Call Home

Classes, like types, contain multiple members. In classes, though, the members can be program procedures (subs, functions, and properties), as well as variables of differing data types. The sub and function members of a LotusScript class are known as *methods* and, like any other subs or functions, perform some kind of script instructions. Overall, classes are true OOP structures and, next to user-defined data types, are like 500-channel cable TV next to a vintage 1945 radio.

To add to the versatile features of the OOP class structure, you can *extend* (a programmerese word that means *enhance*) classes to create new classes. Through the OOP process of *inheritance,* you can use one class as a base for creating a new class that you can then extend by adding or modifying class methods and properties.

In the section "OOP at Work" later in this chapter, I talk about what you can do with classes. Although this discussion is pretty abstract right now, the point is that classes are a key structure in OOP. As the basic building blocks of OOP, objects not only make up classes (as member variables, subs, and so on), but are also *instances* of classes (for example, like you are an instance of the class `HumanBeing`). You put objects into classes, and then you can manipulate the objects by using the properties and methods associated with that class.

So how do you determine what qualifies as an object?

You're a person and probably think that you know what an object is, right? A rock is an obvious object. A toy horse is an object; so is a knitting needle. I don't think of a tree as an object . . . I guess it's too big. And because a dog is living, I don't think of a dog as an object either. But a dog's collar or toenail clippings might be objects.

My neat Lotus SmartCenter dictionary (which is actually the American Heritage Concise Dictionary, Third Edition) calls an object "something perceptible by the senses; a material thing," which is a bit broad and does include a tree or a dog. The dictionary also traces the term *object* to the Latin word *objecere* — to throw, and that

puts us back on the right track again. (You may throw a rock, but probably not a tree or a dog.)

But basically, you can forget about what you always thought of as an object. An object, in script programming, isn't always something you can see, touch, and throw around. An object is more of a module, really, than an object in the traditional sense, but trying to change the name to *Module-Oriented Programming* would just confuse the issue at this point, so I won't. If the object is a mere variable (which it can be), then I don't think of that as a module anyway. Besides, the acronym *MOP* isn't much better than the one that's come to the fore — *OOP*.

Similar to the statement for user-defined data types, LotusScript has a statement for defining classes; the `Class` statement looks like this:

```
[ Public | Private ] Class aclassName [ As abaseClass ]
    definitions and declarations of class members
End Class
```

Essentially, you declare a class in the same way you declare a type. You type the keyword `Class`, and you give the class a name. After you name it, you can fill it up — with variables, subs, and functions (that is, members). And when finished, you put in `End Class`.

Objects: Not Just Rocks Any More

Objects. Classes are objects. The variables, subs, and functions inside classes are objects, too. You have the class objects that are filled with other objects. In OOP, you make your programs out of objects — that's why this word *object* takes the lead in the name *object-oriented programming*.

In programming, an object is . . . an object is. . . . Whew! An *object* is a building block in the hierarchical structure of a larger program. Any of the LotusScript ingredients you're familiar with can be an object — a class, a sub, a function, or a variable.

A scripting object does have something in common with the everyday idea of an object, too. That is, you can recognize and work with a scripting object as a single entity. Think of a script activity as throwing a rock, where the outcome depends on what direction you throw the rock, how hard you throw it, how big the rock is, and what it hits. Similarly, the effect of working with a script object depends on the characteristics of the object and the activity you involve the object in.

The gist of OOP

The gist of OOP, according to a scripting friend of mine, is that you define objects to handle your program activity instead of writing line after line of code. You give those objects what my friend calls *color, shape,* and *mass.* (That is, you give them distinguishing characteristics.) After you define an object, you can use it over and over again. And you don't need to start scripting from scratch to pull together all the object's distinguishing characteristics each time you need to use that object.

In the case of objects that are classes, you give them *methods, properties,* and *events.* This chapter has a section on methods and one on properties, and the next chapter talks about events. A *method,* I found after some initial searching, is just another name for a sub or function. *Properties* are special structures, acting as variables, that you can retrieve in the script and assign values to. (And, because those values help determine an object's features, the scripting term *property* may begin to relate to what you and I think of as a property, namely, a characteristic.)

Becoming comfortable with the scripting terms *sub* and *function* is hard enough without having to deal with this different name — *method* — that means the same thing. A method, in everyday usage, is *a way that you do something.* In programmerese, though, *method* is another word for *procedure.* (I guess, to a programmer, the way you do anything is with a procedure.) I see one advantage to using the different terms, though. You can be reasonably certain, when you hear people talk about methods instead of subs and functions, that they're talking about OOP classes and related matters, and not simple LotusScript scripting.

Digging for OOP objects: Geology 101

We can all think of an object as a rock or a chair, but delving into the LotusScript OOP universe uncovers a new vein of objects. In this new vein, every identifiable scripting item has the potential to be an object. I devote the rest of this section to exploring the objects that can belong to a class.

The objects that make up a class are called *members.*

Mining the member variables

How do you create member variables in a class? You declare them. You may
declare the class variables with the keywords Public or Private; however,
you omit the Dim keyword for variables that are members of a class. Notice the
following example:

```
Class CustomerData
    firstName As String
    lastName As String
    ssNum As String*11
End Class
```

Excavating for methods (subs and functions)

In the OOP world of class definitions, subs and functions have a different
name — *methods*. They're still subs and functions, though. Fortunately, you
create methods (subs and functions for classes) in the same way that you do
for simple scripting. You can see Chapters 12 and 13 for more information about
working with subs and functions.

One of the main benefits of creating a class is that you then have a standard
definition that you can use to create specific instances (objects) that have the
characteristics of the class. You don't have to create the characteristics from
scratch over and over again. Because you create specific instances from
classes, use them for a while, and then get rid of them, LotusScript classes
contain special methods that initialize (Sub New) and delete (Sub Delete)
objects of a class.

You can use the following special elements in class definitions:

- **Sub New:** When you create an instance of a class by using the New keyword in the Set statement, the New method (generally referred to as the
  constructor) initializes values for that class instance (object).

  ```
  Set newObject = New className1
  ```

- **Sub Delete:** When you issue the Delete keyword followed by the name of
  the class instance that you want to delete, the Delete method (referred to
  as the *destructor*) removes that instance of the class from memory.

  ```
  Delete newObject
  ```

- **Me:** When inside a member procedure, you use the Me keyword to refer to
  the class object itself. That is, the construction Me.memVar1 refers to the
  value currently assigned to the memVar1 member of the current instance of
  the class.

  ```
  Me.memVar1 = "This object's value for memVar1"
  ```

The following class definition includes the methods `Sub New`, `Sub Delete`, and `Sub SwitchColors`:

For example, you could create a class `teamData`. Within the class you could create properties (the variables), create subprograms (methods) with the constructor sub, and then delete the subprograms with the destructor sub.

```
Class teamData
    'declare member variables in the class
    firstName As String
    lastName As String
    scoringAverage As String

    ' Define a constructor sub to create a new instance of the
            class
    Sub New (fName As String, lName As String, sAverage As
            String)
        firstName = fName$
        lastName = lName$
        scoringAverage = sAverage$
    ' statements then appear here
        fName$=Mario
        Print fname
    End Sub


    ' Define destructor sub to get rid of new instance when no
            longer needed

    Sub Delete
        Print "Now deleting the text object."
    End Sub
End Class
```

Get*ting and* Set*ting member properties*

You can include a LotusScript property as a member of an OOP class. In Chapter 12, I talk about properties as a form of procedure. In this section, I want to talk about properties as they relate to classes. Close examination of LotusScript properties leads to the discovery that properties actually act as variables in both universes — in scripts and in OOP class definitions.

As a separate entity in a script, properties are separate blocks of code that assign (`Set`) and retrieve (`Get`) the value of a variable. In an OOP class definition, properties have this same structure, but only work with objects that belong to that class. Properties contribute a value to the script in both cases.

Here is an example of a property `Get` statement. The variable `neededInt` from the `Main` sub gets its value from the `Property Get` sub.

```
Sub Main
   ' These statements assign the value of neededInt to X
   Dim neededInt As Integer
   Property Get propInt As Integer
      propInt% = neededInt%
   End Property
   x = propInt%

End Sub
```

Following is an example of a property `Set` statement. The `Property Set` procedure works in reverse from the `Property Get` procedure — instead of getting a value from the property procedure, it gives a value to be used inside the property procedure.

```
Sub Main
   ' These statements assign the value of x to neededInt
   Dim neededInt As Integer
   Property Set propInt As Integer
      neededInt% = propInt%
   End Property
   propInt% = x

End Sub
```

OOP at Work

Something about OOP must be really cool; otherwise, why would so many people be so excited about it? Granted, these excited people may belong to the class `Nerds`, and the rest of us may not be doing cartwheels about the wonderful capabilities of classes and objects. Nevertheless, I'm beginning to see what some of the excitement is about for those who are ready to work with classes. The OOP structures save tremendous amounts of work (because you can reuse your code) and keep you from making mistakes (like typos) at the same time.

Suppose that you are working on an application that requires some basic input and output (I/O) activities with files. You have better things to do than spend six months working on I/O routines, but at the same time, you know that your application needs these activities. Now suppose that a coworker scripting in another application has created a class that performs such I/O.

Well, you don't have to redo all that scripting. You can simply copy the class (that does the file activities) from the other application and use it in your own. (You could use the Windows Clipboard. Open both applications — the one with the code you want to use, and the one you want to use it in. Cut the desired class from the one, and paste it as a class into your new application.)

But this copying is legitimate pilferage — nobody thinks of you as a plagiarizer for doing it, and you don't have to waste your time redoing all that code from scratch. You can use your coworker's class exactly as it is, or you can make modifications or enhancements by *extending* the class.

Extending classes: Knocking them off

After you or your cohort create a class, other scripters can borrow the class, maybe add a few enhancements, and use it over and over again. Knocking-off a class in this way is known as *extending* the class or *deriving* from it. (To you and me, extending something is stretching it . . . like extending the hamburger with a little Hamburger Helper. In the language of OOP programmers, though, to extend is to *copy and enhance*.)

The class that you extend from is called the *base class,* and each new class that you extend to is called a *derived* class. The derived class *inherits* all of the properties and methods from its *parent* class, or *superclass*. Then you can add new properties and methods, and change the old ones if you want.

Extending a class in OOP is a lot like copying a document that you've created in your word processor, leaving much of the original document intact, yet making changes as well. For example, suppose that you had a base class called HumanBeing that had these member variables:

- ✔ HairColor
- ✔ EyeColor
- ✔ Height

And suppose the class HumanBeing had these member methods:

- ✔ DailyOccupation
- ✔ SleepingHabits
- ✔ EatingHabits

LotusScript contains syntax that enables you to easily extend a class like HumanBeing. You can create the following derived classes, which all start with the same properties and methods that are members of the HumanBeing class:

  ✔ AirlinePilot

  ✔ Parent

  ✔ SouthAmerican

  ✔ MusicalGenius

To derive a new class from an existing one, you use the `Class` statement with the `As` option. The syntax looks like this:

```
[ Public | Private ] Class newClass As abaseClass
    theclassBody
End Class
```

The following example shows how to derive the class `Parent` from the class `HumanBeing`:

```
Class Parent As HumanBeing
```

Then, you may want to add to the inherited methods of the new class `Parent` (which are `DailyOccupation`, `SleepingHabits`, and `EatingHabits`) by adding a method called `CarPooling`.

Knocking off existing classes surely is the most powerful feature of OOP and is also a way for people to get an awful lot done without doing an awful lot of work — a very attractive approach, I might add, for us lazy scripters.

Enhancing classes: New variables, properties, and methods

When creating a class based on another class (that is, when deriving a class), you can add new member variables, properties and methods, or you can modify (redefine) the members that you inherited from the original base (parent) class.

The methods (subs or functions) and properties within a class definition are LotusScript procedures that are used only with objects belonging to that class.

You may be interested to know that, if you redefine methods or properties from the parent class, the original methods or properties become *overridden*. You can still get to the original inherited members, by using a special technique in dot notation; see the section, "Accessing members outside of class: using dot notation," for more information.

Accessing members outside of class: Using dot notation

In theory, at least, the technique for getting to a class member from outside the class you're in doesn't sound too difficult. You just need to use the member's full name, and that shouldn't be hard. You use a technique called dot notation. The main thing to remember about dot notation is what comes first — that is, the order of the elements that make up the member's full name.

To reference a class member by its full name, think of the last-name-first rule. For example, because George I is a member of the Tudor family, you would refer to him (in dot notation) as `Tudor.georgeI`.

You type the name of the class first, a dot (or period), and then the name of the specific class member.

Similarly, if you want to refer to a member of a particular object (or instance of a class), you type the name of the object, a dot, then the name of the member.

If you have to go through a series of classes to get to the one containing the member that you're addressing, you type dots and class names until you get there. (I like the fancy terminology the manual uses to say the same thing. "You access any object by traversing the containment hierarchy that connects objects with other objects." Wow! *Traversing the containment hierarchy* — cool!)

Oh, and you can use dot notation with types, too. The section "Naming your type and its elements" earlier in this chapter talks about using dot notation to refer to a type's member variables.

Leave it to totally left-brained types to take a simple term like *dot notation* and confuse matters by calling one variation *dotdot notation*. (I can bring myself to say "dot," but not "dotdot" — that sounds too much like machine talk.) You can use *dotdot notation* to call an overridden property or method in a superclass (or base, or parent class). In dotdot notation, you literally type in two dots in a row, like this:

```
abaseClassName..apropertyName
```

Some day you may need to do dotdot notation, but probably not yet. Anyway, you can say you heard about it here.

OLE Automation and DDE

Lots of Windows applications are very proud to support Object Linking and Embedding (OLE) and Dynamic Data Exchange (DDE) — methods for using more than one program together at the same time. In some cases, you can use LotusScript to create and manipulate objects in non-Lotus products that support OLE and DDE. You use dot notation to refer to objects in other products.

You can find examples in the Lotus manuals and Help files. I just want to point out here that you can write scripts that connect with non-Lotus products. That's enough for this *. . . For Dummies* book, though. If you are ready to actually step through the inter-application sharing process, you'll have no problem following along with the examples in the LotusScript Help files.

The point, then, is that when working with other Lotus programs or even non-Lotus programs, you use object structure and dot notation to get to objects in strange places — such as, in Freelance Plus when you're working in 1-2-3, or even in Microsoft Word when you're working in 1-2-3. You see simple examples of dot notation, for example, when you record your own scripts in 1-2-3 and other programs. If you cut a selection in 1-2-3, you generate this line of code:

```
Selection.Cut
```

1-2-3 knows that you are referring to the current worksheet and doesn't put in the complete address. You are actually using dot notation to refer to the Cut command in the current worksheet. If you know the address for any object, you can refer to it by typing the class names to that address with dots in between.

OOP doesn't mean *oops* at all — not the way it does to people who, you know, stumble and feel uncertain about things. People who go rushing into OOP are likely to find themselves muttering, "Oops! I made a mistake. I shouldn't be in here." OOPs is pretty advanced. In this chapter, you may have gotten a small taste of it — enough, I hope, to feel a little bit comfortable with this style of programming that is taking over the programming world.

Understanding OOP helps you understand how to use OOP in various Lotus products and how to have those products work together. The rest of this book (except for The Part of Tens) talks about using LotusScript with various Lotus products.

Test your newfound knowledge

An object is

1. A stone or something like that — anything you can throw. Even a dog's toenails.

2. Just about anything in manifest creation, when thought of as a unit.

3. A building block in the hierarchical structure of a larger program.

4. All of the above.

To make a derived class in LotusScript, you can

1. Get a bunch of people together, draw up a constitution, and declare yourselves the New Bourgeoisie or something.

2. Knock off an old class (not knock off as in *kill*, but knock off as in *replicate* — called *extend* in programming).

3. Ring a bell, start lecturing, and hope a bunch of objects show up for class.

4. Find somebody with a lot of class and clone him or her in a laboratory.

Chapter 15

Attaching to Events: In Our Main Event

. . . .

In This Chapter

▶ Looking for exciting events in the wonderful world of scripting

▶ Doing what scripters do with events — attaching to them

▶ Naming the event — the key to attaching

▶ Looking for benefits of attaching scripts

. . . .

*Y*ou don't create LotusScript scripts to use them as hot, stand-alone programs; instead, you use them as hot scripts that automate Lotus applications — Lotus Notes, Lotus 1-2-3, and the rest of the SmartSuite. Although figuring out how to create the scripts themselves is important (Chapters 2 through 14 discuss various aspects of creating scripts), the real power of scripts comes from how they work with the Lotus programs.

I don't blame you a bit if you're wondering, "These scripts are great, but how do I get them *inside those Lotus programs?* How do I hook a script into, say, Lotus 1-2-3 so that the script actually runs at the right time? That is, how do I make sure that my script executes when some 1-2-3 user needs it?"

And the answer is this: You attach your scripts to *events*. This chapter shows you how.

What Is an Event?

I think of an event as a big deal happening out there in the world — Wrestlemania, a big stock car race, a ten-ring circus, a gathering of political poobahs, things like that. In programming, an event doesn't have to be that grand; an event can be as simple as a user clicking the mouse button.

When you're talking about programming, an *event* is the occurrence of some interaction between a person and a computer. That is, if the person using a program clicks a button in the interface, clicks to place the cursor in a table, or starts typing, that's an exciting action in the small world of the program. In fact, any one of these actions is a major event, and you can attach a script to it.

Setting Up Your Script to Run

Suppose that you are a bomber (not with dangerous bombs, of course, but with little smoke bombs or something). Suppose, also, that the only way to use your harmless explosives is to attach them to automobile ignitions. The ignitions, in turn, serve as detonation devices. If left unattached and undetonated, your bombs just sit there harmlessly and never smoke. That is, someone has to turn over the ignition with your device attached before — blam — the smoke bomb goes off (causing annoyance, but not hurting anybody).

Similarly, a script in a Lotus program is pretty ineffectual in and of itself. Like the smoke bombs, your scripts must be attached to something (an *object*) and associated with some kind of trigger (an *event*) in order to work. You actually have various ways to run a script:

- ✔ You can run a script from within the LotusScript Script Editor; Chapter 2 and various examples throughout the book show you how. Running a script from the Script Editor is great for making sure that your script works as you're creating it.

- ✔ And you can run a script from within a document or worksheet. You can use the menus and choose Edit➪Script & Macros➪Run.

- ✔ You can create a custom button or icon for your script and run it by clicking the custom item. Doing this is handy when you use the script a lot.

- ✔ You can attach a script to an object/event pair that triggers the script to run when the corresponding event occurs. Attaching a script to an event trigger is the primary way to execute (that means *run,* not *put to death*) your scripts.

Identifying an object for attachment

An event is a little something that happens in a program — something like the user typing input or clicking the mouse. And that event is related to some object in the program: a spreadsheet cell, a drop-down list, a button, or so on. You attach a script to this object/event pair. Then when the event happens — blam — the script goes off.

I think that looking at an example can help clarify the object/event pair concept. I used Lotus 1-2-3 97 for the following example, but you can find objects to attach your scripts to in any program that has LotusScript. Use these steps to take a brief glimpse at a list of objects:

1. **Choose Edit⊏Scripts & Macros⊏Show Script Editor to open the IDE for LotusScript in Lotus 1-2-3 97.**

2. **Click the down-arrow at the right of the Object text box in the IDE to see the drop-down list of objects.**

   You see a list of objects — probably a rather brief list at first. Figure 15-1 shows a sample drop-down Object list.

In whichever Lotus program you're using, the items in this Object drop-down list are the things that you can attach scripts to. The objects in themselves, however, don't trigger the scripts to run. The scripts (like the smoke bombs in the prior analogy) go off only when something (the event) *happens* to the objects.

Attaching your script to an event

The documentation on LotusScript does confess that, when you create a script for an event, you're really creating it for a single object/event pair. Because talking about *hooking up to object/event pairs* could get a little wordy, I'll refer to *attaching to events,* and leave it at that.

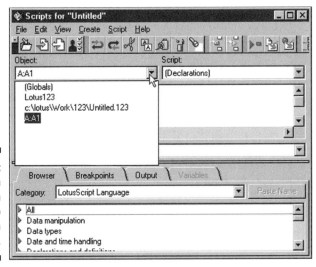

Figure 15-1:
You can attach scripts to objects in this list.

After you identify an object that you want to associate with your script, you need to determine what event accompanies that object and then create the script for that event. You accomplish this script attachment through a series of dialogs and InfoBoxes in the Lotus product that you happen to be working in. Basically, you do the following to attach a script to an event:

- ✔ In your document (spreadsheet, presentation, or so on), select the object (like a merge field or cell) that you want to attach a script to.

- ✔ Identify the object by giving it a name.

- ✔ Open the IDE (Integrated Development Environment) and select the named object; then the associated event appears.

- ✔ Enter the LotusScript statements and functions that you want to make up your script.

The Example: Attaching to an Event in Word Pro

As is almost always the case in scripting (and indeed, I should say, in life) actually doing something is a much better way to understand it than simply talking about it. So I encourage you to try attaching a script to an event in Lotus Word Pro — you can even follow the example in this section.

Suppose that you wanted to add a reminder to a SmartMaster so that anyone who creates a document with that SmartMaster gets the reminder. (By the way, a *SmartMaster* is a Lotus template that preformats your documents. Much of the work of defining objects, events, and scripts are already done in the LotusScript SmartMasters.) You can attach your reminder script to an event in the SmartMaster. For the example in this section, I use a SmartMaster for an invoice form in Word Pro. Then I create a message box reminder (the script) that pops up when someone clicks in the form field that's preformatted to hold the customer name.

Naming an object so that you can find it later

Before you can attach to an object, you have to give the object a name. This *have to* stuff always makes me uncomfortable, but LotusScript needs to have a name for the object so that it can know what it's referring to. And because so many items in each document can have names, LotusScript waits for you to name the ones you're going to use. (Just imagine that LotusScript is a kindergarten teacher with 30 kids to watch. If the teacher didn't know the names of the

Naming ranges and stuff

If you've gotten into the habit of using Lotus 1-2-3 or Freelance Graphics, you may be used to naming cells or ranges. The advantage to giving names to ranges is that you can use the names instead of cell addresses, and the names are a whole lot easier to remember.

For example, a range in Lotus 1-2-3 may have the address A:A1.A:B4 (really intuitive, don't you think?), but you can name this range something like *Results* (which is easy to remember).

After you name a range, you don't have to remember its address anymore. You can use the name, instead of the address, in references like formulas — which is the type of thing that appeals to users, because it's easier and more intuitive.

And scripting gives you another reason to name objects such as ranges. You have to name your objects something so that you can attach a script to them.

students, handling them could get so confusing that he or she might just throw in the towel and bolt the room. Actually, with much respect to kindergarten teachers, working with 30 kids can be overwhelming even when you do know their names.)

1. **In Lotus Word Pro, choose File⇨New Document.**

2. **In the New Document dialog box, click the Create from any SmartMaster tab. Then select Form in the Select a type of SmartMaster list box and invoice1 in the Select a look list box.**

3. **Click OK.**

   You now have a blank SmartMaster form on-screen, with objects in it just waiting for some scripter to come along and attach a script or two. Don't disappoint everyone; attach a script!

4. **Click in the cell where you plan to attach the script.**

   I'll use the To cell, where you see `Click here to type Recipient's Name`, as shown in Figure 15-2.

   Now you have to identify the To cell as an object that you can find later in the Script Editor. This step is key in the whole process of attaching scripts — it's the single thing that experienced programmers will pick up right away. Sound the trumpet: *To attach a script to an object, you have to . . . name the object.*

Click in this cell

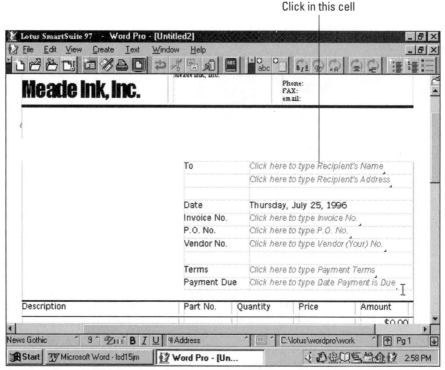

Figure 15-2:
Click the
object
where you
want to
attach a
script.

5. **In the main menu, choose Table⇨Cell Properties to bring up the InfoBox with Table Cell showing in the title bar.**

Make sure that you're in the InfoBox for a Table Cell and not for, say, Text. That is, after Properties for in the title bar of the InfoBox, you should see the words *Table Cell*. The first time I tried to name this cell, I was in the InfoBox for Text and couldn't find what I was looking for.

6. **Click on the Misc. tab.**

The Misc. tab appears; see Figure 15-3.

7. **Type in a name for the cell.**

I typed in **custName** for this example.

8. **Click the X in the upper-right corner to close the Lotus InfoBox.**

When you complete these steps, you've named a selected object — in this example, a table cell in a SmartMaster form. This seemingly obscure act gives LotusScript what it needs to be able to hook a script onto the cell.

Notes/FX field checkbox

Misc. tab   Name field

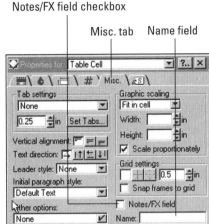

Figure 15-3:
You name
an object
in this
dialog box.

Attaching the script to your named object

All those steps for naming an object (see previous section) may seem like a lot of trouble. And sometimes you find objects already named and available in a document. But many times, you need to name an object before you can attach a script to it.

After you name your object, use these steps to attach a script to it:

1. **Click the Show Script Editor SmartIcon.**

   The Script Editor appears, and if it isn't displayed already, you have to find the object that you just identified — in this example, the To cell named *custName*.

2. **Click the down-arrow next to the Object drop-down list box.**

   You can see the list of available objects in Figure 15-4.

   You should find any objects that you've named in this list. Sometimes, the object's name falls under an expandable category in the list, and you may need to expand the list to see your object.

   In this example, you click on the expansion arrow next to !Body to show the list of objects in the Body category of objects for the SmartMaster form.

Sharing information with Notes F/X fields

When you're naming an object in the Properties for InfoBox, you can click the Notes F/X field check box to make this named object available for use in Lotus Notes as well. I won't go into all the details here, because it's beside the point I want to make. Basically, using the Notes F/X field feature is another example of the integration between Lotus products.

I read about a cool example of this sharing in the Lotus Help files. Suppose that you have, say, a table cell in Word Pro that gives the total price for a contract. You make the cell a bookmark named `TotalPrice` and mark it as a Notes/FX field in the Properties for Table Cell InfoBox. Then through Lotus Notes, you can display the total contract price, maybe in a report that many users

reference or in a database that a bunch of people use daily. If that table cell (the contract price) changes in Word Pro, it automatically changes in Notes, too.

If the price changes in Notes, for that matter, it changes in Word Pro also. This linking and sharing can become a gotta-have-it feature for brokers and other aggressive types in your company who want to spend their time on the phone doing business, instead of at their desks doing drudge work. So, they can have the latest, updated contract price at their fingertips in Lotus Notes (which they're using all the time), instead of having to open a Word Pro document to track down that price. And best of all, they know that the contract price, in either location, is the same!

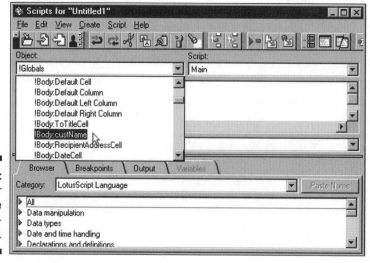

Figure 15-4:
Finding your object in the Object drop-down list.

3. **Click the name of your object to select it from the list.**

In this example, click !Body:custName.

You've selected an object to attach to. You also have to make sure that you have the right event in control. The script that plays each time someone places the insertion point (clicks) in the named cell is Enterlayout (not because of anything you've done, but just because this Word Pro SmartMaster associates the event of clicking the form cell with the script Enterlayout).

4. **Click the arrow next to the Script drop-down list box and select the script associated with your object/event pair.**

For this example, click on Enterlayout (if it's not displayed already). Your IDE should look similar to Figure 15-5, with the Enterlayout sub showing in the Script Editor.

After completing these steps, you've attached the associated script to the object/event pair in the Word Pro form document. You can now add LotusScript code that executes when a user triggers your script. That is, when a user clicks in the To cell of the SmartMaster invoice1 form.

Writing the attached script

You can add your reminder to the user as a message box. You can see Chapter 3 for another example of a script that uses a message box. Try using the IDE Browser panel and follow these steps to complete your script:

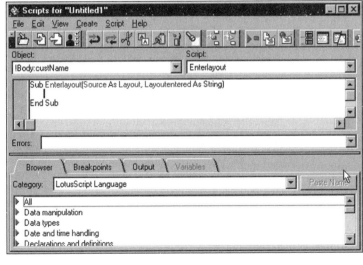

Figure 15-5:
The Script
Editor
shows the
associated
script and
object.

1. **Click on the Browser tab in the IDE; then click the arrow next to All.**

   A list of all LotusScript statements appears.

2. **Locate the LotusScript statement that you want by beginning to type the statement.**

   After you type just the first letter — *M,* in this case — LotusScript highlights the first command that matches, MessageBox.

3. **Click the Paste Name button.**

4. **Type in the rest of the statement elements to complete your script line.**

   Your sub, with the Messagebox statement, should look like this:

```
Sub Enterlayout(Source As Layout, Layoutentered As String)
   Messagebox "Always use complete name."
End Sub
```

5. **Click the X in the upper-right corner to close the Script Editor.**

You may want to save your document as well, although you can run the Script even if you don't.

Trying out the attached script

Now you can try out your attached script. Go back to the document that's linked with your script and find out whether you can run the script.

1. **In your document, activate the event that you've associated with your script.**

   In this example, click in the To cell, where you see Click here to type Recipient's Name, in the Word Pro form. (If the cursor appears in that cell already, click outside the cell and then click in it again.)

   The message box, which admonishes you "Always use complete name," comes up. See Figure 15-6.

2. **Click OK to close the message box.**

Your attached script has done its thing!

After you know a couple of key tricks, then, not all that much is involved in attaching your scripts to events in Lotus products. You have to know where to find the events (by clicking on the list box for Object in the Script Editor). You need to know how to name an object that doesn't have a name already (by using the Lotus Properties InfoBox to name the object). And of course, you need to write the script.

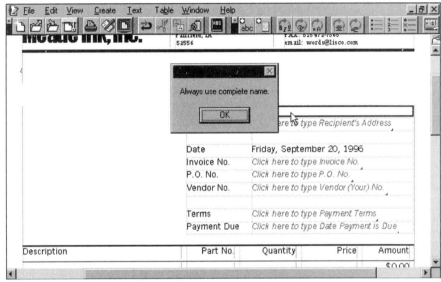

Figure 15-6:
Clicking in
the right cell
can activate
your script.

Looking at the Benefits of Attaching Scripts

Although the process of attaching scripts to events may be a little thing, writing and attaching useful scripts, which help out other users that activate them, can be a big thing. The following list identifies some useful things that you can do with attached scripts:

  ✔ Provide a helpful reminder for filling in complete information.

  ✔ Supply a pick-list of valid input items.

  ✔ Check the validity of information put into a field.

  ✔ Ask for additional input that you may use in a script.

The other users that benefit from your scripting prowess may wonder, "How the heck did somebody get that neat message in here?" But you know how you did it, of course. For the others, just let them wonder.

Test your newfound knowledge

In the exciting world of scripting, an event is

1. Wrestlemania coming to town

2. A major political debate

3. A user typing or clicking

4. A symphony featuring a really famous soloist

To attach a script to an object, you

1. Use Crazy Glue. It doesn't last that long, but it holds tight at first.

2. In the Script Editor, click on the name in the Object box and then write the script.

3. Ask the object, politely, to hold onto the script real tight for a long time, until it just gets so attached to it that it won't let it go.

4. Use the old stand by — chewing gum. Although a little messy, chewing gum can attach anything to anything. Surely it can attach an event to an object.

Chapter 16

Scripting Word Pro: Click Here at Your Own Risk

. . . .

In This Chapter

▶ Writing code mindlessly by recording as you work

▶ Fastening a script to something really useful — a SmartIcon

▶ Getting your scripts to go off on cue

▶ Looking over the objects in Word Pro (and seeing what's where)

. . . .

*L*otusScript, as a programming language, is the same whether you're using Lotus Word Pro, 1-2-3, Approach, Notes, or whatever. Subs are still subs. Functions are still functions. The If statement works the same way. Such uniformity is the beauty of Lotus's achievement in offering a standard scripting language across its product line.

If LotusScript is the same for all products, what good are this chapter on Word Pro and the chapters that follow for the other Lotus products? What's the difference for the different products?

The main difference in LotusScript between products is the OOP (object-oriented programming) structures — that is, the classes, objects, and the relationships between the two within that product. Chapter 14 introduces the basic concepts and structures of OOP, including class hierarchy and naming conventions that are important to understanding LotusScript objects.

Also, you find differences between what the Lotus applications do and, therefore, what you may want to do with them when you use scripts. In Lotus 1-2-3, you automate how you work with tables of data. In Freelance Graphics, you automate how you work with slides and overheads. And in Word Pro, of course, you're likely to want to create a convoluted Gothic novel, populate it with pictures, and use it on your Web site.

This chapter gets you started in using LotusScript with Word Pro (but doesn't offer all that much help with your Gothic novel).

Recording Scripts: Hey, My Own Studio

Recording your own scripts is quite a handy capability, even for experienced scripters. You can record scripts in all the Lotus products that use LotusScript. By recording a script, you can get down the basics (keystrokes and mouse clicks) of what you want to do and then (with experience) clean up the code and adapt it in various ways. I talk about recording scripts early in this book — in Chapter 2, that is.

As I see it, the capacity to record your keystrokes and mouse clicks as scripts is pretty much a prerequisite for any program that expects to have lots of people scripting in it. Anything you can do in the program, you can record.

As an example, suppose that you want to create a script that searches your Word Pro document for a certain word and puts that word into bold type. You don't have to start from scratch — coding the commands for Find and everything. You can step through the menus, keystrokes and mouse clicks and have Lotus Word Pro record the script as you go. Follow these steps to try out recording a script:

1. **Type some text into an open Word Pro document.**

   For example, type these words: **We need to go out and find a bunch of monkeys and train them.**

2. **Place the cursor back at the start of the line.**

   Now you're set up and ready to record your script.

3. **Choose Edit⇨Script & Macros⇨Record Script.**

   Figure 16-1 shows the menu selections that you use.

   The Record Script dialog box, as shown in Figure 16-2, comes up and asks you to enter the name for your script.

4. **In the Record Script dialog box, enter a name for the script that you want to record.**

   For the example, I don't type in a new name but just leave the name Main.

5. **Click OK.**

   The cursor turns into a circle with a bar across it. In the lower-right corner of the screen, a message in red says Recording . . . .

6. **Go through the program keystrokes/mouse clicks that you want to follow for the script.**

   For the example, do the following:

   - Click the Edit menu.
   - Click Find & Replace Text to get the Find & Replace dialog box.

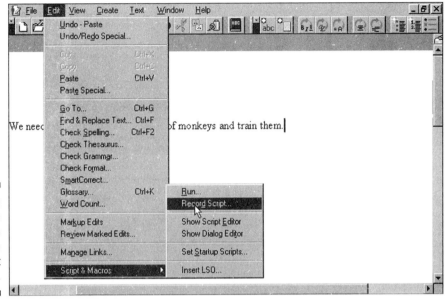

Figure 16-1:
Use these
menus to
start the
script
recorder.

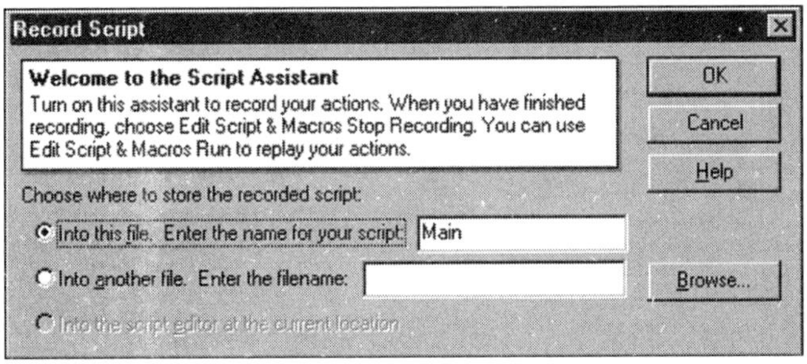

Figure 16-2:
Enter a
name for
your script.

- Type the word **monkeys** in the Find text box.

- Click the Find button.

- When Word Pro highlights monkeys on-screen, click the B icon in the status line at the bottom to bold the highlighted word. (Figure 16-3 shows the screen with the word highlighted and in bold.)

- Click Done.

7. To stop recording, choose Edit⇨Script & Macros⇨Stop Recording.

The Script Editor comes up, showing the script you've recorded; see Figure 16-4. The script you record is almost never perfect. You almost always need to tweak this or that to get the script just right. Sometimes you even make a typing mistake or put in an extra command as you go along.

Recording a script

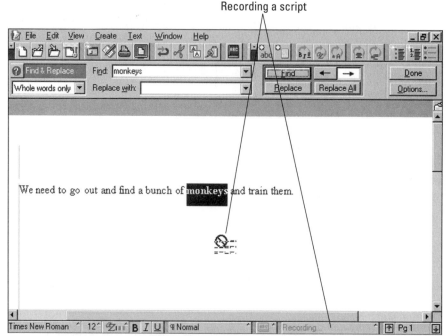

Figure 16-3:
Certain on-screen elements show that you are recording a script.

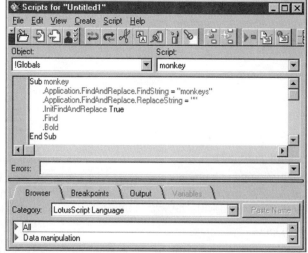

Figure 16-4:
When you record a script, you see the generated code in the Script Editor.

8. **In the script editor, choose** File⇨Save Scripts. **In the resulting Save As dialog box, type in a name for your document, select a folder, and click** Save **to save the script along with the associated document.**

   For this example, I typed the name **monkeys** in the File name box, chose the my_scripts folder in the Save in box, and clicked Save. Word Pro saves the script and document in the folder you choose. (Remember where you save it, because you may want to locate the script if you follow along later in the chapter and assign the script to a SmartIcon.)

Recording a script is a fast way to get a script that does about anything you can do in Word Pro. And don't be ashamed of automating your scripting in this way; you don't always have to script from scratch!

Playing Back Scripts: Where's the Playback Button?

You can play back a script manually, by choosing from the menus. Suppose that you want to play back the script from an existing Word Pro document. First make sure that you open the document containing the script. If you're following the example that I started in the previous section, open the document saved with the name monkeys and unbold the word *monkeys* so that you can see the script doing something when you run it. Then follow these steps:

1. **In Word Pro, choose** Edit⇨Script & Macros⇨Run.

2. **In the Run Script dialog box, choose Run script saved in the current file and click the name of the script from the drop-down list.**

   For the example, Figure 16-5 shows the script name `Main`.

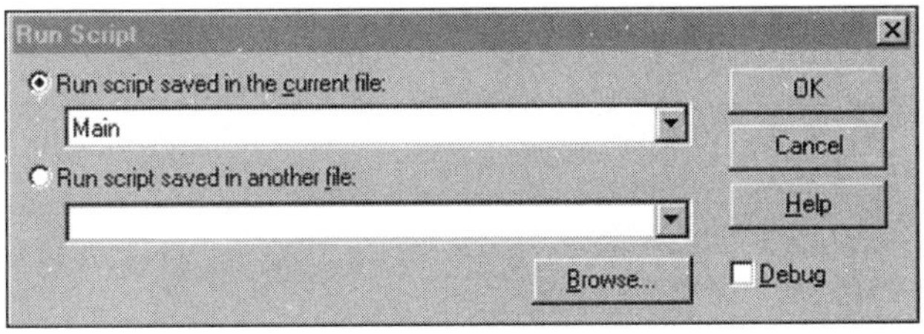

Figure 16-5:
Choose the name of the script you want to run.

3. **Click OK; the script executes.**

   In the example, the script finds the word *monkeys* and bolds it.

Running scripts from the menus isn't too hard, but the fun of scripting comes when you put the scripts in various clever places. One nice thing to do is to associate a script with a SmartIcon. Then you can *trip* the script into action with just a click of the SmartIcon.

Attaching to a SmartIcon

SmartIcons are great for people who don't want to remember much (and have their minds too full of things to be able remember much more anyway). If you attach your script to a SmartIcon, you don't have to remember how you made the script or anything. Just click on the SmartIcon to get it to execute.

You can't attach to one of the standard Word Pro icons. If you tried to attach to the Open SmartIcon for example, you could throw Word Pro into an identity crisis — should it Open, or should it search your document and bold the word *monkeys* (or do whatever your new script tells it to do). To keep its program out of such dilemmas, Word Pro requires you to attach to a fresh icon (that is, an icon that's not used for some other purpose).

Use these steps to attach your script to a SmartIcon:

1. **Choose File⇨User Setup⇨SmartIcons Setup.**

    The SmartIcons setup dialog box appears, as shown in Figure 16-6.

2. **Click Edit Icon.**

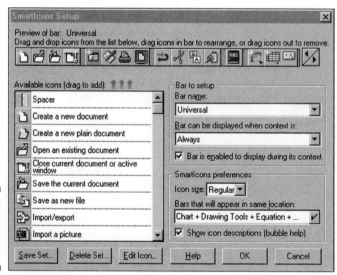

Figure 16-6:
SmartIcons
Setup
dialog box.

The cool Edit SmartIcons dialog box comes up, where you can choose an icon that you want to use.

3. **Click on the scroll arrow next to Available icons you can edit or copy, until you see icons with no assignment.**

   If you see the picture of a monkey, choose that. (Just kidding.) To follow the example, click on the picture of a cassette tape.

You can have a field day designing your own icons and everything. That's a topic for a book with more of a graphics flavor than this one, though. You may want to look at my *Word Pro For Windows 95 For Dummies* book, also published by IDG Books Worldwide, Inc. Or, you can just play around by clicking on mouse colors in the Mouse Button colors box and dragging in the Picture editor to create an icon. The main concern in this book, though, is scripts.

4. **Click the Attach Script button in the lower-left corner of the Edit SmartIcons dialog box.**

   Another dialog box comes up where you can choose the script that you want to attach to the icon.

5. **Select the script you want to attach to the icon.**

   For the example, the script is called Main, in the Word Pro document monkeys, which I saved in the folder my_scripts.

6. **Click Open.**

   Control returns to the Edit SmartIcons dialog box, and the name of the script appears in the Attached Script box at the lower-right.

7. **In the description box, type a description, which subsequently appears in the Bubble help when you put the mouse pointer over the icon.**

   Type in **Find monkeys** for the example.

8. **Click Save to save the connection.**

9. **Click Done to return to the SmartIcons Setup dialog box.**

10. **Drag the icon onto the Preview of bar near the top of the window so that you can test it out.**

    You find your new icon at the bottom of the Available icons (drag to add) list box.

11. **Click OK.**

The script is now attached to the SmartIcon. You can use the SmartIcon as you do any other SmartIcon. That is, to activate any SmartIcon's function — in this case, to run your script — click on the SmartIcon. If you want to test out this new icon, unbold the word *monkeys*. Then put the cursor on the line of text somewhere in front of *monkeys* and click on the SmartIcon to see whether the event of clicking the icon runs the attached script. You can refer to Chapter 15 for more information about attaching scripts to objects and events.

Attaching to a Frame

Scripts attached to SmartIcons are fun, I admit. But scripts become even more fun when you put them in various parts of the document and have them pop up as a help to users while they work.

For example, suppose that you wanted to attach a script to the SmartMaster news2.mwp (a newsletter template), as shown in Figure 16-7. Specifically, you may want to set up the ALSO INSIDE frame so that Word Pro automatically saves the newsletter document each time a user clicks on that frame. You can add this saving feature by attaching a script to the ALSO INSIDE frame. After all, the users may have typed in a lot of newsletter information by the time they click this frame, which makes saving the document a great idea.

First, set up the Script Editor to attach the script to the Frame object and to the Mouseup event. (You can see Chapter 15 for more information on identifying objects and events.) Follow these steps:

1. **Start a Word Pro document with a SmartMaster that contains frames.**

   To follow this example, use the news2.mwp SmartMaster.

2. **Click the frame to which you want to attach a script.**

   After you click the frame, you can tell that it's active by the black handles that appear on the frame's border. For the example, I clicked on the frame at the right that says ALSO INSIDE.

3. **Click the Show Script Editor SmartIcon (if you have it on your toolbar) or choose Edit⇨Script & Macros⇨Show Script Editor.**

   The IDE window for script editing appears. Because you've already selected the frame, its name !Body:Frame3 appears in the Object list box.

4. **Select an event that can activate your script from the Script drop-down list box.**

   Select Mouseup to follow the example.

5. **Type in the LotusScript commands that you want to associate with your chosen object and event.**

   For the example script, I typed the command .Save. Figure 16-8 shows the completed script.

6. **Save your script and choose File⇨Close Script Editor to close the IDE.**

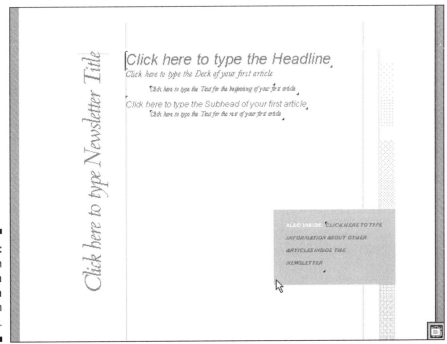

Figure 16-7:
You can attach a script to a frame in SmartMaster.

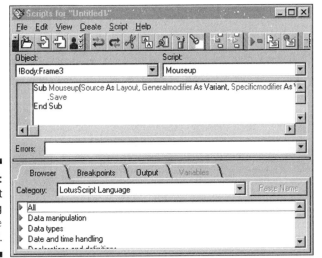

Figure 16-8:
The script containing the .Save command.

Now, every time a user clicks on the frame that you've attached to, your script runs. In this SmartMaster example, the script automatically saves the user's document. Try it out yourself a few times, if you've followed the example. Just click outside the ALSO INSIDE frame, then click in the frame again, and Word Pro saves the document.

If you want to make the change permanent, for other users, remember to save the document (with the frame and its attached script) as a SmartMaster, not just as a document, in the Save As dialog box.

Attaching to a Click Here Block

Click Here Blocks are, in themselves, a form of automation. When you create SmartMasters that are used by others, you can put in Click Here Blocks to guide the other users on where to input information — anything from their name to, you know, anything.

Recognizing that people who create Click Here Blocks probably do a lot of scripting as well, Word Pro makes attaching scripts to Click Here Blocks easy. Follow these steps and try it:

1. **In a blank Word Pro document, choose Create⊏>Click Here Block.**

   The Create Click Here Block dialog box comes up, as shown in Figure 16-9.

Figure 16-9:
Create Click
Here Blocks
with this
dialog box.

```
┌─ Create Click Here Block ──────────────────────────────────[x]─┐
│                                                                  │
│  Create Click Here Block                          ┌─── OK ───┐  │
│  Click Here Blocks are 'hot spots' that tell you where to insert │
│  text or data. You can use them as guides when    ┌─ Cancel ─┐  │
│  creating shared documents or a SmartMaster.                    │
│                                                   ┌── Help ──┐  │
│  Insert Click Here Block with these options:                    │
│  Behavior: [Standard - Insert typed text        ▼] ┌─ Script...┐│
│  Prompt text: [Click here to type Text          ]  ┌─Options...┐│
│  □ Bubble help text: [Click here to type Text    ]              │
└──────────────────────────────────────────────────────────────┘
```

2. **You can fill in the Behavior, Prompt text, and Bubble help text for your Click Here Block.**

3. **Click the Script button.**

   Word Pro opens the LotusScript IDE with the Script Editor ready for your input. The appropriate object and event for the script to attach to are already displayed.

4. Type in the lines of LotusScript code that you want to include in your script.

To follow this example, type this line:

```
Messagebox "Remember to check passport."
```

5. Save your script and choose File⇨Close Script Editor from the menu bar to close the IDE.

Whenever a user clicks a Click Here Block with an attached script, the script executes. In the example, the user sees a message box with the admonition, `Remember to check passport.`

Attaching to other stuff (not)

You can attach to Click Here Blocks, then, right from the menus. Can you do the same thing with other Word Pro items on the Word Pro Create menu — frames, tables, charts, drawings, equations, or whatever?

No, you can't. The Script button in the Create Click Here Block dialog box (as shown in Figure 16-9) probably shows a coming wave of the future for Word Pro. Some day you may able to attach scripts to lots of things with the click of a button. For now, though, you can't. I looked, and I didn't see Script buttons in the dialog boxes for those other document parts.

Attaching to a key

Word Pro is overflowing with *accelerator keys* — keyboard combinations that you can use as short-cuts to get things done faster. You find shortcut keys for getting around the document, for example, and shortcut keys for the commands on the menus. Obviously, you *can* attach scripts to keys . . . but at this time, you can't do it from the Word Pro menus.

Perhaps using shortcut keys for running your scripts has fallen into a bit of a developmental lag. Now, I worry about this, because Microsoft Word lets you attach macros to keys (though Microsoft's performance there is hardly flawless). In Ami Pro, the precursor to Word Pro, you could choose from a dialog box to attach your macros to keys.

In LotusScript Word Pro, however, attaching scripts to keys is pretty tricky. You can do it, but it involves .lss files (that is, you must save your scripts as files with the .lss extension) and tricky key addresses and lines of code. By the next version of the product — the projected Word Pro '98 — you should be able to use a dialog box to attach your script to a key. Perhaps the most useful thing to know right now is that, no, you are not crazy. You can't yet attach your script to a key using menus and dialog boxes.

Importing Ami Pro macros

It may be that Ami Pro — Word Pro's predecessor under Windows 3.1 — is beginning to ride off into the sunset, but it's not riding as fast as you might think. All kinds of Ami Pro loyalists are out there. (I know, because they continue to buy my books on the subject.)

Even those who do move over to Word Pro sometimes hold a strong loyalty to the old product. Chances are that if someone is a loyalist, that person delved deeply enough into Ami Pro to use macros (predecessors of Word Pro scripts).

Word Pro has made what I consider a reasonable accommodation for all those Ami Pro macro lovers. You can ask Word Pro to covert the Ami Pro macro, and it tries. According to the *Do It With Lotus SmartSuite For Windows* newsletter (published by IDG Newsletter Corp. in Boston), Word Pro succeeds about 50 percent of the time in actually converting the macro to a LotusScript script.

Follow these steps to do the conversion:

1. **From the Word Pro main menu, choose Edit⇨Script & Macros⇨Run.**

   The Run Script dialog box appears, as shown in (Figure 16-10).

2. **In the Run Script dialog box, select the option labeled Run script saved in another file.**

3. **Use the Browse button to locate your macro or, if you know the name, type in the name of the Ami Pro macro that you want to run in Word Pro.**

Figure 16-10:
The
Run Script
dialog box.

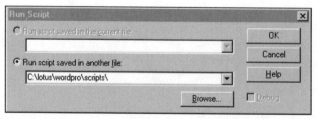

4. **Click OK.**

   A warning comes up to tell you that your chosen macro will be converted to the Word Pro format. Then, Word Pro does its best to run the macro.

In the Ami Pro macro that I tested, copyright.smm, Word Pro succeeded in converting the macro and put the copyright symbol into my Word Pro document. Of course, I chose a really simply macro to test out.

Lots of the old Ami Pro macros don't even apply anymore. Sometimes, the functionality that belonged to the macro is built into Word Pro anyway. For example, I previously used an Ami Pro macro that would tile the screen horizontally. The Word Pro command on the Window menu — Tile Top-Bottom — does the tiling much better than the Ami Pro macro ever did. And macros that apply to Windows 3.11 or to DOS are passé in many cases.

When Word Pro converts a macro file, the file goes through a complete religious conversion (or something similar). After you've converted the macro, it doesn't work as an Ami Pro macro anymore. If you plan to use the macro as a macro again, back it up first (or you must reinstall to get it back). Of course, burning your bridges and getting on with scripting may be a good idea anyway. Ami Pro macros were good for their time, but now scripting's time has come.

Object Structure: "Whosis Is inside of Whatsis?"

The day is dawning, perhaps sooner than many of you like, when you must come to grips with the OOP (object-oriented programming) structure of scripting in Word Pro (and the other Lotus products).

Everything in Word Pro is connected to everything else, in an object-oriented way. You can see Chapter 14 for a quick introduction to OOP, the style of programming where everything is related to everything else in ever-widening circles . . . like the ever-expanding cosmos around us. (Sorry, I'm getting carried away by rhetoric.)

Looking at Word Pro Classes

In OOP, you find objects, and you find classes. Objects are specific instances of classes. Classes belong to other classes (in that ever-expanding universe). Fortunately, Word Pro objects do coincide with actual Word Pro elements that you recognize. If you're familiar with Word Pro, you're familiar with the terms *Page*, *Frame*, *Table*, and *Cell*.

Each object has a name in Word Pro. `!Body:Default Page` is the name for one specific page layout, `!Body:Default Frame` is the name for a specific Frame, `!Body:Default Table` is the name for a specific Table layout, and `!Body:Default Cell` is the name for a specific cell layout.

The OOP name is the complete address for the Page, Frame, Table, or Cell object. You use the complete address if you want to refer to an object in a script. Of course, you don't have to memorize and remember these OOP names. You can find them through the IDE. Try these steps:

1. **In a new Word Pro document, open the Script Editor, by clicking the Script Editor SmartIcon or choosing <u>F</u>ile⇨Script & Macros⇨Show Script <u>E</u>ditor.**

   The IDE window appears.

2. **Click on the list arrow next to the Object drop-down list.**

   You see a list of objects in Word Pro, as shown in Figure 16-11.

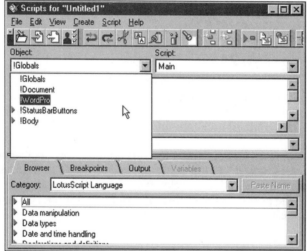

Figure 16-11: The drop-down list of objects in Word Pro.

3. **Click the arrow next to !Body to expand the list of objects under that category.**

   Figure 16-12 shows the expanded list of !Body objects.

As objects of a Word Pro class, each object (you know, a specific Frame or a Cell or a Page) has all of its own properties (the OOP kind), methods, and events. When you run Word Pro, the program knows everything about each active object. Word Pro knows all the properties and methods that belong to an object (like a Frame) in the first place. And it knows any changes that you've made, such as putting a fancy border around the frame.

When you know the address for any object, you can get to it and use it. The next section talks a little about those addresses.

Understanding containment hierarchy: Who's the boss?

Control. The evolution of this new scripting language is all about control, really. With Ami Pro macros, you didn't have it (control, that is). With LotusScript, you're *The One*. You can get to almost any object in any Lotus program or in Windows and use it in your script. It's a scary proposition, but power is power. Control is control. LotusScript gives it, and you may as well relish it.

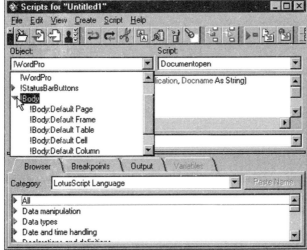

Figure 16-12:
A list of objects contained in another object.

When you write a script, you can get to and control many Word Pro structures — frames, cells, or whatever — because these structures belong in what LotusScript fondly refers to as the Word Pro *object model*.

The objects aren't all just lined up side by side. Objects are inside of classes. Classes are inside other classes. When an object is contained inside another object, it has the properties of the larger one. Lotus refers to the relationship of classes to other classes and objects as the *containment hierarchy*. (That term has a nice ring, don't you think?)

In the IDE, you can see immediately what object is inside of what class. Just click the Object drop-down list, as shown previously in Figure 16-12. For example, you can see in the figure that the `Default Page` is inside the class `!Body`.

To get to any object, the easiest thing, of course, is to click its name in the Object drop-down list in the IDE. Sometimes, however, you may want to refer to an object as you're typing in a script. To do this, you can type its address using dot notation. (See Chapter 14 for more information about dot notation.) To reference a page object, you may see an address like the following:

```
.Documents("mydoc.lwp").Divisions("!Body").Foundry.PageStyles(Default
Page))
```

The next section explains terms like `Foundry` and tells a little more about addresses like the one in this example.

Traversing the containment hierarchy

Typing the whole notation for each object for each reference would be confusing and hard. The dot notation is a series of class names — classes followed by a dot (.) followed by contained classes. Within some classes are specific instances of that class in parentheses, as in this structure — `.Documents ("mydoc.lwp")`.

For example, the complete dot notation for a Click Here Block object named `ClickHere1`, may be as follows:

```
.Documents("mydoc.lwp").Divisions("!Body").ClickHeres("ClickHere1")
```

Whenever you are scripting inside a particular document, Word Pro knows that you're working in the current division of the document, so you only need to type the object name, like this:

```
.ClickHeres("ClickHere1")
```

If you want to refer to an object in a different division, then you have to type the name of the division. I'll mention, too, in the interest of completeness, that you also need to type the word `.Foundry`. A *Foundry* is the Word Pro class where Word Pro stores all the contents of a particular document. Suppose you were in a division named `Background` and wanted to get to the division named `Body`. You would type this:

```
.Divisions("Body").Foundry.ClickHeres("ClickHere1").
```

The objects that you want to work with are there inside other classes. If you type the right dot notation, you can refer to them.

Word Pro has established flexibility as an ideal with LotusScript. The program doesn't hide all kinds of features and say, "Sorry, buddy, you can't go there." You can use the object containment hierarchy to change all kinds of things, such as an object in the !Body division of a document. Of course, tinkering with Word Pro is like tinkering with your car. If you're going to take your car (or Word Pro) apart, you better be careful, and you better know how to put it back together. Otherwise, something may not run right!

A certain natural protection in Word Pro keeps most people from fiddling with the program's inner essence, even though much of that is now accessible. The protection is this: You have to know how to get to things before you can change them. And probably, the people who know how to get to those inner structures are also those who won't break them or who know how to fix them if they do.

Test your newfound knowledge

To record a script in Word Pro, you just

1. Flip on the VCR and put in a special code; then hook up the VCR to your hot Pentium PC, and *Eureka*!

2. From the Edit menu, choose Script & Macros, then Record Script.

3. You don't. Labor unions have formed and lobbied congress to prevent random automatic recording of scripts by nonunion users.

4. You wrap cord around the script to cord it. Then, you wrap it again to *record* it.

Containment hierarchy is

1. An international cartel whose main objective is the restraint of trade

2. The opposite of the liberation lowerarchy

3. A nonsense term thrown in here to confuse you

4. The relationship of Word Pro objects to each another — who's in charge and who's inside of what

Chapter 17
Scripting Approach: Let's Modify Our Approach

. . . .

In This Chapter

▶ Recording scripts in Approach

▶ Turning macros into scripts at the push of a button

▶ Slipping scripts into Approach macros

▶ What's inside of where in the Approach object structure

. . . .

*1*n its handling of scripts, Lotus Approach has a leg-up on both 1-2-3 and Word Pro. For one thing, it has a nicely written booklet about itself that the other products can't yet match. Secondly, Approach is very good at translating macros into scripts — better than its sister products. Best of all, Approach is very, very good at making its contents available to other members of the Lotus SmartSuite. And sharing its valuable data is an outstanding quality, to be sure, for a database product.

Approach, like Lotus 1-2-3, had a sophisticated macro language of its own before LotusScript came along. Now, asking for an advanced macro system to step aside is asking quite a lot — even if a better system (like LotusScript) comes along. I liken the situation to asking an aging Hall of Fame ballplayer to step aside for a youthful replacement.

With this new scripting language, Approach has to scramble to incorporate all the capabilities that it offers in its macro language while, of course, offering all the advantages of LotusScript — such as using object-oriented (OOP) structures to expand areas of control in Approach.

At the moment, as Approach evolves to offer the full scripting language, Approach offers macros and LotusScript side by side.

Whereas in 1-2-3 97, you can record scripts but not macros, in Approach 97, you can record both macros and scripts. You can also convert a recorded macro to a script.

Recording a Script

You often do certain things (such as searching for a record) repeatedly when you're working with your database. Scripts are a great way to automate repetitive tasks. The following steps show you how to record a script:

1. **Start Approach and open an existing database or SmartMaster or create a new database.**

   For the example, I use a Video and Actor SmartMaster Application. The database comes up, with the name video.apr.

2. **Choose Edit⇨Record Transcript from the Approach main menu.**

   The Record Transcript dialog box appears, as shown in Figure 17-1.

3. **Click the radio button next to As script.**

4. **Type a name for the script in the drop-down list box.**

   For the example, I typed in the name **Wildflower**.

5. **Click Record.**

   Approach is now recording your actions like keystrokes, mouse-clicks, and so on. You can do whatever you want to test out the script recorder. To follow the example, do the following:

   • On the video.apr Main Menu, click Find Menu.

   • In the Find Menu screen, click the arrow next to Video Title, and click Wildflowers.

   • Press Enter. A screen appears showing the file and information about it.

6. **Choose Edit⇨Stop Recording from the main menu when you're finished with the actions that you want to record.**

   The Script Editor appears and displays the recorded script, as shown in Figure 17-2.

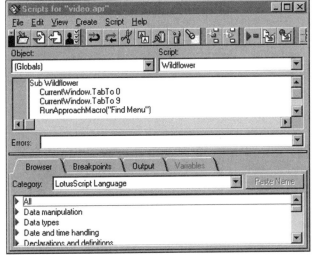

Figure 17-2:
The Script
Editor
opens and
shows the
recorded
script.

As I mention when talking about recording scripts in Chapter 2 and elsewhere, the recorded script may not be exactly what you want. You may have to edit out certain steps that you took by accident. Sometimes, too, the recorded script may not record all the actions you expect it to. But the recorded script is a good start towards a final script, and good starts are nice to have.

Taking the Short Course on Macros

Macros are quite sophisticated in Approach. Certain SmartMasters (preformatted database templates) come with whole sets of macros that can easily be menu choices for working with the database at hand. For example, in the video SmartMaster, Approach has macros for showing a list of actors and the titles of their movies, for finding directors, for listing actors in a selected movie, and much more. With so much invested into macros, Approach has a challenging job in switching to scripts.

Recording a Macro

This book is about scripts, not macros, so this discussion of creating macros is rather half-hearted. If you want to record a macro in Approach, you first choose Edit➪Macros. In the resulting Macros dialog box, you click on New. Now you're ready to define a new macro. Figure 17-3 shows the Define Macro dialog box. Through this dialog box, you can readily name your macro and assign it to a function key (a capability that is most useful and is not always readily available).

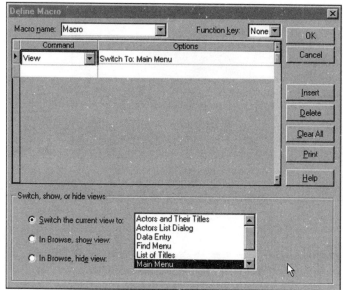

Running a macro

Like a good horse, an Approach macro doesn't have much value unless you run it regularly. To run a macro, choose Edit⇨Run Macro from the Approach main menu. A list of available macros pops up, as shown in Figure 17-4. If the macro that you want to run is assigned to a function key, you can press the function key. If it's assigned to a button or object, you can click that appropriate element.

Unlike 1-2-3 and Word Pro, Approach does not have the Edit Icon button, which you use to assign a script to a SmartIcon in the SmartIcons Setup dialog box (as discussed in Chapter 16). In other words, in Approach, you can't assign a script to a SmartIcon by using menu commands. That's a surprising omission but, hey, all things in time.

You can make do without attaching to SmartIcons, though. You can assign a macro to a button that you design yourself. Click on the Design button, just below the Universal SmartIcon bar in Approach. Then choose Create⇨ Control⇨Button. Click and drag the cursor to create a button of the size and shape you want. Creating a button in Approach is similar to creating a button in the Dialog Editor, as explained in Chapters 8 and 9. The Properties InfoBox appears; you can select the macro to run (or define a new one), give your button a meaningful label, and so on.

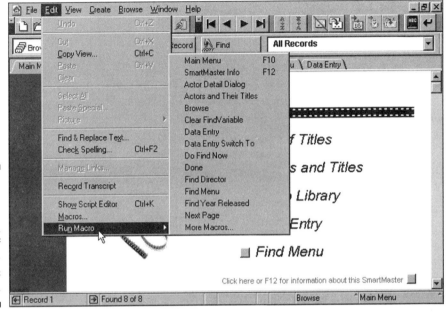

Figure 17-4:
When you
point to
Run Macro,
a list of
available
macros
pops up.

Converting macros to scripts

Not only does Approach allow you to record scripts, the program does an
exemplary job of converting existing macros to scripts. Try these steps:

1. **From the Approach main menu, choose Edit⇨Macros.**

   The Macros dialog box appears.

2. **In the Macros dialog box, click the name of the macro that you want to
   convert.**

   In the example shown in Figure 17-5, the macro Main Menu is selected.

3. **Click the Convert to Script button.**

   Approach prompts you to name the script, neatly converts the macro to a
   script, and opens the Script Editor with the LotusScript code for the
   converted macro showing.

Putting a script into a macro

Because scripts conform to OOP concepts (which I talk about in Chapter 14),
you can use scripts to control many aspects of working with an Approach
database — a good reason to evolve into a scripter instead of a macro writer.

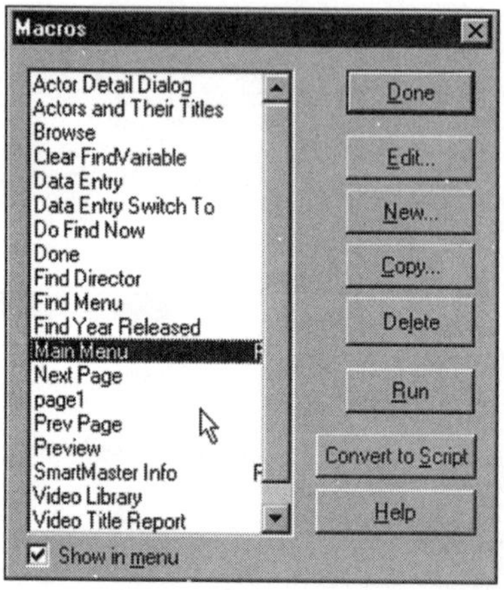

Figure 17-5:
Select the
macro that
you want to
convert.

But Approach offers a compromise for users who want to evolve gradually to scripting or just continue using macros. You can put a script into a macro, as follows:

1. **From the Approach main menu, choose Edit⇨Macros.**

   The Macros dialog box appears.

2. **In the Macros dialog box, click New.**

   Now the Define Macro dialog box appears.

3. **In the Macro name text box of the Define Macro dialog box, type a name for the macro.**

   Figure 17-6 shows the macro name `run_script`.

4. **From the Command drop-down list box, select Run.**

5. **From the Run macro drop-down list box, select the script that you want to run.**

   Although the list box is labeled Run macro, you can choose a script by name from the drop-down list.

6. **To close the Define Macro dialog box, click OK; then click Done in the Macros dialog box.**

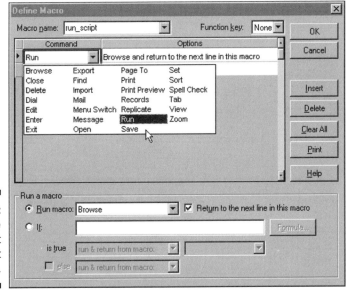

Figure 17-6:
Select the
script that
you want
to run.

Finding Objects in Approach: Of Needles and Haystacks

I may not be right, but I'm guessing that you're more likely to use your OOP (object-oriented programming) knowledge when dealing with Approach than when dealing with other Lotus products, like Word Pro or Freelance Graphics. That is, Approach is a database program, which naturally lends itself to the idea of relationships among items of data — and relationships are an OOP basic.

Using OOP structures to work with your data is a pretty advanced topic, so I don't give you all the details and how-tos. But I can tell you that a strong OOP structure is there in Approach and point you in the right direction.

The containment hierarchy

The idea of objects belonging to classes, and classes inside of classes, is a basic OOP concept. You may want to check out Chapter 14 in this book. But the diagram in Figure 17-7 shows which Approach classes are inside of which other ones — the increasingly familiar *containment hierarchy*.

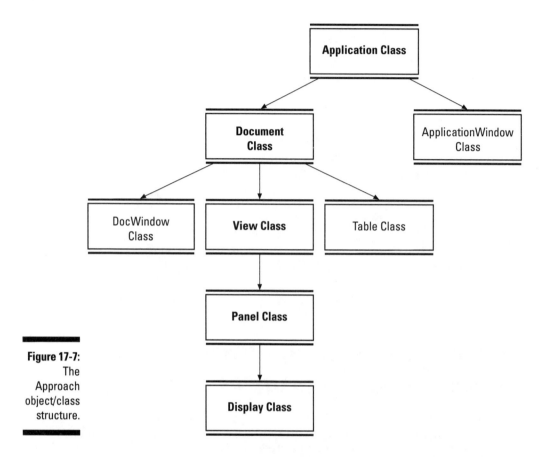

Figure 17-7:
The
Approach
object/class
structure.

Some of these classes, possibly of interest to the more technical among you, don't actually have any objects of their own — the Display, Panel, and View classes. They are just there as a way to help organize everything else, a noble enough calling, really.

Approach objects you may use the most

You probably shouldn't play favorites among your objects or anything, but you may use some objects more often than others. For example, you can use Button objects and attach scripts to them. You use Radio Buttons for allowing users to make one choice (and only one) from a set of options in a dialog box. Table 17-1 gives a list of the objects you may use most often.

If Approach is so great, why does everybody use Microsoft Access instead?

I've been wondering about something, so I thought I'd share my thoughts with you: Approach, which Lotus calls, "The High-Powered Database The Whole Team Can Use," is quite the Cadillac of database programs. It has great SmartMasters that give you professional, predefined databases before you even start. Approach lets you use dBASE, Paradox, and Lotus Notes data without even converting it. And you can share data back with Lotus Notes.

Look at this other cool stuff. When viewing a database report, you can drag a crosstab to get a different view of the data (the way you can in an Excel PivotTable). You can drill down behind a crosstab or chart record to see the specific records underneath. And, of course, you can use LotusScript. Approach is so neat that it raises an obvious question: "If this product is so great, how come everybody uses Microsoft Access instead?"

For that matter, you could just as easily say the same things about Word Pro — "Wow. This product is incredible. Why does Microsoft Word have all the market share?" The new 1-2-3, too, is a dream package, but how will it ever win back its following from the likes of Microsoft Excel?

The answer probably has to do with the ability of Microsoft to usurp complete markets on the strength of its operating systems. Microsoft Access is no junk, either, nor are Microsoft Word and Microsoft Excel. Of course, many other development and marketing issues have impact, too.

Well, I digress. One or two additional thoughts, if I may — maybe LotusScript, which Microsoft cannot yet match, will be the astounding capability that brings the market streaming from Microsoft back to Lotus. Lotus, of course, sees Notes as its flagship product now and, hand-in-hand with that, the concept of Team Computing. LotusScript makes a nice contribution to both Notes and to Team Computing, though, so it just may do its part to help the SmartSuite products (Approach, Word Pro, 1-2-3, and Freelance Graphics) get a little recognition.

Table 17-1	Approach Objects
Object	*How You Can Use It*
Button	Attach scripts to it
DropDownBox	Give a list of choices
FieldBox	Get input from users
Form	Set up a view for a single record
ListBox	Give a list of choices

(continued)

Table 17-1 *(continued)*

Object	How You Can Use It
RadioButton	Offer one choice from a group of choices
Report	Present data from multiple records
TextBox	Display a message
Worksheet	Display records in a grid of columns and rows

.LSX files

Hard core scripters are going to want to know how to get to Approach data to use it in scripts for, say, 1-2-3 or Word Pro (or, of course, Lotus Notes). Approach has three objects whose purpose is to let you get at data: Connection, Query, and ResultSet.

You use the .LSX file DBENGN01.LSX to get to such data-related objects. If you're familiar with Windows .DLL files (dynamically linked libraries), you may be ready for Lotus .LSX files as well. Both give scripters access to data. You declare the .LSX file under Declarations (in the Script drop-down list in the LotusScript IDE).

Test your newfound knowledge

How do you convert a macro to a script?

1. Send the macro to classes and hope that it comes to the realization that, "Yes, I truly want to be a script."

2. Use the Convert to _S_cript button in the Macros dialog box.

3. Beat it ruthlessly with a stick.

4. Just pretend that it is a script. Before long, you'll believe that it is, and that's practically as good as having it really be a script.

How do you get at Approach data when scripting in, say, 1-2-3.

1. Get behind the computer, and poke around gently in the serial port.

2. Use an .LSX file.

3. Call it using a special *900* number that you download from the Lotus Web Page.

4. You can't get to it. It's impertinent even to ask.

Part V

Claiming More New Territories: Scripting Other Lotus Products

The 5th Wave — By Rich Tennant

"Hey, wait a minute - why does your scripting group have a coffee budget of $250,000?"

In this part . . .

*W*hen you're on a roll, you may as well continue with what you're doing. Part V continues the adventure that began in Part IV — that is, you get an introduction to scripting in several more Lotus products. In this part, you see uses for LotusScript in Lotus 1-2-3, Freelance Graphics, and Lotus Notes.

Chapter 18

Scripting 1-2-3: Secrets of Successful Celling

. . . .

In This Chapter

▶ Making a fancy script just by clicking stuff (recording the script)

▶ Executing the script with a click of a key

▶ Executing the script with a click of a button or a SmartIcon

▶ Hiding your script behind a cell

▶ Watching scripts get along just fine with old style 1-2-3 macros

. . . .

*A*utomating is a way of life in 1-2-3 — more so, I dare say, than in Word Pro or Freelance Graphics. Users of word processing and graphics programs are *words-and-pictures* people; spreadsheet users are *numbers* people. Numbers people are more likely than words people to be programmers. (We call programs "languages," but we should call them "mathematical systems.")

What I'm really getting at is that *programming* is more or less a way of life with spreadsheet users anyway, more than with word processing users or graphics users (maybe more than with users of any other office product). Think about it. To do anything at all, spreadsheet users have to type in formulas. Formulas are very, very simple programs, aren't they? They're codes that get things done.

Somewhat advanced spreadsheet users begin to use functions — which are simply customized, stored formulas. Functions offer a bit more advanced programming than formulas. People who use formulas and functions find themselves customizing their worksheets quite routinely. For them, creating macros, which contain both formulas and functions, is a natural next step. For the newest version of 1-2-3, people can write scripts with LotusScript instead of using macros (though the macro language is still in 1-2-3, too).

Recording a Script: The Easy Way Out

If you know a series of steps that you want to put in a script, but maybe aren't sure of all the LotusScript syntax and keywords for doing it, recording the script is a good way to go.

Suppose that you had a sample worksheet, like the one shown in Figure 18-1, and you wanted to record a script that selects columns D and E and converts them to currency format. (You may need such a script, because perhaps you are planning to create a series of worksheets, and you know that, over and over again, you need to convert the columns to currency format.)

Try recording a script with these steps:

1. **From the 1-2-3 main menu, choose Edit⇨Scripts & Macros⇨Record Script.**

   The Record Script dialog box, as shown in Figure 18-1, comes up.

2. **In the Script name text box, type a name for the script.**

   In the example, I type in the name **columns**.

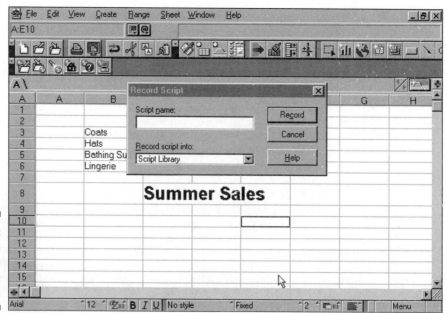

Figure 18-1:
Type a name
for the
script in this
dialog box.

3. **Under Record script into, you can select an option from the drop-down list.**

   The example selects Script Library.

4. **Click Record.**

   Stop recording and Pause or restart buttons appear near the upper-left of the worksheet window, as shown in Figure 18-2.

5. **Go through the steps (keystrokes, menu selections, and mouse clicks) that you want to record.**

   To follow the example, hold down Ctrl. Click on the Column headers for D and E to select the columns. Right-click and choose Range Properties. In the Lotus InfoBox, click the tab labeled # and then click Currency.

6. **Click the Stop Script Recording button.**

   The columns change to a currency format, and the script pops up in the Script Editor. See Figure 18-3.

Stop script recording   Pause or restart script recording

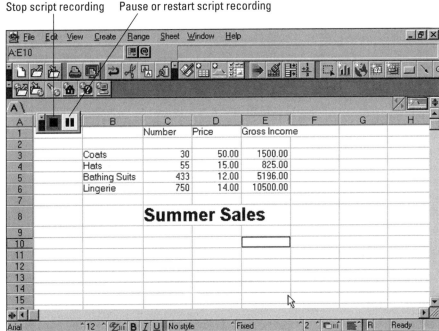

Figure 18-2: In 1-2-3, the recording buttons appear when you start recording.

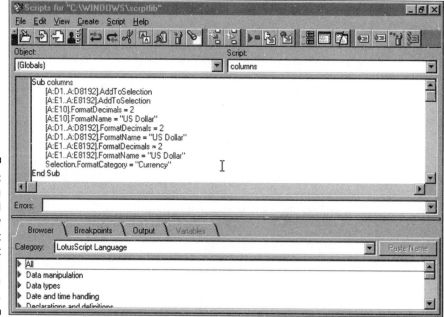

Figure 18-3:
You can record all this fancy script without typing a single command.

Before LotusScript in 1-2-3 97, 1-2-3 had macros. Unlike Word Pro, which has dropped its former macro language, 1-2-3 still makes its macro language available. If you are a confirmed user of 1-2-3 macros and want to keep using them, you can hardly be blamed. Mastering something like a macro language is hard, and having mastered it, who wants to take on another one?

But can you record a macro? No, you can't. You have to use LotusScript to take advantage of that easy feature. If you choose to record a series of steps, the only choice you get is to record a script. Maybe Lotus is sending a subtle message to people: "Use LotusScript."

Playing Back a Script: A Push-Button World

After you have a script in the IDE, you can play it back in the ways discussed in Chapter 2, and throughout this book. As one way, you can choose Edit⇨Scripts & Macros⇨Run to bring up the Run Scripts & Macros dialog box, as shown in Figure 18-4.

Figure 18-4:
Choose
your scripts
and macros
from this
dialog box.

You can use faster, more automated ways to run scripts, too. If you're going to automate, you may as well find the fastest way to play back the script you've recorded — perhaps by assigning the script to a key or a button.

Assigning a script to a key

The teams would probably have to deny it publicly, but I suspect competition among the development teams for the various Lotus products. Competition would come naturally, even though all the teams belong to the Lotus SmartSuite team now.

In the race between the 1-2-3 and the Word Pro development teams, 1-2-3 has scored a point over Word Pro in the arena of playing back scripts. In Word Pro, you can't just use menu selections to assign a script to a key, but you can (hooray!) readily do so in 1-2-3. Follow these steps to assign a script to a key in 1-2-3:

1. **From the 1-2-3 main menu, choose Edit⇨Scripts & Macros⇨Global Script Options.**

   The Global Script Options dialog box appears, with some fairly cool options. See Figure 18-5. You can add the script to the Actions menu, and you can assign it a keyboard shortcut. You even get to write the Help text for the menu command.

2. **In the Scripts drop-down list box, click on the script that you want to assign to a key.**

   In this example, I select the script named `columns`.

3. **Click the Edit Options button.**

   The Edit Script Options dialog box, as shown in Figure 18-6, appears.

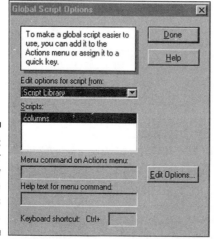

Figure 18-5: Make your script handy to use with this dialog box.

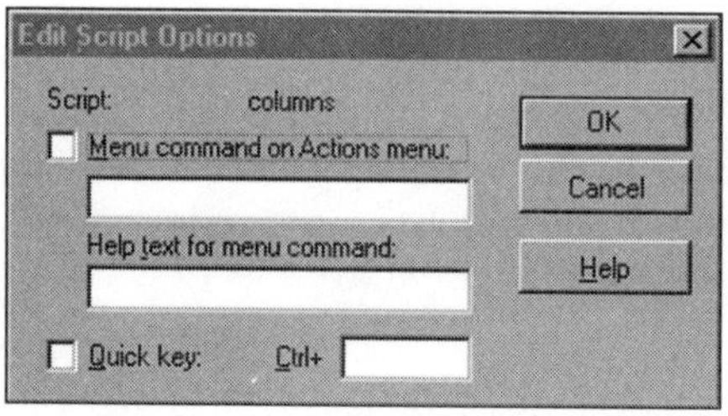

Figure 18-6: Use this dialog box to assign a key to a script.

4. **Check the Quick key check box.**

5. **In the Ctrl+ text box, type the shortcut key that you want to use for your script.**

   Type the letter **m**, for example.

6. **Click OK to close the dialog box; then click Done.**

Assigning a script to a button

For some time, 1-2-3 has offered the option of attaching macros to buttons, which are not the same as SmartIcons. (They aren't as pretty to look at as SmartIcons, but they are easy to use. And they get the job done.) Buttons are easy to drag around on the screen to wherever you're working, and you don't have to try to figure out which SmartIcon on the bar is the one you're looking for.

Don't create a button and then assign an existing script to it. Use a SmartIcon to do that. If you want to use a button, first create the button and then write the script to go with it.

Creating a button with attached script

When you create a button, 1-2-3 selects the button and displays the Script Editor, which contains an empty Click script for the button. You can use these steps to create buttons pretty quickly:

1. **With a 1-2-3 worksheet open, choose Create⊃Button from the 1-2-3 main menu.**

2. **Click and drag in the worksheet to create the size and shape button that you want. Then release the mouse button.**

   The button appears with small, black squares called *handles* on its borders. The Script Editor opens up, as shown in Figure 18-7, ready for you to write your script.

3. **In the Script Editor, type in the LotusScript statements for your script.**

   This example creates a simple message box that comments on seasonal sales. I typed in the following script line:

   ```
   Messagebox "Winter sales are better."
   ```

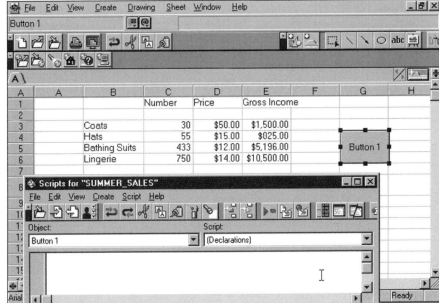

Figure 18-7: When you create a button, 1-2-3 shows the Script Editor and invites you to attach a script.

4. **After completing your script, click the appropriate control at the upper-right of the Script Editor window to close or minimize the Script Editor.**

5. **Click in the worksheet so that the button you created is no longer selected.**

   When the button is not selected, the handles around its border disappear.

6. **Click the button that you created on the 1-2-3 worksheet to run the attached script.**

Anytime you want, you can run the script just by clicking the button that you created.

You can drag the corners of your button later to reshape it, and you can move the whole button around like a sack of recyclables. Also, you may want to change the name of the button to something meaningful. Right-click the button to select it and choose Drawing Properties from the shortcut menu. In the resulting Lotus InfoBox, type a descriptive name for the button in the Text box.

Yo, can I attach to a SmartIcon instead?

If you are accustomed to using buttons in 1-2-3, you can keep right on doing so in the newest version. If you prefer SmartIcons, well, that's all right. You can assign scripts to SmartIcons. The steps are the same as for Lotus Word Pro (where, to be sure, the process probably came from in the first place anyway — the Word Pro development team likes flashy Windows capabilities such as SmartIcons).

These are the steps for attaching a script to a SmartIcon in 1-2-3:

1. **Choose File⇨User Setup⇨SmartIcons Setup.**

   The Edit SmartIcons dialog box appears.

2. **Click Edit Icon.**

   Clicking this button is the key step, and you may not guess it unless you read it somewhere.

3. **Create an icon or edit one from the Available icons you can edit or copy.**

   If you decide to work with a standard icon, you have to edit it in the Picture editor to differentiate it from the standard 1-2-3 icon.

4. **Save and name the new icon.**

5. **Click Attach Script.**

   The Attach Script dialog box appears.

6. **Choose the Script you want to attach to the icon from the Script name drop-down list in the Attach Script dialog box.**

7. **Click Attach to return to the Edit SmartIcons dialog box.**

8. **Enter the icon's bubble help in the Description text box.**

9. **Click Save.**

10. **Click Done to return to the SmartIcons Setup dialog box.**

    The new icon is at the bottom of the list in the list box labeled Available icons (drag to add). If you want, you can drag the icon to the Preview of bar shown near the top of the screen. Click Save Set to have your new icon displayed as you work.

11. **Click OK to close the SmartIcons Setup dialog box.**

Attaching a script to a cell: Hey, I'm in jail.

1-2-3 makes attaching scripts to different elements easy. You can attach to named ranges, as in the example from Word Pro in Chapter 15. You can attach to single cells. You can attach scripts to all kinds of things. After you attach to an object, you also choose an event to go with it. When 1-2-3 LotusScript sees the object and event together, that's the trigger — the script goes off.

Suppose that you want to caution users when they click a particular cell for entering data that should be reported only in increments of ten. Follow these steps to attach a warning script:

1. **Place the cursor in the cell you want to attach a script to.**

   I clicked cell A:C4, for the example.

2. **Open the Script Editor in one of the usual ways, such as by clicking on its SmartIcon.**

   Notice that the Object drop-down list box shows the current cell address as the Object, as shown in Figure 18-8. You need to choose the event that you want to associate with this Object and this script.

3. **In the Script drop-down list box, select Cellcontentschange.**

4. **In the Script Editor window, type in the LotusScript statements and functions that you want in your script.**

   To follow the example, type this line:

   ```
   Messagebox "Please use increments of 10."
   ```

5. **Click the X at the upper-right of the Script Editor window to close the Script Editor.**

Whenever you change the contents of the cell, the script runs, and the message box appears, as shown in Figure 18-9.

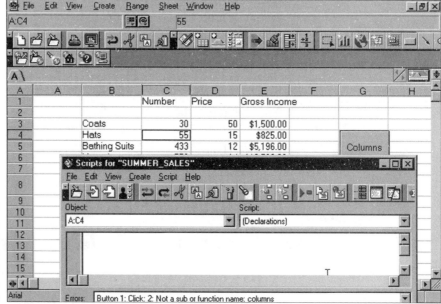

Figure 18-9:
You can
attach a
helpful
message
to a cell.

Please use increments of 10.

OK

If you can name a 1-2-3 element, you can probably attach to it. Other objects that you can attach a script to in 1-2-3 are named ranges, worksheets, and graphic objects, such as drawings, charts, and maps.

Hooking up to the Internet

If you're a big lover of the Internet, 1-2-3 comes with a special toolbar and capabilities for interfacing with the Internet. You can even create a button that comes with its own LotusScript code for connecting with an Internet site. Just follow these steps:

1. **Click the down-arrow to the left of the Universal SmartIcon bar to see the list of SmartIcon bars. Then select Internet Tools to display the 1-2-3 Internet Tools toolbar.**

2. **Click the button (shown in the margin) whose Bubble help says Create a button with a link to a URL.**

   The Create a link button dialog box appears.

3. **In the Create a link button dialog box, type in the text to appear on the button and the URL to link to.**

   For example, I type in **Lotus Web Site** for the text and `www.lotus.com` for the URL.

4. **Click OK.**

   1-2-3 creates the button and generates the LotusScript code for the associated script.

5. **To take a look at the LotusScript code, select the URL-linked button and choose Edit↪Scripts & Macros↪Show Script Editor.**

   The Script Editor appears with the script for the button showing, as in Figure 18-10.

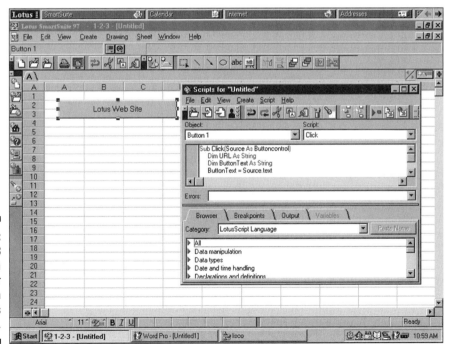

Figure 18-10:
1-2-3 generates a script for a button that links to a URL.

Macros and LotusScript: An Easy Alliance

In Word Pro, the old macro language is gone. Kaput. You can try to import Ami Pro macros and have a 50/50 chance of success, but in Word Pro, you can't run the old Ami Pro macros. Well, imagine the havoc in 1-2-3 if all the devoted macro users flat out couldn't use their old 1-2-3 macros or had only a 50/50 chance that they would work.

Well, that hasn't happened. Macros coexist with scripts. You can execute any old 1-2-3 macro that you want. You can go happily along, living in a world of macros and just ignore LotusScript, if you want. And some experienced macro users may do just that. You can even use the two (macros and scripts) together. You can call a script from a macro, as follows:

1. **Put the cursor in the cell where you want to have the macro.**

2. **Type {.**

   This little curly brace tells 1-2-3 that a macro is about to happen.

3. **Type in your macro keywords and commands and include the name of the script.**

4. **Type a curly brace { at the end to close the macro.**

When you run the macro, you'll run the script inside it as well.

Test your newfound knowledge

What's the difference between a macro and a script?

1. Macros are the *old* 1-2-3 programming language; scripts are the *new and preferred* one.

2. Macros start out in a cell, with an open brace ({) to show they're there; scripts live in the Script Editor and don't use the brace.

3. Macros don't have a very good name. Only programmers know what macros are. Scripts have kind of a nice name.

4. All of the above.

How do you attach a script to a cell?

1. In a firm, steady voice, tell it, "Get over to that cell, and stay there."

2. Place the cursor in the cell, open the Script Editor, choose the event you want, and type the name of the script.

3. Masking tape is good.

4. Call the police and report the script for a misdemeanor of some sort.

Chapter 19

Scripting Freelance Graphics

● ●

In This Chapter

▶ Seeing why LotusScript in Freelance Graphics is so far mostly for smarties

▶ Writing a script and attaching it someplace cool

▶ Assigning scripts to SmartIcons better than any other Lotus product

▶ Poking around a little in the object-oriented structure

● ●

*L*otus Approach, 1-2-3, and Word Pro all had healthy macro languages in earlier versions before coming out with LotusScript in their SmartSuite 97 versions. Freelance Graphics — what can I tell you? — didn't. Maybe this fact reflects what I talk about in Chapter 17 — that words-and-pictures type people (like you and me) tend to use Word Pro and Freelance Graphics, where numbers people (nerds) feel a strong affinity for 1-2-3 and Approach.

Freelance Graphics has never had a macro language before, and I believe, *nobody has ever missed it.* Now Freelance is playing a little catch-up with regard to its scripting language by including LotusScript now. You can turn the prior deficit into a virtue and say, "In Freelance Graphics, you don't have to hassle with trying to convert your old macros over to LotusScript. And you don't have to confuse yourself by having the old macro language coexist with the new scripting language as you gradually convert everything to LotusScript."

You *can* turn the macroless history of Freelance Graphics into a virtue, but I think that's a bit of a stretch. The fact is that scripting has just never been center stage (or even in the wings) with Freelance before, for better or worse. But now Freelance is gaining sophistication by association because it has the same scripting language as truly deep-down nerdy products like 1-2-3 (and *nerdy,* here, is a term of praise, so please don't write and complain).

LotusScript for Smarties

I think that the designers of Freelance Graphics had programmers in mind with its version of scripting, if you want to know the truth. In Freelance, you can't record a script from the menus — which is my technique of choice. You *can* do things like the following:

- ✔ Create custom dialog boxes to automate common tasks (a programmer-type task)
- ✔ Create scripts to bring in data from other Lotus applications (yup, also for advanced-type people)
- ✔ Automate documents with content topics like those in the Business Plan presentation (that comes with Freelance) and in other content-rich presentations

You can do a lot with LotusScript in Freelance Graphics, and if you're a LotusScript smartie (or have a smartie friend to do the really hard stuff), then you can have a lot of fun creating and running the scripts and maybe modifying them here and there.

Writing Scripts in Freelance: The Script Editor

To create a script in Freelance Graphics, you first start the program and choose a SmartMaster. The example I show in this chapter uses the Business Plan SmartMaster and the content page called *Mission Statement*. You can choose these elements when you start Freelance Graphics, or choose them by clicking File⇨New Presentation. I saved my sample file with the name *mission*.

1. **From the Freelance main menu, open the Script Editor; you can click the Script Editor SmartIcon or choose Edit⇨Script⇨Show Script Editor.**

    The Script Editor comes up, as shown in Figure 19-1.

2. **In the Script Editor menu, choose Create⇨Sub.**

    A dialog box in which you can name the sub appears as shown in Figure 19-2. You can replace the default name Sub1 with a more descriptive name for your script.

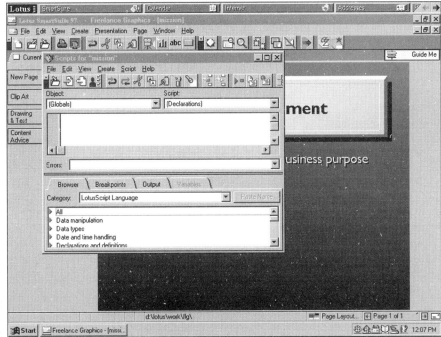

Figure 19-1:
The
Freelance
Script Editor
when it first
comes up.

Figure 19-2:
Name your
sub here.

3. Click OK.

Freelance returns you to the Script Editor. The name of the sub is in place
(for the example, the name is Reminder), and the script-to-be awaits your
typing. See Figure 19-3.

4. Type in your variables and other LotusScript statements.

For the example, I typed in a simple message box statement:

```
Messagebox "Make this a strong selling point."
```

5. Press F2 to check the Script and F5 to run it.

The message box pops up. See Figure 19-4.

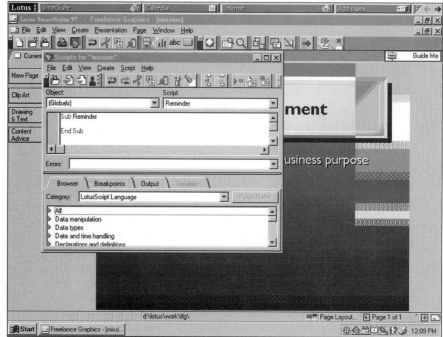

Figure 19-3:
The Script Editor right after you name the sub.

Figure 19-4:
This message box comes up when I run the sample script.

Attaching to a click here . . .

Often, you want to attach scripts to elements in the document. For the example, you can attach the message box to the Business Plan SmartMaster's Click Here block that says `Click here to describe your business purpose.` Follow these steps:

1. **In the Object drop-down list box, choose TextPlacementBlock1.**

2. **In the Script drop-down list box, choose Clicked.**

3. **Type in the LotusScript statements that you want in the script.**

   Figure 19-5 shows the completed script with `Messagebox` statement.

Choose the object here   Choose the script here

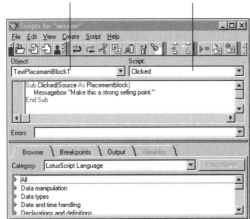

Figure 19-5:
This script is
attached to
a *clickable*
element.

If you try to test this script (which is attached to a click-here element in the SmartMaster template) in the usual way — that is, by pressing F5 when you are in the Script Editor, you get the error message `Cannot run procedure`. That doesn't mean your script doesn't work, though. It just means that, in this case, you have to run the script from the document, not from the Script Editor. The next section, "Running the attached script," tells you how to run your script.

Running the attached script

To run the script attached to the click-here element, close or minimize the Script Editor, then click the click-here element in the document. The attached script runs — in this example putting up the message box as shown in Figure 19-6.

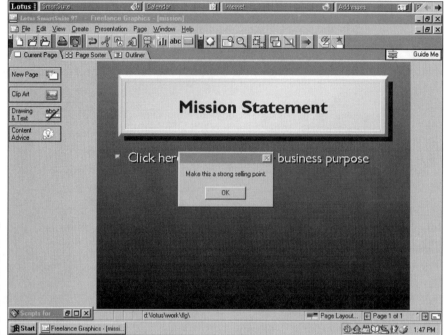

Figure 19-6:
When you
click the
click-here
element, the
script runs.

Recording scripts in Freelance Graphics: "Huh? You mean, I can't?"

Recording a script (by having LotusScript automatically make script statements out of your keystrokes and mouse clicks) is often useful, and after you
record it, you can work with the script to make changes. Although you can
record a script in Lotus 1-2-3 and Lotus Word Pro (and you may have a habit of
doing so), you can't record a script yet in Freelance Graphics. It's my impression that developing a process like that takes a while to do. If you look at
the drop-down menu for Script (see Figure 19-7), you find no choice for
Record script.

You can't record Scripts in Freelance Graphics, but you can *write* them, and
that's pretty good. LotusScript is in the product, so Lotus has every right to
toot its horn about having LotusScript across the whole product line.

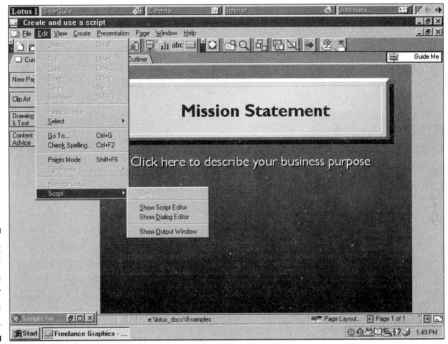

Converting Macros: "Huh? There Aren't Any?"

Converting macros from previous versions of the product is quite a major concern with other Lotus products — Word Pro, 1-2-3, Approach, and especially Lotus Notes. However, converting macros presents no problem whatsoever with Freelance. You couldn't write macros in Freelance before, so you don't have to worry about having any bothersome old macros to convert!

Assigning Scripts to SmartIcons

You might expect a visual product like Freelance to be unusually good at a visual activity — like assigning scripts to SmartIcons — and it is unusually good. (In Approach, by contrast, you can't even assign scripts to SmartIcons at all, though you can assign macros to buttons.)

Use these steps to assign a script (one that you've already created) to a SmartIcon in Freelance Graphics:

1. From the main menu, Choose File➪User Setup➪SmartIcons Setup.

The SmartIcons Setup dialog box appears, as shown in Figure 19-8.

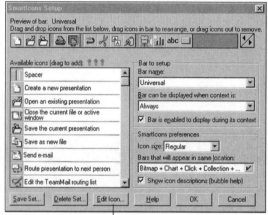

Figure 19-8: Start with this dialog box to assign a script to a SmartIcon.

Click here

2. Click the Edit Icon button.

Figure 19-9 shows the extremely nifty Edit Icon dialog box that comes up. Choose a SmartIcon for attaching your script. This dialog box helps you have a field day adapting existing SmartIcons or creating new ones using nice colors. You can even see a neat preview of the button as you create it, a feature I haven't seen in the other Lotus products. Freelance has, hands down, the best Edit Icon box I've seen.

The Edit Icon dialog box even has excellent Help for your creative process. Just click on the Help button in the dialog box if you want guidance on creating a custom icon.

3. Click the Attach Script button.

The Add Script dialog box comes up. From this dialog box, you click the Browse button to navigate to the script you want to attach to the SmartIcon of choice.

4. Click Open in the Browse dialog box and then click OK in the Add Script dialog box to complete the script attachment.

For your SmartIcon to be useful after you've attached the script, you must drag the SmartIcon onto the Universal SmartIcon bar or to another icon bar that you have on-screen.

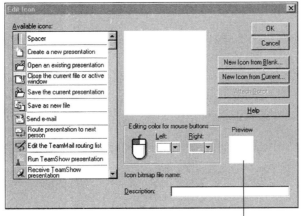

Figure 19-9:
The nifty
Edit Icon
dialog box in
Freelance
Graphics.

Previews show up here

Looking at the Freelance Object Structure

For serious scripters who want to use object-oriented programming elements (OOP) to navigate to various objects in Freelance, the object structure is important. (See Chapter 14 for an introduction to OOP.)

In Freelance, the top object is an *abstract class* (that is, a class with no objects) named BaseObject. The next level of objects are Application, Document, Page, DrawObject, and a number of others. Some of these objects contain other objects. For example, DrawObject contains TextBlock, Table, Chart, OLEObject, PlacementBlock, Media, and Selection.

If you think about the terms for Freelance Graphics objects as words in English, instead of as scripting objects with names, they do make quite good sense. A *chart,* for example, is *drawn* as a visual representation of information. Or in scripting terms, Chart is an object of the class DrawObject. In addition, you know that a chart is just one type of visual representation of information. You can have other drawn items such as tables (Table) or images (OLEObject) that also represent information.

To refer to any of the objects while scripting in Freelance, you use *dot notation,* which is a naming convention that uses the hierarchical relationship of elements in OOP to identify a specific object. I explain dot notation briefly in Chapter 14, and you can see it in use throughout the scripting code in this book. (I mean, there's no tome on the subject even in Chapter 14. If you get into this OOP stuff heavily, you can use the Lotus help files, too.)

To use dot notation to refer to an object, you have to know the *containment hierarchy*, that is, the genealogical relationship of the objects and classes to each other. Following are three of the most important OOP containment relationships in Freelance Graphics:

- ✔ Each instance of Application has a variable called ActiveDocument that refers to the current document.

- ✔ Each instance of Application has a variable called Document that refers to all open documents.

- ✔ Each instance of Document has a variable called ActivePage that refers to the current Page.

The point here, really, is that, thanks to LotusScript and to OOP, you can reference any object in Freelance, use it in programs, even change its properties if you want. However, I see this natural protection: The only scripters that are really able to get into the program itself and make changes probably know enough so that they don't do a lot of damage.

Be careful when you delve into the OOP hierarchy (of Freelance Graphics or any other Lotus product) while scripting. The program's objects are exposed, and there's no guarantee that you can't do some damage by poking around with these objects.

Test your newfound knowledge

How do you use the Script Recorder in Freelance Graphics?

1. Hey, what are you talking about? The same way you'd use any Script Recorder, of course.

2. Put your fingers over some of the holes and blow on it.

3. This is a trick question, because Freelance Graphics doesn't yet have a Script Recorder.

4. Connect it up to your TV.

How do you convert a Freelance macro into a Freelance Script?

1. Hey, what are you talking about? The same way you'd convert any macro to a script, of course.

2. Go up to its door and keep talking until you get it to convert.

3. This is a trick question because Freelance Graphics didn't have macros in earlier versions.

4. You can't convert a Freelance macro. It's just too darn stuck in its ways.

Chapter 20

Scripting Lotus Notes:
A World of Its Own

L otus Notes presents a bit of a culture shock if you come to it after working first with the Lotus SmartSuite programs. It's a complete universe of its own . . . almost a way of life.

Also, Lotus Notes has an important distinction from all the SmartSuite programs. When IBM bought Lotus back in '95 in its highly publicized hostile takeover, the computer giant wasn't particularly after Freelance Graphics or Organizer (not according to the *Wall Street Journal* articles I read). IBM was buying Lotus Notes and its certifiable genius of a developer — Ray Ozzie.

Lotus Notes itself is a little hard to define, even for Lotus. It's a database, but you shouldn't confuse it with, say dBASE or Paradox. Lotus Notes is a database of information and business tools. It's mail. It's inventory tracking. It's information management. It's team computing. It's a whole corporate lifestyle.

Because Lotus Notes is such a universe unto itself, the fact that it implements LotusScript in its own unique fashion isn't surprising. When it comes to doing LotusScript in Notes, well, you don't just open the Script Editor and type in scripts the way you do in the other products. You work a little differently. You create an object — like a button — and then you access a scripting pane for that object.

Whatever small differences between scripting in Notes and scripting in SmartSuite may exist, the LotusScript language is much the same in Notes as in the SmartSuite products like 1-2-3. You still use the `Dim`, `Messagebox`, and other LotusScript commands. The Notes environment is a bit distinctive . . . that's all.

Getting Set to Write a Script

As in the SmartSuite programs, Notes scripts are *event-driven*. When some triggering activity takes place, the scripts go off. That is, they run, or execute, as a result of the activity occurring. To use a script, you create an object such as a button (which I use for this chapter's example) or a Notes Agent and attach the script to it.

Before scripting, you go through some preparations. If Shakespeare was going to write a script, he had to grab his quill pen and a sheet of paper. Eugene O'Neill, to write a script, had to roll a sheet of paper into his typewriter. Everybody has to go through some kind of preparation to write a script. To script in one of the other Lotus programs, you have to start up the program and open the Script Editor. To script in Notes, you have to start with a database. Here's how to do it: First, of course, start up Lotus Notes itself. Figure 20-1 shows the Notes workspace that I see when I begin a session (though yours needn't look exactly the same as mine shown here).

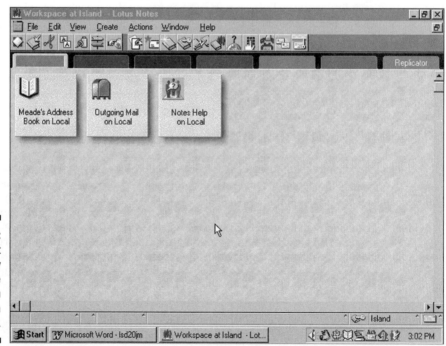

Figure 20-1:
Here's what Notes may look like when you start a session.

Just as you work in a document in Word Pro or a worksheet in 1-2-3, you work in a database in Notes. Use these steps to create the database for writing a sample script:

1. **From the Main menu, choose File⇨Database⇨New.**

   The New Database dialog box comes up and asks for a bit more information, as shown in Figure 20-2.

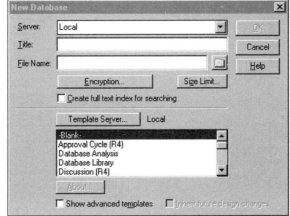

Figure 20-2:
Fill in this dialog box information when creating a database.

2. **Type in a title for the database and a filename.**

   In the example, I type **A Quick Script** in the Title text box and **QUICK.NSF** in the File Name text box.

3. **In the list box in the lower half of the New Database dialog box, select a template for your database.**

   The example uses the template named Discussion (R4).

4. **Click the Inherit future design changes check box to deselect this option.**

5. **Click OK.**

6. **When the About document opens after Notes creates the database, choose File⇨Close to close it.**

After you follow these steps, you find yourself inside a Notes database, and you're ready to get going with scripting. Figure 20-3 shows the database as you're about to begin.

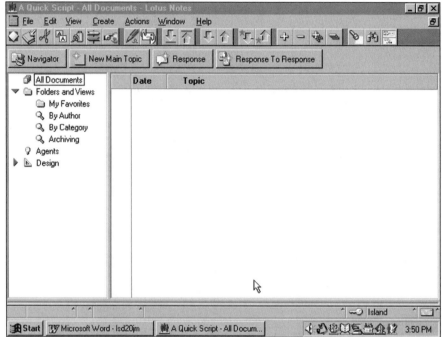

Figure 20-3:
A sample
Notes
database
before you
create your
script.

Creating a Button: Where's the Buttonhole?

In Notes, you don't just work within a database. You work within a Main Topic. You can follow these steps to create a Main Topic for your session:

1. **Click the New Main Topic button near the top of the screen, below the SmartIcons.**

   The Main Topic document opens, as shown in Figure 20-4. Notice that the various fields in the document are denoted by a pair of symbols that look like corners of a frame.

2. **Type in a brief description for the main topic.**

   For the example, I typed in **Quick scripts can be useful scripts**.

3. **Press Enter (or click in the Category field) and type in a category name.**

   In the example, I type in **Scripting**. The Category field has an arrow to the right, indicating that a drop-down list may be available. If you have an existing category name that you'd like to use, click this arrow and choose keywords from the resulting drop-down list.

4. **Press Tab, or click in the Body field.**

Body field   Type description here   Category field

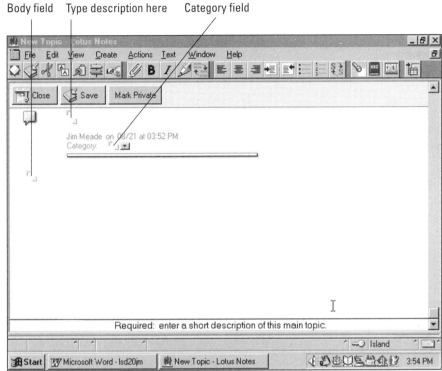

Figure 20-4:
A blank
Main Topic
document.

After you're in the body of the main topic document, you can create the interface element that you want to attach your script to. In the example, I create a button for my script with these steps:

1. **From the main menu, choose Create⇨Hotspot⇨Button.**

   A Lotus Properties InfoBox appears (see Figure 20-5), and at the bottom of the screen, the programmer's pane appears. (This pane is not quite the familiar LotusScript IDE yet. This pane is for creating macros. In a moment, the example brings you to the scripting pane.)

2. **In the Properties InfoBox, type a label into the Button label text box.**

   For the example, I type in **Print the title**, which describes what I intend for the attached sample script to do.

3. **Click Save to save the document with the labeled button and then close the InfoBox.**

   You're almost ready to start scripting. Your main topic document has a newly created button — just waiting for you to attach a script — in the document body.

Figure 20-5:
Fill in the
properties
for your
button here.

Scripting the button

After setting up your Lotus Notes database, starting your main topic document, and creating your button, you're ready to let LotusScript take over. To switch into scripting mode, you perform a single click:

1. Click the Script option button in the programmer's pane.

Now, this is no small happening. The Notes equivalent of the IDE is now available, and you're ready for some scripting. Figure 20-6 shows the programmer's pane after you choose the scripting option. (Although the version shown here, from Notes 4.0, is not identical with the IDE in the SmartSuite programs, I have to believe that it will, one day, be identical.)

2. To display the familiar Browser for the LotusScript language, click the Show browser check box (so that an _x_ appears in the check box) in the programmer's pane.

Figure 20-7 shows the Lotus Notes programmer's pane with the Browser displayed. In the version we're using for this book, the Browser is at the right, rather than at the bottom as it is in the other programs. You point and click to select the LotusScript language topics and commands that you want — as in the other Lotus programs that we cover in the book. Best of all, the information that you need is available through the Browser.

The programmer's pane is ready for you to write your script and attach it to the button, but you may want to double-check to be sure.

3. Make sure that the Define and Event list boxes display the correct elements for your scripting activity.

In the example, the Define list box shows `Print the title (Button)` and the Event list box shows `Click` as the event.

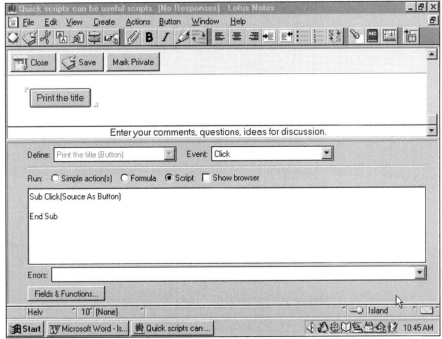

Figure 20-6:
The programmer's pane after you choose the Script option.

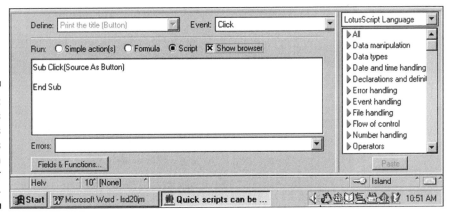

Figure 20-7:
The Lotus Notes programmer's pane with the Browser displayed.

4. Type in your LotusScript statements.

Following is the sample script used in this example along with an explanation of the script lines that I added:

```
Sub Click(Source As Button)
    Dim my_DB As NotesDatabase
    Set my_DB = New NotesDatabase( "", "quick.nsf" )
    Messagebox( my_DB.Title )
End Sub
```

- **Line two:** (Dim . . .) declares the variable my_DB as an instance of the class NotesDatabase.

- **Line three:** (Set . . .) sets the value of my_DB so that it refers to the filename quick.nsf on the local computer.

- **Line four:** (Messagebox . . .) gets the title of the database that my_DB represents, and prints it in a dialog box.

Running a script: Isn't there an easier way?

If you've been using the Script Editor in other programs, you may be planning to execute the script in one of the familiar ways — by choosing from a menu or by pressing F5. To try out the Notes script, though, you don't use a familiar method, but instead, you go through a more complicated process.

Use these steps to compile the script (translate the code into usable form) and then run it from the main topic document.

1. From the main menu, choose File⇨Close.

If there are errors in the script, you see them at the bottom of the programmer's pane. Check your typing, and try again. For more information about finding script errors, check out Chapter 5.

2. Click Yes when asked, "Do you want to save your changes?"

You return to the view pane for the database, as shown in Figure 20-8. You can see that my main topic document shows up in the database view.

3. Choose File⇨Open and specify the filename of the document that you saved with your attached script.

You can also double-click the file name or click it once and press Enter to open the document that you saved.

4. Click the button (or whatever interface element that your script is attached to) to run the script.

In Figure 20-9, you can see the message box that the script creates.

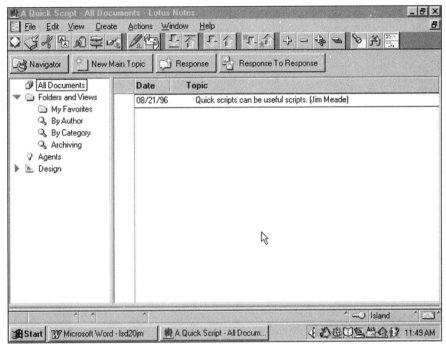

Figure 20-8:
The view pane for the database you're in.

5. **Depending on what you wrote your script to do, you can respond appropriately or simply view the results of your script.**

   In my example, I click OK to close the message box.

Figure 20-9:
The results of running my script.

Editing a script: Hey, call rewrite!

Scripting is more about rewriting and debugging than about writing scripts in the first place, as I discuss in Chapter 5 and in lots of other places in this book. Chances are, you're just going to have to get back to the script you've created and make changes to it.

Suppose that you want to edit the script for the button in the document used as an example in this chapter — filename quick.nsf. You can follow these steps:

1. **Open the document with the script attached, if it's not open already.**

2. **Click the Edit Document button near the top of the screen to put the document into edit mode.**

If you're experienced with Lotus Notes, then, fine, you won't forget to put the document into Edit mode. If you aren't experienced, though, then this is just the kind of step that can get a novice scripter to thinking, "Oh, man, this thing is broke. What's the matter here? I should have called in sick today." Putting the document into Edit mode is one of those elusive little steps, easily forgotten, that can drive you nuts and cause you to think of turning to some other line of work . . . something having nothing to do with computers.

3. **Activate your script to get access to the appropriate menu for editing your interface element.**

For the example, click the Print the title button once. (In this case, the script executes. Click OK to close the message box.) Now, a new menu item — Button — appears on the main menu, as shown in Figure 20-10.

Button menu

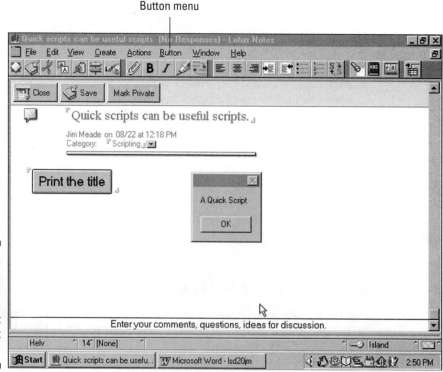

Figure 20-10:
Click the button, and you're almost ready to edit the script.

A word to Lotus Notes formula lovers

If people who have spent time developing Approach macros are likely to be attached to their macros (as I speculate in Chapter 18 that they must be), then think how Notes formula programmers must feel! Lotus Notes, a large, corporate database program, is much more ambitious than Approach.

The message for established Notes programmers is a simple, "Not to worry." You can use formulas with more Notes elements than you can use scripts with (at least in Notes 4.0). The previous Lotus Notes formula language exists intact. It's just that now those who want to work in LotusScript have the option to do so.

4. **From the main menu, choose the appropriate menu for editing your interface element.**

   For the example, choose <u>B</u>utton⇨<u>E</u>dit Button. The programmer's pane comes up at the bottom of the screen, and the button InfoBox comes up, too. Close the InfoBox, to give yourself more room, then edit the script to your heart's content. Figure 20-11 shows the reopened programmer's pane with script.

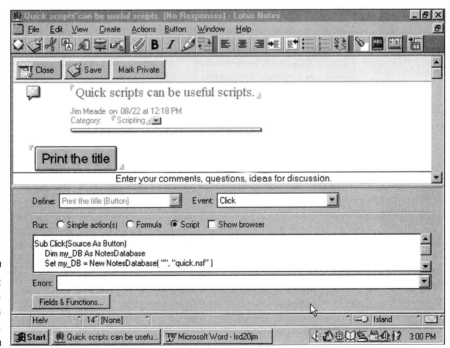

Figure 20-11: Back at the programmer's pane again.

Other Things That You Can Script, Besides Buttons

Obviously, buttons aren't the only things you can script in Lotus Notes, even though this chapter steps you through the steps of writing a script for a button. You can also script Agents, Actions, Events, and other Hotspots.

But Notes does have some elements that work with attached formulas instead of attached scripts. If you want to automate a SmartIcon, for example (and you may well want to), you have to use a formula, not a script. And if you want to attach code to a formula, such as a Selection formula, you attach a formula, not a script.

For the time being, formulas and scripts coexist, and they have to do so peacefully. The point here is that you can attach scripts to more than just buttons . . . of course.

Checking Out the Object Structure

Lotus Notes — when it's well-used — is an incredible compendium of useful information. All kinds of stuff resides in Notes databases. When you're scripting, you may want to get to all kinds of Lotus Notes elements.

To get to Lotus Notes program elements, you use object-oriented programming (OOP) naming conventions (that is, dot notation), and you refer to *objects* by referring to the *classes* (a grouping of like objects in OOP) that the objects belong to. (See Chapter 14 for a rundown of basic OOP information.)

To help you in making such references to OOP objects, Notes provides a complete description of its object structure — that is, of the classes in Notes and what they contain. You can display the object structure from within the Browser, or you can get to it directly from the Notes Help files. Try looking at it with the Browser:

1. **From the programmer's pane, click Show browser.**

2. **In the drop-down list box at the top of the Browser, click the arrow at the right to display the choices; then click Notes: Classes.**

   Figure 20-12 shows the Browser with entries for Notes: Classes. In this figure, I maximized the Browser window to show as much of it as possible, therein blocking out the programmer's pane entirely.

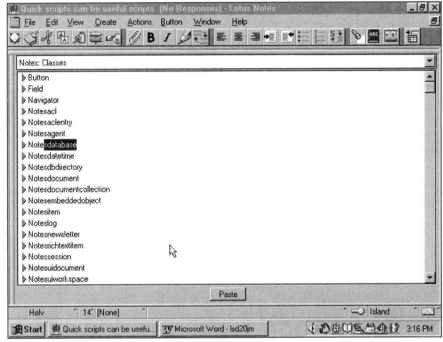

File   Edit   View   Create   Actions   Button   Window   Help

Notes: Classes

▶ Button
▶ Field
▶ Navigator
▶ Notesacl
▶ Notesaclentry
▶ Notesagent
▶ Notesdatabase
▶ Notesdatetime
▶ Notesdbdirectory
▶ Notesdocument
▶ Notesdocumentcollection
▶ Notesembeddedobject
▶ Notesitem
▶ Noteslog
▶ Notesnewsletter
▶ Notesrichtextitem
▶ Notessession
▶ Notesuidocument
▶ Notesuiworkspace

Paste

Helv   14 [None]   Island

Start   Quick scripts can be usefu...   Microsoft Word - lsd20jm   3:16 PM

Figure 20-12:
The
Browser,
showing
object
structures in
Lotus Notes.

You can refer to the Notes objects by class and use the reference in a script. For example, if you wanted to refer to a particular field in a Notes database, you would begin your reference with the class name `Field`. For an example of a script that uses a reference to a program element, see Chapter 2. For a discussion of naming OOP objects with dot notation, refer to Chapter 14.

GOOD TO KNOW

V+

Test your newfound knowledge

What is Lotus Notes anyway?

1. A database

2. Team computing

3. Mail

4. All of the above and more

When is the programmer's pane a programmer's pain?

1. Early in the morning, when you have to use it and you aren't in the mood yet

2. Late in the afternoon, when you haven't had your afternoon coffee, and you aren't in the mood yet

3. When you want to do some scripting, and you can't find a way to get to it

4. All of the above and more

Part VI
The Part of Tens

The 5th Wave

In this part . . .

*F*or Dummies books don't have things like lengthy
catalogues of boring references, but sometimes
having brief lists of useful information gathered into a single
place can be nice. And I don't see why you can't have a little
fun while you're looking over these lists, too! I suggest that
you review Part VI as follows: Pretend that you're back at
the lodge, your scripting journey is completed, you're
hoisting a few refreshing beverages and recalling the
highlights of the trip. . . .

In Part VI, you find a list of the most-used LotusScript
statements — quite helpful, perhaps, because you have
scores of statements to choose from. You find out, too, some
of the statements you may never need. (I find a perverse
attraction to such a list . . . I just do.) You discover some
guidelines for writing good scripts. And (my personal
favorite), you find definitions of confusing BASIC terms
presented in language that you *can* understand.

Chapter 21

Ten LotusScript Statements That Get You a Long Way

1 don't know about you, but I like to get started quickly on figuring out new things and pick up the fine points as I go along. But I also like to have my new projects *work* as soon as possible. Suppose that you're going to start up a boat and cruise safely around a small lagoon. You need a few safety instructions, and you need to know what button to push and what lever to use to steer. You can learn the fancy things (like pulling water skiers and hopping waves and stuff) much easier after you have the feel of driving the boat.

Likewise, in scripting, you run into an overwhelming number of statements and functions. Turn on the LotusScript online Help or the IDE Browser listings, and you see scores of them. Figure 21-1, for example, shows just the LotusScript statements and functions that start with the letter *C*.

What if you want to know just a few statements and functions? Maybe you want to know the absolute minimum to get you by — you're interested in writing scripts that work, not scripts that impress anyone with their cleverness. This chapter provides you with a few essentials.

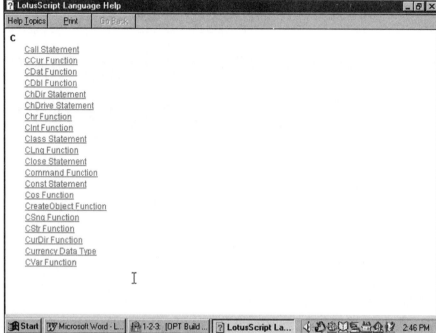

Figure 21-1:
With so
many
statements
and
functions,
you get
sensory
overload
just contem-
plating
them.

This chapter, to beginning scripters, is like a language phrase book for travelers in foreign countries. Maybe the voyagers don't speak the foreign language fluently, but they can say, "Where is . . . ?", "Restaurant," "Room," and "Thank you." The natives may not think that such tourists are great conversationalists, but those tourists can survive. The rest of the chapter lists the ten gotta-have-'em LotusScript statements, with syntax and maybe an example.

Using Dim

Having researched the topic of *most important LotusScript statements* a bit, I've found that you need even fewer statements than I thought to get started scripting. You can do an awful lot of experimenting with LotusScript by using just *four* statements (or in some cases, functions). And really, the big statement to know is this one — humble-looking, misnamed, funny little Dim.

When you write scripts, a primary thing that you do is *Dimension* (Dim) *variables*. That is, you define your script's *variables* (data holders) by giving them a name, a data type, and maybe an initial value. Then, you can run your script to see what values those variables end up with. For more information, you can refer to the whole chapter dedicated to variables (Chapter 6), and you can look at other chapters that deal mainly with variables as well (such as Chapter 7, where you find out how to name variables).

Dim *syntax*

Following is the syntax statement for the Dim statement:

```
{ Dim | Static | Public | Private } DeclareVariable1 [ ,
            DeclareVariable2 ]...
```

And an example:

```
Sub Main
    Dim marbles As String
    marbles = "Do you have any marbles?"
    Print marbles      'Output is Do you have any marbles?
End Sub
```

Dim...as

"Wait a minute here," you have every reason to protest. "You just gave a Dim example." Well, because I feel that Dim is so important, I'm giving example two, and then I may give examples three and four. I think I could probably make some aspect of Dim take up all ten elements of this chapter, but I won't.

Pay special attention to the As portion of Dim in this example. This part of the Dim statement assigns the data type to the variable:

```
Dim x As Single
```

The following are the basic data types in LotusScript:

- ✔ Currency
- ✔ Double
- ✔ Integer
- ✔ Long
- ✔ Single
- ✔ String
- ✔ Variant

LotusScript cares *a lot* about data types. Becoming effective at working with variables, like dimensioning your variables with particular data types, is much more important than moving on to master some LotusScript keyword other than Dim.

Dynamic declaration of variables

Variables are so integral to LotusScript that you can declare them without even using a keyword. LotusScript knows that nothing significant happens in your script unless you declare variables and that many things can happen after you do. Therefore, LotusScript softens its generally unforgiving nature and allows you to dimension variables without even using `Dim`.

Although giving you the syntax for a statement that doesn't exactly exist is difficult, I can show you an example of declaring a variable *dynamically* or, as programmers say, *implicitly*.

```
daysonJob% = 5
```

By naming the variable and giving it a value (that is, *initializing* it), you *declare* the variable. What amazing freedom . . . but you aren't going to find such freedom anywhere else in scripting. But be glad that you get the freedom with variables, the rulers of all LotusScript elements.

%, &, !, #, @, and (of course) $

Not only can you dimension variables dynamically, you can define data types by using mere symbols, instead of spelling out the data type words. The following two lines of code mean the same thing:

```
Dim myCur@
Dim myCur As Currency
```

To use a data type symbol in your variable declaration, place it at the end of your variable name.

Table 21-1 lists the data type symbols and what each stands for. As you script, you recognize that these symbols are as commonplace in the LotusScript language as the articles *a, an,* and *the* are in English.

Table 21-1	Data Type Symbols
Data Suffix Character	**Data Type**
%	Integer
&	Long
!	Single
#	Double
@	Currency
$	String

Programmers love the on-the-run kind of scripting that is represented by dynamic declarations and use of data type symbols. You see, programmers take any shortcuts that the programming languages allow them!

Checking Your Output with Print

As you're scripting along, thinking that you're accomplishing something, whether you're really doing what you intend can be difficult to see. The best way to check your output is with the Print statement.

And the syntax is as follows:

```
Print [ expression1, expression2, expression3, . . . ]
```

The Print statement doesn't print things on your printer, the way a Print command does in your word processor or in other kinds of programs. Don't hold that against Print, though. Print places output in a very valuable place — the Output panel of the LotusScript IDE (Integrated Development Environment).

Using More Than One Sub

"Don't write one big script," the experts all proclaim. "Write lots of little programs." When you write little programs (subroutines), you can isolate your bugs to a small area and work on them there (where the pesky little critters, like cockroaches trapped in a single cupboard, may still refuse to die).

The Sub statement lets you create all those small programs by defining a sub, or subroutine. The syntax looks like this:

```
[ Static ] [ Public | Private ] Sub mySubName [ ( [ argu-
            ment1, argument2, . . . ] ) ]
   [ code lines ]
End Sub
```

I describe the following example in more detail back in Chapter 12:

```
Sub Main
   Call Stand_back
End Sub
```

```
Sub Stand_back
    Messagebox "Stand back, baby!"
End Sub
```

The output of this example is a message box with an OK button and the words *Stand back, baby!*

If you do much scripting, you'll use subs all the time (or else you'll have the longest, most confusing scripts of anybody around).

Creating a Function

Functions are all over the place in LotusScript. The LotusScript Complete Reference (A – Z) in the Help files contains mostly functions. *Functions* are related lines of code that return a value to the calling program (the program that uses the function), whereas Subs don't.

You can use the Function statement to create your own functions, just by naming them and specifying certain elements of the function. You call functions only by name, not with the Call statement (which is the exclusive province of subs).

The syntax for the Function statement is as follows:

```
[ Static ] [ Public | Private ] Function functionName [ ( [
            paramList ] ) ] [ As returnType ]
    [ statements ]
End Function
```

In the following example (see Chapter 13, too), the function SumUp adds the passed parameters (the integers x and y) and returns the result (also as an integer) to the Main subroutine:

```
Sub Main
    x%=1
    y%=4
    Print SumUp (x%,y%)
End Sub
```

```
Function SumUp (x As Integer, y As Integer) As Integer
    SumUp = x + y
End Function
```

When the Main subroutine (that calls the SumUp function) runs, it prints 5 in the Output panel of the IDE.

Talking to Users with Messagebox

You know that you're becoming a true scripter (and not merely a user) when you begin creating message boxes that other users see. "You mean, I made that?" you may ask when you view your own first message box. When you use the Messagebox statement, you give your users some information and wait for their response (like clicking a button or something) so that you know they at least saw the message box.

Even if Messagebox didn't make this exclusive list on its own merits (which it does), it certainly would make the list because of what using Messagebox does for the self-esteem of emerging scripters.

And the syntax looks like this:

```
MessageBox ( yourmessage [ , [ abutton + anicon + adefault +
            amode ] [ , yourboxTitle ] ] )
```

The following example script creates the message box shown in Figure 21-2:

```
Sub Main
    Messagebox "Hey, how you doing?"
End Sub
```

Figure 21-2:
Creating a
message
box is
thrilling for
the novice
scripter.

Getting Feedback with Inputbox

Inputbox is one order of complexity beyond Messagebox (just as a Function is one turn more than a Sub). If simply displaying a Messagebox message to the user boosts your scripter ego, think what gathering data from the user means to your self-confidence and inner happiness. By using Inputbox, you can ask the user for some information and then put that information back into the script. Given Inputbox's high level of accomplishment, recognizing its place in the top-ten list of LotusScript statements to know isn't difficult.

`Inputbox` syntax is as follows:

```
Inputbox[$] ( aprompt [ , [ atitle ] [ , [ adefault ] [ ,
              anxpos , aypos ] ] ] )
```

And finally, an example that uses `Inputbox`:

```
Sub Main
    ' Get a number from the user. Convert the number
    ' from a string into an integer.
    Dim number As Integer
    number% = CInt(Inputbox$("How many do you want?"))
End Sub
```

When you execute the script, you get an input box like the one shown in
Figure 21-3.

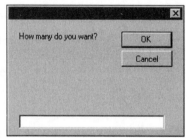

Figure 21-3:
Making an
input box for
the user is
also fun!

Making Decisions with
`If...Then...Else`

As you begin to do *real* work with scripts, you need ways to enable your scripts
to check out a number of conditions and decide which conditions live up to
certain expectations. Using the `If` statement is one of the best ways to do this
decision-making work, so `If` makes my top-ten list, too.

You can use the `If...Then...Else` statement to have your script do something if a condition is met (and, of course, do something else if the condition
isn't met).

And the If statement syntax is as follows:

```
If condition1 Then [ doThisCode ] [ Else [doThatCode ] ]
```

A simple example of an If statement follows:

```
Dim x As Integer
x% = 50
If x% > 0 Then Print "Big" Else Print "Small"
'Output is Big
```

If you agree with me that I've said enough about the If statement, and If you're also ready to stop reading, Then you can go off for a snack, Else you can turn the page to the next list.

Chapter 22

Ten Other LotusScript Statements You May Like, Too

*I*f you've been scripting a little and getting favorable results, maybe the simple, confidence-building statements presented in Chapter 21 aren't so much what you need. Perhaps you feel ready, and you want to do more challenging things in LotusScript. But because of the many statements and functions in the LotusScript Help files, you're pretty hard-pressed to know which ones can be truly useful to you. The list in this chapter may help you decide.

You don't *need* the ten statements that I list here to accomplish a lot of things, but they're among the most substantive of all the available statements and functions. I gathered these recommended statements from experienced LotusScript scripters who have a feel for what you may want to do as you begin to ramp up with your own scripting.

Accomplishing Real Work with Dot *Commands*

The Print statement is very useful — useful enough to secure a place in the top-ten list of most useful statements (Chapter 21). However, Print doesn't display its output anywhere except in the Output panel of the IDE. That location is great for debugging your script (see Chapter 5), but not too useful for accomplishing real work.

To display output in a document, you can use the *dot method* (that is, to precede a command with a period, or *dot*). I discuss one good example in Chapter 2 — .Type in Word Pro. The following is an example of how you use .Type:

```
Dim x As String
x$ = "Buy me a coat."
.Type x
```

You see these words in your document when you run the script containing the preceding .Type example:

```
Buy me a coat.
```

Using the dot method enables you to include all kinds of commands from your current application in your scripts. In this book, I show you the dot method at work when you record a script, as in the Word Pro 97 example from Chapter 16. In the following example, I use the Word Pro 97 script recorder to create a script that finds the word *good* and then formats it as bold and italic.

Separating your dot commands from your LotusScript commands

LotusScript has a Type statement (see Chapter 14), which is completely different from the *dot type* command (.Type). And I want to point out that Type is not at all the same as .Type so that you won't drive yourself crazy (the way I did) by trying to find out information about .Type by reading about Type in LotusScript Help files.

The dot type command, if you're curious, is an old Ami Pro command that has carried over into Word Pro. To read the documentation about .Type, though, you have to go back to Ami Pro. I don't recommend that you go do that. I point out this fact because sometimes I have a hard time knowing when to stop clarifying things....

```
Sub Main
    .Application.FindAndReplace.FindString = "good"
    .InitFindAndReplace True
    .Find
    .Bold
    .Italic
End Sub
```

Notice all the *dot* commands (.InitFindAndReplace, .Bold, .Italic, and so on) in the preceding recorded script. Dot commands enable you to use the commands from your applications and place results in the current document. You notice these dot commands are generated for you when you record scripts, but as you do more advanced scripting, you may create dot commands yourself, without recording.

Branching Off with Select

The If statement (from the list in Chapter 21) is probably more widely used than Select among beginning scripters. You know, If has that popularity thing going for it — most people have heard about If and can't wait to give it a try.

For certain kinds of quite common situations, though, Select is cleaner and more elegant. Many come to prefer Select over If.

```
Select Case selectExpr
    [ Case condition1
        [ dostatements1 ] ]
    [ Case condition2
        [dostatements2 ] ]
    ...
    [ Case Else
        [dostatements3 ] ]
End Select
```

The following is an example of an If statement that tests a series of conditions and determines output accordingly. After the If statement code, I show the same example using a Select statement instead:

```
Sub Main
   Dim candidate As Integer
   candidate = 26
   If candidate = 14 Then
      Print "Jolene comes through!"
   Elseif candidate = 18 Then
      Print "It's your day, Harvey!"
   Elseif candidate = 22 Then
      Print "Frank's a Winner!"
   Elseif candidate = 26 Then
      Print "Johanna emerges on top!"
   Elseif candidate = 30 Then
      Print "Johnson dominates!"
   Elseif candidate = 34 Then
      Print "To Victor belong the spoils!"
   Else
      Print "No worthy candidate today."
   End If   'Output Johanna emerges on top!
End Sub
```

As promised, the following code performs the same function as the preceding If statement by using the more efficient Select statement:

```
Sub Main
   Dim candidate As Integer
   candidate% = 26
   Select Case candidate
   Case 14
      Print "Jolene comes through!"
   Case 18
      Print "It's your day, Harvey!"
   Case 22
      Print "Frank's a winner!"
   Case 26
      Print "Johanna emerges on top!"
   Case 30
      Print "Johnson dominates!"
   Case 34
      Print "To Victor belong the spoils!"
   Case Else
      Print "No worthy candidate today."
   End Select   'Output Johanna emerges on top!
End Sub
```

After you begin to consider If kind of old hat, you're ready for the more precise Select statement. With Select, you can more readily read through the list of choices and see what's there. Also, because you don't have to type in your variable name so often, you're less likely to miskey it when you use the Select statement.

Looping with For

So why did the If statement make the top ten list in Chapter 21, while For slipped to the third position in this second list of ten? Although the list compiler (that is, me) has no hard data to go on, he has the definite impression that For — for all its robustness and widespread usage — simply doesn't have the following of If.

In any case, the For statement is handy for enabling you scripters to set up your scripts to repeatedly execute a statements or set of statements. You can base the number of times the script statements are repeated on a specified number of repetitions.

The syntax for For looks like this:

```
For mycount = startcount To endcount [ Step addcount ]
    [ script statements ]
Next [ mycount ]
```

An example using For:

```
Sub Main
    For count= 1 To 5
        Print "current count =" count
    Next
End Sub
```

When you run the preceding script, you see these results in the Output panel:

```
current count = 1
current count = 2
current count = 3
current count = 4
current count = 5
```

You can also use `While` and `Do` statements the way that you use `For` — to set up your scripts to conditionally and repeatedly execute a statement or set of statements. I talk about all these looping statements in Chapter 11, but, you don't need to go looking there now or anything. . . I'm just mentioning it.

Converting Data Types with `CInt` and `CSng`

Just as scripting has much more to do with juggling variables than any newcomer may expect, juggling variables has much more to do with properly matching data types than any novice would ever dream.

Even though they may appear to mean little to anyone else, `CInt`, `CSng` and other functions for converting data types have great value to scripters who are trying to get their variables to have matching data types. For example, `CInt` converts an expression to a value having the Integer data type and, because `CInt` is a function, returns that value. Likewise, the `CSng` function does its conversion and returns a Single data type value.

The syntax for `CInt` looks like this (and the syntax for `CSng` is very similar):

```
CInt ( expression )
```

Following is an example of `CInt` in use:

```
Sub Main
    ' Do this to convert from Currency to Integer type.
    Dim x As Currency
    x@ = 15.91
    Print CInt(x@)          ' Prints 16
End Sub
```

I'm not saying that these data type conversion functions will become important to you this day or even this month. But my inside sources in the scripting world tell me that these functions will come to matter to you as a scripter. . . and sooner than you probably expect.

Keeping Current with Now

Date functions always seem to have their day. In particular, the Now function figures out the current date and time for the computer system that is running the script. And because Now is a function, it returns the date and time to the script. You can use the Now function, for example, when you want to know the current date and time for display in a message box.

The syntax for Now is quite simple:

```
Now
```

And so is this example:

```
Print Now     'Output is 5/14/96 3:28:21 PM
```

Two other popular date functions are Date and Day. Date returns the date without the exact time (which is the way most of us refer to dates anyway), something like 12/26/97. Day, on the other hand, is another favorite function of programmers. True to its name, this function returns the day of the month by itself; for example, Day returns a *7* if the script supplies a date that refers to the seventh day of the month.

Handling those Errors: On Error

Because of error messages causing all the heartache that they do for end users, compassionate scripters begin to look for ways to cushion their impact. One such method employs the On Error statement, which enables scripters to offer alternatives for handling errors that occur when a script is running.

The On Error syntax looks like this:

```
On Error [ errorNum ] { GoTo alabel  |  Resume Next | GoTo 0 }
```

The following is a simple example. If any error occurs when the script containing this On Error statement is running, script execution continues with the statement following the one that caused the error. When you run the script, instead of getting stuck in a void caused by the error, the script simply bypasses the statement in error and looks to the next statement to continue its activity.

```
On Error Resume Next
```

Working with error messages can become quite involved. Please note that the syntax for the `On Error` statement contains different options for handling errors. By specifying the error number (that is, `errornum`, which tells LotusScript what particular error condition you're interested in), you can recognize each distinct error condition and even provide separate instructions for handling each different type of error (Perhaps you `Resume Next` for one error and `GoTo alabel` for another). Also, instead of using an error number, you can specify an error in the `On Error` statement by using the *constant* (the named variable assigned to the error number by LotusScript) for that error. For example, the next two `On Error` statements refer to the same error in LotusScript (that is, the error that occurs when your script tries to divide by zero):

```
On Error 11 . . .
```

```
On Error ErrDivisionByZero . . .
```

Opening Other Programs with `Shell`

Often, as you prepare scripts for others, you may want to allow your users to make use of other programs. Perhaps you want to list the other available programs on a menu and allow your script users to choose a program from there. The `Shell` function enables your script users to start up other programs.

The Shell function syntax is as follows:

```
Shell ( program name [ , awindowStyle ] )
```

If you want to open up the Windows Calculator program, try using the following example script:

```
Sub Main
    Dim openCalc As Integer
    openCalc% = Shell("CALC.EXE", 1)
End Sub
```

When you run this script, the Windows Calculator starts up, as shown in Figure 22-1.

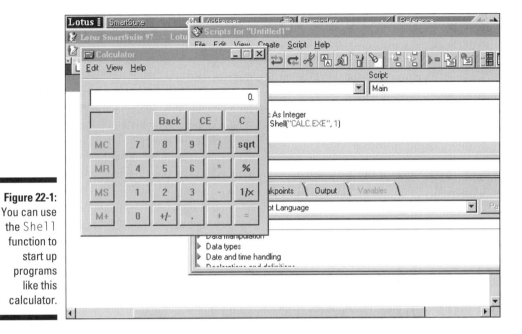

Figure 22-1:
You can use
the Shell
function to
start up
programs
like this
calculator.

Relating to Your Objects with Set

Because you and I now program in a world of OOP (object-oriented programming), we may as well face up to it and use statements like the Set statement. You can use Set to establish a relationship between an object and a variable. That is, you help your objects get oriented in their own little universes. Here's the syntax:

This list shows the syntax for using Set in three ways:

✔ To create an object and assign its reference to variable

```
Set myvar = New aclass [ ( [ argument list ] ) ]
```

✔ To make a copy of an existing object reference to another variable

```
Set myvar1 = myvar2
```

✔ To associate a product object (that is, an object defined by the Lotus software program that contains it) with a variable

```
Set myvar = Bind [ aproductClass ] ( myObjectName )
```

In the following example, I declare workerBee as a variable referring to an object of the class AllBees and then use the Set statement to create a new AllBee object and assign its reference to workerBee.

In your class declarations, put this statement:

```
Class AllBees

End Class
```

Then, in your Main sub, include these script lines:

```
Dim workerBee As AllBees
Set workerBee = New AllBees
```

Making Your Output Look Right with Format

In this esoteric world of programming, encountering an old friend from the world of spreadsheets is comforting. Format is such an entity (an old friend, that is). You can use the Format function to do things like put your output into a date form or display your numbers as currency.

The Format syntax looks like this:

```
Format[$] ( expression [ , theformat ] )
```

The following example defines the variable myMoney as currency, gives myMoney an initial value, and then displays the value of myMoney (formatted as currency) in a message box.

```
Sub Main
    Dim myMoney As Currency
    myMoney@ = 65
    Messagebox "My money amounts to " & Format(myMoney@,
            "Currency")
End Sub
```

Figure 22-2 shows how the resulting message box looks.

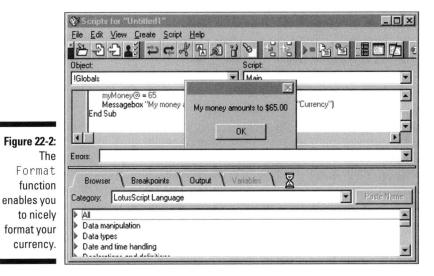

Figure 22-2:
The
Format
function
enables you
to nicely
format your
currency.

Getting Out with Exit

Intermediate scripters find that the Exit statement comes in handy. For example, you can have a script that looks through a collection of choices until it find the one it wants. After the finding the desired choice, the script uses the Exit statement to get out of the statements that look through the choices.

The syntax for the Exit statement is simple:

```
Exit statementblock
```

And I know that you're going to love running this next sample script:

```
Sub Main
   For count = 2 to 99
      Print Format(count, "General Number") & " bottles of
            beer on the wall. . ."
      If count > 5 Then Exit For
   Next
   Print ". . . and so on!"
End Sub
```

The sample script checks the loop count so that it can (mercifully) stop displaying its message in the Output panel — have a look at Figure 22-3.

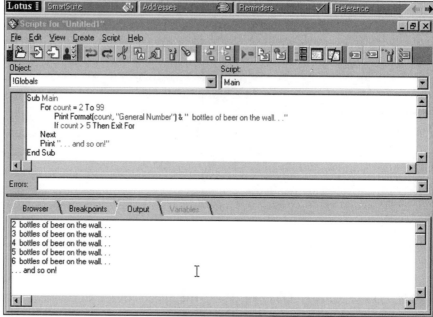

Figure 22-3:
The Exit
statement
allows a set
of script
statements
to stop
executing
under
certain
circum-
stances.

I've heard that intermediate scripters find Exit to be a handy tool. On that
recommendation, I include the Exit statement here, allowing it to barely
squeak in as the last of the other top ten LotusScript statements.

Chapter 23

Ten LotusScript Statements You Almost Never Need

I think that people find reassurance in knowing that relatively useless things exists *out there* in any difficult subject. And, the people just delving into LotusScript are no exception. "Maybe I don't know much about this LotusScript programming language," the novice scripter thinks, "but some parts of LotusScript are so obscure that no one else knows them anyway. Even the great scripters are just like me in that respect."

Actually, in scripting as in working with spreadsheets, I find that *most* functions and statements listed in a complete LotusScript reference are unnecessary for *most* people *most* of the time. (In fact, they're unnecessary for *some* people almost *all* the time.) The list in this chapter could easily be 50 times as long as it is — nevertheless, I checked with a longtime scripter while compiling this list to come up with statements that tend to be used by only a few hearty programmer-types.

Assigning variable values with Let

When you assign a value to a variable, you can use Let, as in this statement:

```
Let firstName = "Horace"
```

However, you don't have to use the keyword Let at all. Let is actually redundant — it's like an extra appendage that is used less and less. People who still use Let may do so because they want to call attention to a variable assignment or, perhaps, because they're creatures of habit.

Retrieving a character code with Asc

This is another pretty useless one for you. You can use the Asc function to find out the ASCII character code for the first character in a string, as in this example:

```
capB& = Asc("B")
Print capB&      'Prints 66
```

Almost nobody ever has to do that.

Using Declare (for calls to C)

You can use Declare to identify a LotusScript function or sub that calls an external function written in C (another programming language). An *external* function is one that does not exist within the LotusScript programming language, but that is defined in a shared library of C routines.

Syntax for the Declare statement (for external C calls) looks like this:

```
Declare [ Public | Private ] { Function | Sub }
  lotusScriptname Lib libraryName [ Alias theAliasName ]
  ( [ argument list ] ) [ As theReturnType ]
```

Well, do *you* have a shared library of C routines — I mean, one that you're aware of? A novice scripter probably doesn't know the C programming language in the first place and probably won't be calling an external C routine.

Compiling with conditions: The %If directive

The %If directive looks much like an If...Then...ElseIf statement (which I list in Chapter 22), but this directive is very specialized. The %If directive, by the way, carries instructions to the LotusScript compiler. Based on the evaluation of product constants (that are already defined by the various Lotus products), the directive causes LotusScript to compile only the statements in the directive that are associated with the product constant.

The %If syntax looks like this:

```
%If productConstant1
    statements
[%ElseIf productConstant2
    statements ]
...
[%Else
    statements ]
%End If
```

Each Lotus product has its own product constants, but using this directive with these products is for advanced LotusScript users and gurus. And I'm not sure that even they have much use for the %If directive.

Looking for product constants with IsDefined

The IsDefined function is a companion to the %If directive (used to identify the run-time value of product constants) and, apparently, is just as inconsequential to the majority of us as the %If directive. Forget about IsDefined.

At least the syntax is simple:

```
IsDefined ( string Expression )
```

Inserting ASCII files with %Include

%Include is another directive, which inserts the contents of an ASCII file (that contains only LotusScript statements) into a script where the directive appears at the time the script is compiled. The syntax for %Include looks like this:

```
%Include afileName
```

You may have occasion to include whole files into other files when you're using your word processor. You probably don't have much occasion to be popping files into other scripts when you're using LotusScript, though.

You ought to get some practical reward for plowing through a chapter like this, which you must be doing if you are reading this tip. So upon further reflection, I have to say that this directive does actually have some usefulness. Sometimes you do want to include, say, a list of constants from somewhere else. This directive — %Include — is in here to see if you're paying attention. It's the exception that proves the rule. Look for occasions to use %Include, and you can make me look silly for putting it in a chapter with directives that you won't ever use.

Converting numbers with Bin

You and I don't have much occasion to convert our numbers to binary. But in case you want to see what kind of results you get, use the following syntax for the Bin function:

```
Bin[$] ( numericExpression )
```

Just because I'm curious, I think that Bin is worthy of an example:

```
Print Bin$(3)      'Prints 11
```

Keeping track with Timer

Timer sure is a handy function — it returns the time that has elapsed since midnight, in seconds.

The syntax is exceptionally simple:

```
Timer
```

And I have a great example:

```
Dim seconds As Single
seconds = Timer
Print Timer               'Output for me is 53252.13
```

Of course, your output will be different if you run this sample Timer script, but what difference does it make? In all the years of your life, have you ever had occasion to know how many seconds have elapsed since midnight?

Representing your numbers in Hex

If you like the Bin function, you'll really get a kick out of using Hex. That's right, you can convert your numbers to a hexadecimal representation by using the Hex function.

Just follow this syntax:

```
Hex[$] ( numericExpression )
```

And for an example:

```
Print Hex$(15)  'Prints F
```

Fine, this prints the hexadecimal representation of the number *15* as *F*, but do you know what that *F* represents? I'm not certain that I do. (Okay, I'm certain that I don't.)

Discovering base eight with Oct

Like Bin and Hex, the Oct function lets you represent your numbers in yet another interesting way . . . this time as an element of a numbering system with a base of eight.

The Oct syntax:

```
Oct[$] ( numericExpression )
```

And the example:

```
Print Oct$(15)      'Prints 17
```

I just don't think that I'm going to be using the Oct function in my scripts right away; how about you?

Chapter 24

Ten Things You Can Do to Write Horrible Scripts

· ·

In This Chapter

▶ Hiding your variables

▶ Giving your variables names that make no sense to anyone

▶ Jamming your statements onto one line

▶ Using large blocks of untested script

▶ Making large scripts with as few subs as possible

▶ Making subs hard to identify by leaving out `Call` statements

▶ Defining your variables without data types

▶ Using arguments without data types

▶ Nesting ifs, nesting nested ifs, nesting nested nested ifs . . .

▶ Looping endlessly

· ·

*W*hen I playfully came up with the idea for this chapter some months ago, I thought that stating the principles of good scripting practice by stating their opposites may be helpful to readers. So (with tongue in cheek, of course) I present this chapter. After all, nobody likes a goody-goody who recites only the rules of right behavior.

I've seen just how ornery a compiler can be when it checks over the scripts that I write, and just the thought of fighting these bad programming principles makes my skin crawl. You can bring yourself hours of correcting and debugging misery by falling prey to just *one* of these practices. And what's really scary is that most of us can pick up these bad practices spontaneously, without reading about them in a book.

I REALLY DON'T WANT YOU TO FOLLOW THESE HORRIBLE SCRIPTING PRACTICES.

Even when you do your scripting right and work very methodically, you can still get error messages.

1. Declare your variables willy-nilly, as you use them.

Bury your variables inside subs and be sure to declare them dynamically, instead of with the Dim statement, so they'll be harder to find. The LotusScript compiler doesn't care how you declare your variables, as long as you declare them before you use them. But if you practice willy-nilly variable declaration, anybody trying to read your script will be thoroughly confused (including you). And you get the added challenge of not being able to figure out later what you intended the script to do or how you wanted it done.

2. Give your variables whacked-out names.

If you want a variable to hold data corresponding to an employee ID, for example, why be a conformist and give the variable a totally unimaginative name, like employee_ID? Instead, why don't you name the variable dog_House. And don't forget that you can mix numbers into the names of variables after you've started off the name with a letter. As an even better idea, try naming your employee ID variable something like s_422_999_go. The compiler won't mind. Why should you? (See Chapter 7 for rules on naming.)

Also, remember that LotusScript keywords all begin with uppercase letters. If you start your variable names the same way, (as in Dog_House) you can make the variable names look just like keywords. Then when people look at your script, they'll have a more difficult time telling which terms are the keywords and which are the variables that you named yourself.

3. Put lots of statements per line and separate them by colons.

If you're programming outside the LotusScript IDE, you can easily put multiple scripting statements on one line. The LotusScript compiler itself is quite liberal with regard to statements per line. As far as the compiler is concerned, you can legally cram any number of statements on a line (as long as you separate the statements with colons). The code can actually work, and the cramped appearance confuses the heck out of people who try to read it.

This confusing practice of putting multiple scripting statements per line is one bad practice that the IDE corrects for you. That is, the IDE places your scripting statements one per line.

Compare this (hard-to-read) script:

```
Dim firstName As String : Dim lastName As String  : Dim age
          As Integer : Dim emp_code As Single
```

With this (easy-to-read) version:

```
Dim firstName As String
Dim lastName As String
Dim age As Integer
Dim emp_code As Single
```

4. Don't test your scripts when you modify them.

As with the preceding bad practice of multiple script statements per line, the LotusScript IDE makes not testing your scripts more difficult to do. That is, because LotusScript tests the validity of each script line as you finish it, you're sort of testing the script as you go. But sometimes you can find ways around it.

Anyway, if you want to write a bad script that causes headaches and aspirin consumption, try to create as big a program as you can without testing anything. Put in lots of statements and functions and go blithely along. Then at the end, you'll face a large, complicated script, and you'll have no idea where to start looking if the script doesn't work right.

5. Try not to use many subs.

Hey, just because subs are available doesn't mean that you have to use them all the time. The IDE creates a separate block for a sub automatically after you declare it, but you can always work with lots of variables and avoid creating subs as much as possible. Try to put all your code into one, giant Main subroutine. Doing this makes your script hard to read and almost impossible to debug later.

6. Don't use `Call` statements for your subs, if you do use subs.

`Call` statements don't work with functions, just with subs. Keeping this in mind, you can suppose that someone may want to look through a script to locate just the subs. Well, if you don't use `Call` statements for your subs, you can make reading your script just that much harder. That is, the person picking out the subs in your script will have difficulty distinguishing them from functions.

7. Don't give your variables data types when you declare them.

The LotusScript compiler is a real stickler for data types. The compiler likes to know whether it's dealing with an integer, a string, a long data type, or whatever. Also, if you declare variables as certain types, you can readily check user input later on to see whether that input is proper. (When your input box asks for a *name*, did the user enter a *number?*)

By not declaring data types, you can create all kinds of confusion. For example, suppose that a function insists on receiving an integer and you haven't declared your variable to be an integer type. Or, maybe your users are putting in numbers when your script asks for their names; if you haven't declared the data types for your variables that accept the user input, your script won't know the difference. All kinds of havoc can come up when your variables don't have data types. Try it, and find out.

8. When you use arguments with functions, don't declare their data types either.

Nothing in LotusScript says that you have to declare the data types of the variables you use as arguments in a function. By the way, arguments declared with data types look like this:

```
Sub SumUp (x As Integer, y As Integer, z As Integer)
```

Well, you can have them look like this:

```
Sub SumUp (x , y , z )
```

The compiler won't tap you on the shoulder and insist that you put in the data type. Confusion may come up later over data types — the bane of any scripter's existence — but, after all, this section is all about methods that create confusion.

9. Use nested ifs instead of subs and nest as many ifs in your script as you can.

LotusScript's IDE comes into play on this *nested if* issue and insists on indenting each If statement that you place inside (*nest*) another If statement. You can do nothing about that, if you're scripting inside the IDE. But, you can boggle the human mind by nesting If within If within If, instead of using subs. The compiler doesn't mind — only humans do, and one intent of bad scripting practices is to find ways to confuse people anyway.

See Chapter 10 for more discussion about nested ifs.

10. Put lots of endless loops in your scripts.

Endless loops make people dizzy. Although I've raised objections to many items in BASIC nomenclature, I see nothing wrong with the term *endless loop,* which I discussed in Chapter 11. This term accurately describes a condition that anybody hates to encounter in a script. Endless loops really live up to this name; that is, they'll continue to run endlessly. The poor script user is forced to press Escape or to use some other means to shut down the script that keeps repeating itself. If you really want to cause user frustration, try to slip in an endless loop, here and there, when you're writing your horrible script.

Chapter 25

Ten Things to Help You Write Pretty Good Scripts

· ·

In This Chapter

▶ Declaring and naming variables appropriately

▶ Organizing your LotusScript code

▶ Testing your code as you go along

▶ Dividing your scripts into logical routines

▶ Identifying your script elements for the human eye

▶ Using programming structures efficiently

· ·

Chapter 24 presents good programming principles in a satiric way, and looking at them that way is fun. After all, nobody likes a "do-it-this-way" lecture all the time. However, with all joking aside, cutting straight to the core of the information can be nice, too.

So, for those who aren't in the mood to fool around, I present the ten principles of good programming, written straight. If you want an explanation of the bad things that result from not adhering to these principles, you can refer to the list in Chapter 24.

Xerox this list and keep it by your computer.

1. Declare your variables at the beginning of the script.

When you declare your variables at the beginning of the script, you can readily find them for review later. See Chapter 6 for all kinds of variable information. Chapter 7 talks about variables, too.

2. Give your variables meaningful names.

Make sure that your variable names reflect the data that you're using them to hold. That is, call the variable that holds a customer's name something like `custName`. You may want to begin variables with lowercase letters, too, so you can tell them from LotusScript keywords. In Chapter 7, I talk a lot about naming elements in LotusScript.

3. Put one script statement per line.

If you follow this scripting principle, your scripts are much easier to read and debug.

4. Test changes to your script right away.

Test any new subs or modifications to existing subs as you go along. Nipping any errors in the bud is easier than finding and fixing them later in a large script. See Chapter 5 for further discussion of checking and debugging your scripts.

5. Use lots of subs.

Having lots of smaller subs (instead of one long, complicated script) makes programs easier to decipher, debug, and maintain.

6. Use `Call` statements for your subs.

LotusScript lets you access your subs by name only, but using the `Call` statement helps you differentiate subs from functions (which are also called by name). When you use `Call` statements for your subs, your scripts are simply easier to read.

7. Give your variables data types when you declare them.

The "Type mismatch" error message seems to be LotusScript's favorite. During script debugging — when you're trying to match up data types and get rid of that pesky mismatch error message — having declared data types with your variables at the outset really helps.

8. Declare data types for the arguments that go along with your functions.

Declaring data types for *arguments* (the variables that you pass around with your functions) is quite important for helping your functions know what to expect! And, as in tip 7, declaring data types simplifies debugging.

9. As much as possible, use subs instead of nested ifs.

As far as the LotusScript compiler is concerned, you can nest If statements inside If statements to your heart's content. But you may find — when you come back to your script later to figure out what you've done — that all those nested ifs are confusing. Experienced scripters tend to use subs instead of nested ifs, when possible.

10. Avoid endless loops.

Obviously, you want to avoid endless loops — you know, those situations in which your script gets stuck repeating a For, While, or Do loop, with no means of escape. Your program simply doesn't work when you have an endless loop. See Chapter 11 for the discussion of loops.

Be especially careful to have a line of code that changes the value of a condition in a While loop.

Chapter 26

Ten Common Error Messages —
and What They Mean
in Plain English

. . . .

In This Chapter

▶ Looking at a type mismatch

▶ Dealing with an instance member that does not exist

▶ Handling a class or type name not found

▶ Finding errors in spelling and punctuation

    `Unterminated string constant` ("You forgot the 't' in 'String.'")

    `Not a sub or function name: Endif` ("You need a space in End If.")

▶ Facing the unexpected

    `Unexpected: Bogart; Expected: End-of-Statement, Operator`

    ("You left off the quotation marks.")

    `Unexpected: Print; Expected: End-of-Statement`

    ("You have to put Print on a separate line.")

    `Unexpected: day; Expected: Identifier`

    ("You can't use a keyword as a variable.")

    `Unexpected: Code; Expected: (;End of Statement; ,;AS;LIST`

    ("You can't have any spaces in variable names.")

    `Unexpected: &; Expected: Statement`

    ("You forgot the line continuation character.")

. . . .

Computer error messages in other programs (like word processors, games, and stuff) have begun to take on a more human character. The compiler error messages in LotusScript, though, give you that zesty feeling of being right there in the pioneering days of . . . something. In this chapter, I thought that I'd have fun by looking at the real error messages that come up and comparing them with what the messages might say if compilers spoke English.

After all, lots of error messages are the result of the scripter making simple mistakes in punctuation and layout. And besides being fun, seeing the error messages' English translation has the added benefit of showing that extremely threatening error messages often require extremely simple fixes. This list may help you feel less threatened by error messages and may help you realize, too, that *you* don't have to find what the error message says it's looking for. An error message may ask you for a statement when all you really need to do is take the space out of a variable name.

The LotusScript compiler is very good at finding errors in the first place. But for telling scripters what they need to do to fix those errors, I must say that the compiler just isn't that skilled at communicating. As the title of this chapter suggests, I show you some common LotusScript compiler error messages and tell you what they really mean.

Type mismatch

A type mismatch error is probably the most common LotusScript error message. You see this message when your script attempts to use a variable as a data type different than the type you defined. Look at the following example:

```
Dim starName As String
starName% = "Humphrey Bogart"
```

The preceding script lines contain an error (dealing with the variable starName) that causes a type mismatch error. To correct the error, change the data suffix character for starName from % (integer) to $ (string) to match the data type established in the Dim statement (As String).

The error message says Type suffix does not match data name: starName. Myself, I'd prefer a message that said, "Hey, if you define a variable as a string, you can't turn around and say it's an integer."

Instance member does not exist

A second very common error message comes around as you begin to work with OOP (object-oriented programming) structures. The following example shows an error that triggers the Instance member does not exist error message.

```
Class RealClass
    '...
End Class
Dim myVariable As Variant
Set myVariable = New RealClass
Print myVariable.Anything
```

In this example, the last script statement is illegal because `Anything` is not defined as a member of `RealClass`. You can declare `Anything` as a member of the class, but the easiest way to correct the error is to delete the `.Anything`.

Instead of the phrase `instance member does not exist`, I'd like the message to say, "Woops, you haven't defined *Anything* as a member of the class `RealClass`."

Class or type name not found

Running into intimidating error messages because you make a simple typing error is common. Suppose that you typed this:

```
Dim starName As Sring
```

You'd get the following error message: `Class or type name not found: Sring`.

I'd rather have the message say, "Sorry to distract you . . . you forgot the t in `String`." I know that asking for the error messages in English is too much, but the compiler always seems to assume the worst, for even the most minute things.

Unterminated string constant

Often, simple mistakes bring error messages in highly elevated, very serious technical language. For example, suppose you typed this line:

```
star$ = "Humphrey Bogart
```

You'd get the following error message: `Unterminated string constant`. And that sounds like a terrible thing, very hard to fix.

A good translation of the error message is, "Oops. You forgot the quotation mark at the end." I suppose that designing a compiler to be so specific about typing omissions would be difficult, but "You forgot the quotation marks" as an error message would certainly be less unnerving.

Unexpected: Bogart; Expected: End-of-Statement, Operator

Suppose you leave off both quotation marks when initializing a string variable in your script line — like this:

```
star$ = Humphrey Bogart
```

Then you get this error message: Unexpected: Bogart; Expected: End-of-Statement, Operator.

Personally, I would rather have the error message say, "Woops. You left off the quotation marks around *Humphrey Bogart*." If I read this English translation of the error message, I'd have a much easier time fixing the problem. (And it wouldn't make me feel so guilty and incompetent.)

Not a sub or function name: Endif

You find many opportunities in scripting for leaving out the small things. Just look at this other startling error message that I encountered recently: Not a sub or function name: Endif.

You see, I had inadvertently written a script that looked like this:

```
If . . .
   Print "You did GREAT!"
EndIf
```

My upcoming request is, of course, too much to ask, but wouldn't a message like "You've almost got it right. You just need a space in the middle of End If." have been so much nicer? After all, End If is a legitimate command, and I wasn't trying to put a sub or function there anyway (as the error message suggested).

Unexpected: Print; Expected: End-of-Statement

Suppose you get a little careless while you're scripting and put a command where LotusScript doesn't expect it. For example, maybe you're using some If . . . Then structures, like this:

```
If Score < 75 Then
. . .
```

When you get to the Else portion of the script, suppose that you type this line:

```
Else     Print "You did GREAT!"
```

Then you get this error message: `Unexpected: Print; Expected: End-of-Statement.`

Well, the statement ends all right; however, another statement follows it on the same line. I'd find a message like this more helpful, "Hey, you have to put the `Print` command on a separate line." Sometimes, the compiler's words seem so far from stating the actual problem.

Unexpected: day; Expected: Identifier

Suppose you typed this script line to define a variable:

```
Dim day As Double
```

You'd get this error message: `Unexpected: day; Expected: Identifier.`

"Well," you wonder, "what kind of identifier were you looking for?" A more helpful error message might say, "Sorry, buddy. You've inadvertently used a LotusScript keyword as a variable name. You have to change the name a little bit to have your script work."

Unexpected: Code; Expected: (;End of Statement; ,;AS;LIST

You may also run into this perplexing error message; suppose you typed this line:

```
Dim movie Code As Double
```

You'd get the error message: `Unexpected: Code; Expected: (;End of Statement; ,;AS;LIST.`

Trying to figure out the script problem on the level of the compiler's actual message may cause a bit of head scratching. So, I'll show you the English translation: "Hey, you can't have any spaces in variable names like `movieCode`." I suppose that the compiler can't figure out that a simple space (between `movie` and `Code`) caused all its difficulties. On the other hand, you and I have a hard time figuring out what the compiler means — what with all those parentheses and semicolons flying around.

Unexpected: &; Expected: Statement

Suppose that you typed these lines in your script:

```
Messagebox frstName$ & " owes "
   & Format(applyLoan@ * applyInterest!, "Currency")
```

The LotusScript compiler wouldn't like the code and would give you this error message: Unexpected: &; Expected: Statement.

If you take the error message at face value, you may try to think of a statement to add in to make everything work. But if the compiler were a little psychic, it could say to you, "I think you meant to put an underscore (_) at the end of the first line." (The _, of course, is the *line continuation character*.)

When you fix the script error, your lines of code look like this, and the error message goes away:

```
Messagebox frstName$ & " owes " _
   & Format(applyLoan@ * applyInterest!, "Currency")
```

Chapter 27

Ten Definitions of Confusing LotusScript Terms (A - L)

In This Chapter

▶ Discovering the half-English language of BASIC

▶ Getting specific with meanings in LotusScript

*T*he maddening thing about many BASIC terms is that they are a form of what I'll call *half-English,* which is a close relative of pidgin English. That is, BASIC terms are everyday words, *but they don't have everyday meanings.* For example, the BASIC half-English may use the word *animal* as if it meant only *male mongoose,* or the word *weather* as if it meant *rainy July day in the Amazon.*

General everyday words that you and I always thought we knew suddenly take on very specific meanings in LotusScript (and, I hasten to add in fairness, in all forms of BASIC). I'm thinking, in particular, of terms like *property* and *procedure,* but I know lots of other examples.

Well, the list in this chapter (and the one in Chapter 28) help you keep your sanity by reassuring you that, yes, the meaning you previously knew for these terms is a valid meaning everywhere else. However, you also need to accept the meanings of the terms as constrained by the narrow, literal, mathematical mind of the LotusScript compiler.

In this chapter and the next, I help you find out what these selected terms mean to LotusScript. Use these definitions as your flashlight to illuminate the corners of the compiler's mind. You'll find a meaning that you recognize, and you'll gain the special understanding that helps you along with scripting.

Argument

An argument, anybody knows, happens when two people get into a fight and yell stuff at each other that they don't necessarily mean . . . not in LotusScript, though.

In the study of logic, an argument is the minor premise in a syllogism, and I suppose that definition helps to justify how the term *argument* is used in scripting. In LotusScript, an *argument* is information that the script needs to get its work done. The arguments for a sub or function appear in parentheses after the sub or function name, as in the following example:

```
Sub Sum (x As Integer, y As Integer, z As Integer)
```

The arguments in this example are the variables x, y, and z (the stuff in parentheses).

Comment

In the case of the term *comment*, English and half-English (spoken by the LotusScript compiler) converge pretty well. When you or I make a comment, we may make a more or less informal expression of our reaction to something, as in phrases, "That movie is pitiful. I wouldn't take my dog to it." or "That restaurant has great food. I would take my dog to it."

In LotusScript, *comments* are lines of text used mainly to explain script code to a human who reads the code. If you follow the right syntax for creating LotusScript comments, you can say whatever you want.

You can enter a one-line comment in your script by doing either of the following:

- ✔ Type ' (single quotation mark) at the beginning of a line and then enter the comment line.
- ✔ Type Rem at the beginning of a line and then enter the comment text.

You can add a comment to an existing line of script by doing either of the following:

- ✔ Adding a colon and then a Rem statement like

```
y=6 : Rem Use a colon to separate statements.
```

- ✔ Typing ' (single quotation mark) and then putting in the comment like

```
y=7     'No colon needed when you use a single quote.
```

You can enter a block of comment lines by using the %Rem...%End Rem directives and following these steps:

1. **Type** %Rem **at the beginning of a new script line.**

2. **Enter the lines of comment text.**

3. **To end the comment block, type** `%End Rem` **at the beginning of a new script line.**

For example:

```
%Rem These lines illustrate the fact that
you can put about anything you want into comment
lines in a script.
You can whack in characters like $, &, and ^. Whatever
you put in, the compiler doesn't read it anyway.
It lets you get away with violent crime between
the Rem and End Rem statements.
%End Rem
```

Condition

For the word *condition,* common sense English and specialized, mathematical compiler half-English are not too far apart. In English, a *condition* is a . . . situation, a state of affairs. In `If` statements and loops in LotusScript, the compiler often looks to see if one condition is true before going ahead to do something.

Look at the syntax for the `If` statement:

```
If condition Then [ statements ] [ Else [ statements ] ]
```

And then look at the following script lines:

```
If grade < 75 Then
    Print "Your grade is unsatisfactory."
End If
```

In the preceding code, the condition that must be satisfied in order to `Print` is the condition that `grade < 75`. In LotusScript, then, *condition* means more or less what you and I expect it to mean: "Meet my conditions, or forget about going ahead with the deal."

Constant

In LotusScript, a *constant* is a variable. That idea takes some getting used to. If you're thinking about the meaning of constant in English, you think, "Well, which is it — constant (unchanging) or variable (ever changing)?"

In half-English compilerspeak, though, a *constant* is simply one special type of variable. All rules that apply to variables apply to constants as well, except that after a constant's value is set in the script, the script can't change that value.

For example, suppose you have a constant variable named `minWage` (for minimum wage). After you set the minimum wage to use in the script, you want `minWage` to have that same value everywhere in the script. You declare `minWage` as a constant with the `Const` statement (whose syntax looks like this):

```
[ Public | Private ] Const constantName1 = expression1
    [, constantName2 = expression2 ]. . .
```

For example:

```
Const minWage! = 4.50
```

The preceding script line defines the constant `minWage` as currency and sets its value to $4.50.

Event

An *event,* in real life, is something that happens — usually something exciting or even monumental, like a WWF wrestling match or a circus. An *event* in LotusScript, although hardly as exciting as a circus, is also something that happens within one of the Lotus programs.

Events trigger scripts. For example, clicking on a button is an event, and the occurrence of the event can cause a script attached to that button to execute.

Expression

An *expression,* to the rest of us, is a few choice words strung together; expressions can often be quite colorful. "Cold as a well-digger's feet" is an expression, for example. In LotusScript compilerese, an expression is also a collection of letters, numbers, and symbols strung together, but this collection can be a little harder to decipher than an expression in English.

A LotusScript expression is a combination of operands (variable names, numbers, and so on) and operators (computational symbols, comparison operators, and so on), as in the following example:

```
1 < 2
```

In the preceding expression, 1 and 2 are operands, and < is the operator. Together, the operand and operators make up the expression.

Function

A *function,* as you and I probably think of it, is what my dictionary calls a person's assigned task or duty. Looking at what the term *function* means in mathematics can be helpful in understanding the specialized, half-English meaning of function in LotusScript. In the mathematical sense, a *function* is "a variable so related to another that for each value assumed by one, there is a value determined for the other."

In this case, the meaning of function in mathematics *is* the meaning in LotusScript. *Functions* are script subroutines that return a value to the calling program. (Subs that aren't functions don't have the power to return any values, so really, a function is a quite privileged and influential sub.) See Chapter 13 for more discussion about functions.

In the following example, the function Sumup returns the sum of the arguments x and y to the script that calls it.

```
Function Sumup As Integer
    Sumup = x + y
End Function
```

Identifier

Identifiers are sequences of letters, digits, and underscores used to name LotusScript components. In short, they're names. Usually, identifiers name variables, and follow these rules:

- ✔ The first character of the identifier has to be a letter.
- ✔ The remaining characters in the identifier (after the first character) can be letters, digits, or underscores.
- ✔ Identifiers can't include spaces.
- ✔ Identifiers can be no more than 40 characters long.

If you're really interested in finding out more about identifiers, you can look in Chapter 7.

Initialize

Several English words — initiate, initiation, initiative — have meanings that relate to the meaning of initialize in BASIC's half-English. That is, all these terms have something to do with starting out. When you *initialize* a variable in LotusScript, you give it an initial (or starting out) value.

But in BASIC, *initializing* seems to me to have more to do with giving a value than with starting out, and that's why I think *initializing* belongs in this list of confusing terms. (Perhaps the term *valuizing* would be more descriptive, except that no such word exists, and the last thing we need is one more jargon term to deal with.)

If a script is going to deliver a value for a variable at the end, it has to have a value for the variable at the beginning — hence, initializing has to happen. You don't always have to initialize variables yourself; LotusScript can initialize a variable to a default value based on its data type. The following script lines define xyz as a string variable and initialize it to the value End of alphabet.

```
Dim xyz As String
xyz$ = "End of alphabet"
```

Keyword

Keywords are identifiers (you know, *names*) that LotusScript reserves for its own use. LotusScript uses the keywords to name its own statements, built-in functions, constants, and data types. Some examples of keywords:

```
If, Dim, Integer, True
```

You can find a complete listing of keywords in LotusScript's own documentation.

If you try to use Dim (or any other keyword) as a variable in one of your own scripts, you get an error message from the LotusScript compiler. You have to come up with variable names that LotusScript hasn't used already.

Lexical Element

The term *lexical element* isn't really an entity in LotusScript itself, but you come across it in discussions about the language. In English, *lexical* refers to vocabulary, as opposed to grammar. LotusScript seems to have a similar distinction in mind. The LotusScript *lexical elements* are all the pieces and parts that make up LotusScript statements. Subs, functions, keywords, variables, and constants are all such pieces and parts (that is, lexical elements). You then have to follow LotusScript's rules of syntax (the grammar) to make LotusScript statements that work in the script.

One thing is very clear to me, though. English is a whole lot more natural-sounding and a million times more forgiving than these scripting languages. About the biggest *error message* you run into if you use English lexical elements incorrectly is a disapproving look from somebody who's a stickler for correctness. Most of the time, people know what you mean, and they let you murder the king's English however you like.

Chapter 28

Ten More Definitions of Confusing LotusScript Terms (M - Z)

Chapter 28 continues with LotusScript term definitions where Chapter 27 left off (that is, at letter M). As in Chapter 27, I remind you of a common English definition and try my hardest to relate that definition to the specialized meaning of the term as used by LotusScript. So, read on to enjoy this next batch of enlightened definitions for LotusScript language terms.

Member

This term — *member* — is at risk of being politically incorrect in the '90s. This term has an air of exclusivity about it. The meaning of the term in LotusScript is more or less what it is in English; a *member* is one of the individual elements that, taken together, compose a group. However, the political connotations of this term in LotusScript worry me — can only certain variables be members of a class, and others cannot? The whole idea of having classes, which has a faint smell of social stratification about it, is politically risky these days.

With such higher considerations aside, the fact is that, in LotusScript, a *member* is a variable, function, sub, or property that *belongs* to a particular class. And by belonging, a member derives its identity from and helps to make up the super-structure called the *class*. Both *member* and *class* apply to object-oriented programming (OOP) structures and are of little concern to you until you embark upon working in the OOP universe.

The following example shows the relationship (in a syntax fashion) of members to the class definition through the `Class` statement:

```
[ Public | Private ] Class className1 [ As baseClass1 ]
    classBody1
End Class
```

A *member* of the class is an element that is listed within *classBody1*.

Method

The term *method* is a classic example of the reason that I felt compelled to compile this list of definitions in the first place. A *method,* as anybody who speaks English knows, is a technique of some sort — you know, an *approach* for doing something. In LotusScript, though, *method* has a highly specialized meaning: A method is a function — a script routine that returns a value to the calling program.

As near as I can tell, applying the name *method* to a function only creeps in during discussions of classes and OOP (object-oriented programming), as in the phrase "a class and its methods." I'm guessing that OOP discussions outside of LotusScript use the term methods and that the term has slipped into LotusScript while the language's creators had their minds on much higher issues (issues other than avoiding confusing double names for things like functions).

Procedure

My CD-ROM dictionary says, in general, that a procedure is a way of performing or effecting something. It goes on to say, more specifically, that a procedure is an act composed of steps. When programmers want to do anything, they do it with a program. To them, therefore, a procedure is a program. And, conversely, a program is a procedure. I suppose that some such thinking must be how BASIC languages got the idea to use the term *procedure* as they do.

Throughout the programming world, a *procedure* is a program. Likewise in LotusScript, a procedure is a script. More specifically, you can think of procedures as named sections of a script that you can invoke by name, and programmers love procedures because they're reusable. That is, because scripts can call the same procedures (blocks of code) from different places in the script, using procedures can eliminate having to repeat lines of code.

LotusScript refers to different structures that consist of blocks of code — like subs, functions, and properties — as procedures. Chapters 12 and 13 have more information about these different structures.

Property

To you and me, property is stuff that we own, like a house and a suitcase. And sometimes, property refers to a characteristic such as brown hair or blue eyes. And in some programming environments, like Microsoft Visual Basic, property has a meaning that makes sense — for example, the color, size, or location of an object that you create in a dialog box is a property.

In LotusScript, though, the term is downright confusing. A *property* is a procedure that behaves in a specialized way. You use a property in OOP (object-oriented programming) primarily for the clandestine manipulation of variables. You can tell from this description that, in LotusScript, working with properties is an advanced feature, but you can refer to Chapter 12 for a bit more information.

Routine

In English, a routine is something you do that is commonplace and repetitive, as in the phrase "part of her daily routine." A *routine,* throughout the woolly world of programming, is a program. In LotusScript, therefore, a routine is a script.

Many times, programming routines are thought of as discreet parts of what can be a larger program. You may also want to refer to the definition of procedure, which discusses blocks of code that can be used repeatedly. You can think of such code blocks as routines.

The term *routine* probably earns its greatest distinction in LotusScript by being a term best known, not for itself, but for its children — subs (which is short for *subroutines*). This situation is one of those instances like famous boxer Roy Jones, Jr. — where the offspring is illustrious while the parent remains relatively obscure. In fact, I notice that Mr. Jones, the offspring, has recently dropped the *Jr.* from his name, much as subroutine tends to drop routine from its name. For those who don't follow boxing (and, I understand, many people don't anymore), Jones (the younger) is an undefeated middleweight division boxer who tends to dispose of his opponents in the early rounds. Most potential opponents go to great lengths to avoid confrontation with the man who, some say, would be a worthy opponent even for a truly famous heavyweight boxer like Muhammad Ali.

Script

A *script* is what actors follow when making a movie or creating a play, although they love to deviate from it. In LotusScript, a *script* is a program. Other names for a script are application, function, procedure, property, routine, and sub . . . although some of these names (such as function) are specialized and don't have as broad a meaning as does the simple term *script*.

Statement

In English, a *statement* is something that you say, sometimes with great emphasis, as in the phrase, "He's making a statement with that nose ring." In LotusScript, a statement is one step in the control flow of a script. Many times, a LotusScript statement corresponds to a single line of code. But LotusScript has specialized statements — like `If . . . Then . . . Else If` and `Select` — that take up more than one line.

Sub

In everyday parlance, a *sub* has come to be known as a pretty good sandwich — on French bread with cold cuts and onions — and in Philadelphia is referred to as a *hoagie*. In LotusScript, a *sub* is a program within a program. For more information about subs, see Chapter 12 and also the definitions for *procedure, routine,* and *script*.

A sub differs from a function (another program within a program) in that the sub doesn't return a value back to the program that calls it, but a function does.

Variable

Variables are so important to scripting that they shouldn't be in the same list with terms like *routine* and *property* and *method*. Variables *sound* kind of unimportant, unless you happen to be a mathematician and are accustomed to thinking of variables as useful. And, variables sound kind of flaky, too — as if they change all the time.

Variables are the absolute heart of what you do when you script. You define variables and find out their values. End of story.

If you want a formal definition of variable, you can say that a *variable* is a script element that is uniquely named and defined as a container for storing data. Chapter 6 is devoted to the discussion of variables, but most other chapters in the book end up talking about them, too.

Variant

A *variant* is a confusing little term for English-speakers who are coming to LotusScript for the first time. You have to get to the term's sixth letter (the *n*) before you realize that it's *variant* and not *variable* (and *variables*, I uphold, are of earth-shattering importance and not to be confused with *variants*).

Actually, a *variant* is a type of variable — one that has no assigned data type. Data types, such as Integer, Currency, or Single, tell the script what kind of data the variable is supposed to contain. Good scripters tend to look askance upon the practice of leaving variables as variants, most of the time. You can refer to Chapter 6 for further discussion of variants, data types, and variables.

Index

IDG BOOKS WORLDWIDE REGISTRATION CARD

Title of this book: **LotusScript® For Dummies®**

My overall rating of this book: ❑ Very good [1] ❑ Good [2] ❑ Satisfactory [3] ❑ Fair [4] ❑ Poor [5]

How I first heard about this book:

❑ Found in bookstore; name: [6]   ❑ Book review: [7]

❑ Advertisement: [8]   ❑ Catalog: [9]

❑ Word of mouth; heard about book from friend, co-worker, etc.: [10]   ❑ Other: [11]

What I liked most about this book:

What I would change, add, delete, etc., in future editions of this book:

Other comments:

Number of computer books I purchase in a year: ❑ 1 [12] ❑ 2-5 [13] ❑ 6-10 [14] ❑ More than 10 [15]

I would characterize my computer skills as: ❑ Beginner [16] ❑ Intermediate [17] ❑ Advanced [18] ❑ Professional [19]

I use ❑ DOS [20] ❑ Windows [21] ❑ OS/2 [22] ❑ Unix [23] ❑ Macintosh [24] ❑ Other: [25]_____
(please specify)

I would be interested in new books on the following subjects:
(please check all that apply, and use the spaces provided to identify specific software)

❑ Word processing: [26]   ❑ Spreadsheets: [27]

❑ Data bases: [28]   ❑ Desktop publishing: [29]

❑ File Utilities: [30]   ❑ Money management: [31]

❑ Networking: [32]   ❑ Programming languages: [33]

❑ Other: [34]

I use a PC at (please check all that apply): ❑ home [35] ❑ work [36] ❑ school [37] ❑ other: [38]_____

The disks I prefer to use are ❑ 5.25 [39] ❑ 3.5 [40] ❑ other: [41]_____

I have a CD ROM: ❑ yes [42]   ❑ no [43]

I plan to buy or upgrade computer hardware this year: ❑ yes [44]   ❑ no [45]

I plan to buy or upgrade computer software this year: ❑ yes [46]   ❑ no [47]

Name: Business title: [48]   Type of Business: [49]

Address (❑ home [50] ❑ work [51]/Company name:)

Street/Suite#

City [52]/State [53]/Zipcode [54]:   Country [55]

❑ **I liked this book!** You may quote me by name in future
IDG Books Worldwide promotional materials.

My daytime phone number is _____

IDG BOOKS

THE WORLD OF
COMPUTER
KNOWLEDGE

❏ YES!

Please keep me informed about IDG's World of Computer Knowledge.
Send me the latest IDG Books catalog.